COLOSSIANS

Brazos Theological Commentary on the Bible

COLOSSIANS

CHRISTOPHER R. SEITZ

BrazosPress

a division of Baker Publishing Group
Grand Rapids, Michigan

Published by Brazos Press
a division of Baker Publishing Group
P.O. Box 6287, Grand Rapids, MI 49516-6287
www.brazospress.com

Printed in the United States of America

Library of Congress Cataloging-in-Publication Data
Seitz, Christopher R.
    Colossians / Christopher R. Seitz.
       pages cm. — (Brazos theological commentary on the Bible)
    Includes bibliographical references and index.
    ISBN 978-1-58743-301-6 (cloth)
      1. Bible. Colossians—Commentaries. I. Title.
BS2715.53.S45 2014
227′.7077—dc23   2014003268

14 15 16 17 18 19 20   7 6 5 4 3 2 1

For Elizabeth

Ἐνδύσασθε τὴν ἀγάπην, ὅ ἐστιν σύνδεσμος τῆς τελειότητος

Revêtez-vous de l'amour, qui est le lien de la perfection

CONTENTS

SERIES PREFACE

Near the beginning of his treatise against Gnostic interpretations of the Bible, *Against Heresies*, Irenaeus observes that scripture is like a great mosaic depicting a handsome king. It is as if we were owners of a villa in Gaul who had ordered a mosaic from Rome. It arrives, and the beautifully colored tiles need to be taken out of their packaging and put into proper order according to the plan of the artist. The difficulty, of course, is that scripture provides us with the individual pieces, but the order and sequence of various elements are not obvious. The Bible does not come with instructions that would allow interpreters to simply place verses, episodes, images, and parables in order as a worker might follow a schematic drawing in assembling the pieces to depict the handsome king. The mosaic must be puzzled out. This is precisely the work of scriptural interpretation.

Origen has his own image to express the difficulty of working out the proper approach to reading the Bible. When preparing to offer a commentary on the Psalms he tells of a tradition handed down to him by his Hebrew teacher:

> The Hebrew said that the whole divinely inspired scripture may be likened, because of its obscurity, to many locked rooms in our house. By each room is placed a key, but not the one that corresponds to it, so that the keys are scattered about beside the rooms, none of them matching the room by which it is placed. It is a difficult task to find the keys and match them to the rooms that they can open. We therefore know the scriptures that are obscure only by taking the points of departure for understanding them from another place because they have their interpretive principle scattered among them.[1]

As is the case for Irenaeus, scriptural interpretation is not purely local. The key in Genesis may best fit the door of Isaiah, which in turn opens up the meaning of Matthew. The mosaic must be put together with an eye toward the overall plan.

---

1. Fragment from the preface to *Commentary on Psalms 1–25*, preserved in the *Philokalia*, trans. Joseph W. Trigg (London: Routledge, 1998), 70–71.

Irenaeus, Origen, and the great cloud of premodern biblical interpreters assumed that puzzling out the mosaic of scripture must be a communal project. The Bible is vast, heterogeneous, full of confusing passages and obscure words, and difficult to understand. Only a fool would imagine that he or she could work out solutions alone. The way forward must rely upon a tradition of reading that Irenaeus reports has been passed on as the rule or canon of truth that functions as a confession of faith. "Anyone," he says, "who keeps unchangeable in himself the rule of truth received through baptism will recognize the names and sayings and parables of the scriptures."[2] Modern scholars debate the content of the rule on which Irenaeus relies and commends, not the least because the terms and formulations Irenaeus himself uses shift and slide. Nonetheless, Irenaeus assumes that there is a body of apostolic doctrine sustained by a tradition of teaching in the church. This doctrine provides the clarifying principles that guide exegetical judgment toward a coherent overall reading of scripture as a unified witness. Doctrine, then, is the schematic drawing that will allow the reader to organize the vast heterogeneity of the words, images, and stories of the Bible into a readable, coherent whole. It is the rule that guides us toward the proper matching of keys to doors.

If self-consciousness about the role of history in shaping human consciousness makes modern historical-critical study critical, then what makes modern study of the Bible modern is the consensus that classical Christian doctrine distorts interpretive understanding. Benjamin Jowett, the influential nineteenth-century English classical scholar, is representative. In his programmatic essay "On the Interpretation of Scripture," he exhorts the biblical reader to disengage from doctrine and break its hold over the interpretive imagination. "The simple words of that book," writes Jowett of the modern reader, "he tries to preserve absolutely pure from the refinements or distinctions of later times." The modern interpreter wishes to "clear away the remains of dogmas, systems, controversies, which are encrusted upon" the words of scripture. The disciplines of close philological analysis "would enable us to separate the elements of doctrine and tradition with which the meaning of scripture is encumbered in our own day."[3] The lens of understanding must be wiped clear of the hazy and distorting film of doctrine.

Postmodernity, in turn, has encouraged us to criticize the critics. Jowett imagined that when he wiped away doctrine he would encounter the biblical text in its purity and uncover what he called "the original spirit and intention of the authors."[4] We are not now so sanguine, and the postmodern mind thinks interpretive frameworks inevitable. Nonetheless, we tend to remain modern in at least one sense. We read Athanasius and think him stage-managing the diversity of scripture to support his positions against the Arians. We read Bernard of Clairvaux and

2. *Against Heresies* 9.4.
3. Benjamin Jowett, "On the Interpretation of Scripture," in *Essays and Reviews* (London: Parker, 1860), 338–39.
4. Ibid., 340.

assume that his monastic ideals structure his reading of the Song of Songs. In the wake of the Reformation, we can see how the doctrinal divisions of the time shaped biblical interpretation. Luther famously described the Epistle of James as a "strawy letter," for, as he said, "it has nothing of the nature of the Gospel about it."[5] In these and many other instances, often written in the heat of ecclesiastical controversy or out of the passion of ascetic commitment, we tend to think Jowett correct: doctrine is a distorting film on the lens of understanding.

However, is what we commonly think actually the case? Are readers naturally perceptive? Do we have an unblemished, reliable aptitude for the divine? Have we no need for disciplines of vision? Do our attention and judgment need to be trained, especially as we seek to read scripture as the living word of God? According to Augustine, we all struggle to journey toward God, who is our rest and peace. Yet our vision is darkened and the fetters of worldly habit corrupt our judgment. We need training and instruction in order to cleanse our minds so that we might find our way toward God.[6] To this end, "the whole temporal dispensation was made by divine Providence for our salvation."[7] The covenant with Israel, the coming of Christ, the gathering of the nations into the church—all these things are gathered up into the rule of faith, and they guide the vision and form of the soul toward the end of fellowship with God. In Augustine's view, the reading of scripture both contributes to and benefits from this divine pedagogy. With countless variations in both exegetical conclusions and theological frameworks, the same pedagogy of a doctrinally ruled reading of scripture characterizes the broad sweep of the Christian tradition from Gregory the Great through Bernard and Bonaventure, continuing across Reformation differences in both John Calvin and Cornelius Lapide, Patrick Henry and Bishop Bossuet, and on to more recent figures such as Karl Barth and Hans Urs von Balthasar.

Is doctrine, then, not a moldering scrim of antique prejudice obscuring the Bible, but instead a clarifying agent, an enduring tradition of theological judgments that amplifies the living voice of scripture? And what of the scholarly dispassion advocated by Jowett? Is a noncommitted reading, an interpretation unprejudiced, the way toward objectivity, or does it simply invite the languid intellectual apathy that stands aside to make room for the false truism and easy answers of the age?

This series of biblical commentaries was born out of the conviction that dogma clarifies rather than obscures. The Brazos Theological Commentary on the Bible advances upon the assumption that the Nicene tradition, in all its diversity and controversy, provides the proper basis for the interpretation of the Bible as Christian scripture. God the Father Almighty, who sends his only begotten Son to die for us and for our salvation and who raises the crucified Son in the power of the Holy Spirit so that the baptized may be joined in one body—faith in *this*

---

5. *Luther's Works*, vol. 35, ed. E. Theodore Bachmann (Philadelphia: Fortress, 1959), 362.

6. *On Christian Doctrine* 1.10.

7. *On Christian Doctrine* 1.35.

God with *this* vocation of love for the world is the lens through which to view the heterogeneity and particularity of the biblical texts. Doctrine, then, is not a moldering scrim of antique prejudice obscuring the meaning of the Bible. It is a crucial aspect of the divine pedagogy, a clarifying agent for our minds fogged by self-deceptions, a challenge to our languid intellectual apathy that will too often rest in false truisms and the easy spiritual nostrums of the present age rather than search more deeply and widely for the dispersed keys to the many doors of scripture.

For this reason, the commentators in this series have not been chosen because of their historical or philological expertise. In the main, they are not biblical scholars in the conventional, modern sense of the term. Instead, the commentators were chosen because of their knowledge of and expertise in using the Christian doctrinal tradition. They are qualified by virtue of the doctrinal formation of their mental habits, for it is the conceit of this series of biblical commentaries that theological training in the Nicene tradition prepares one for biblical interpretation, and thus it is to theologians and not biblical scholars that we have turned. "War is too important," it has been said, "to leave to the generals."

We do hope, however, that readers do not draw the wrong impression. The Nicene tradition does not provide a set formula for the solution of exegetical problems. The great tradition of Christian doctrine was not transcribed, bound in folio, and issued in an official, critical edition. We have the Niceno-Constantinopolitan Creed, used for centuries in many traditions of Christian worship. We have ancient baptismal affirmations of faith. The Chalcedonian definition and the creeds and canons of other church councils have their places in official church documents. Yet the rule of faith cannot be limited to a specific set of words, sentences, and creeds. It is instead a pervasive habit of thought, the animating culture of the church in its intellectual aspect. As Augustine observed, commenting on Jer. 31:33, "The creed is learned by listening; it is written, not on stone tablets nor on any material, but on the heart."[8] This is why Irenaeus is able to appeal to the rule of faith more than a century before the first ecumenical council, and this is why we need not itemize the contents of the Nicene tradition in order to appeal to its potency and role in the work of interpretation.

Because doctrine is intrinsically fluid on the margins and most powerful as a habit of mind rather than a list of propositions, this commentary series cannot settle difficult questions of method and content at the outset. The editors of the series impose no particular method of doctrinal interpretation. We cannot say in advance how doctrine helps the Christian reader assemble the mosaic of scripture. We have no clear answer to the question of whether exegesis guided by doctrine is antithetical to or compatible with the now-old modern methods of historical-critical inquiry. Truth—historical, mathematical, or doctrinal—knows no contradiction. But method is a discipline of vision and judgment, and we cannot know in advance what aspects of historical-critical inquiry are functions

8. *Sermon* 212.2.

of modernism that shape the soul to be at odds with Christian discipline. Still further, the editors do not hold the commentators to any particular hermeneutical theory that specifies how to define the plain sense of scripture—or the role this plain sense should play in interpretation. Here the commentary series is tentative and exploratory.

Can we proceed in any other way? European and North American intellectual culture has been de-Christianized. The effect has not been a cessation of Christian activity. Theological work continues. Sermons are preached. Biblical scholars turn out monographs. Church leaders have meetings. But each dimension of a formerly unified Christian practice now tends to function independently. It is as if a weakened army had been fragmented, and various corps had retreated to isolated fortresses in order to survive. Theology has lost its competence in exegesis. Scripture scholars function with minimal theological training. Each decade finds new theories of preaching to cover the nakedness of seminary training that provides theology without exegesis and exegesis without theology.

Not the least of the causes of the fragmentation of Christian intellectual practice has been the divisions of the church. Since the Reformation, the role of the rule of faith in interpretation has been obscured by polemics and counterpolemics about *sola scriptura* and the necessity of a magisterial teaching authority. The Brazos Theological Commentary on the Bible series is deliberately ecumenical in scope, because the editors are convinced that early church fathers were correct: church doctrine does not compete with scripture in a limited economy of epistemic authority. We wish to encourage unashamedly dogmatic interpretation of scripture, confident that the concrete consequences of such a reading will cast far more light on the great divisive questions of the Reformation than either reengaging in old theological polemics or chasing the fantasy of a pure exegesis that will somehow adjudicate between competing theological positions. You shall know the truth of doctrine by its interpretive fruits, and therefore in hopes of contributing to the unity of the church, we have deliberately chosen a wide range of theologians whose commitment to doctrine will allow readers to see real interpretive consequences rather than the shadow boxing of theological concepts.

The Brazos Theological Commentary on the Bible has no dog in the current translation fights, and we endorse a textual ecumenism that parallels our diversity of ecclesial backgrounds. We do not impose the thankfully modest inclusive-language agenda of the New Revised Standard Version, nor do we insist upon the glories of the Authorized Version, nor do we require our commentators to create a new translation. In our communal worship, in our private devotions, in our theological scholarship, we use a range of scriptural translations. Precisely as scripture—a living, functioning text in the present life of faith—the Bible is not semantically fixed. Only a modernist, literalist hermeneutic could imagine that this modest fluidity is a liability. Philological precision and stability is a consequence of, not a basis for, exegesis. Judgments about the meaning of a text fix its literal sense, not the other way around. As a result, readers should expect an eclectic use of biblical translations, both across the different volumes of the series and within individual commentaries.

We cannot speak for contemporary biblical scholars, but as theologians we know that we have long been trained to defend our fortresses of theological concepts and formulations. And we have forgotten the skills of interpretation. Like stroke victims, we must rehabilitate our exegetical imaginations, and there are likely to be different strategies of recovery. Readers should expect this reconstructive—not reactionary—series to provide them with experiments in postcritical doctrinal interpretation, not commentaries written according to the settled principles of a well-functioning tradition. Some commentators will follow classical typological and allegorical readings from the premodern tradition; others will draw on contemporary historical study. Some will comment verse by verse; others will highlight passages, even single words that trigger theological analysis of scripture. No reading strategies are proscribed, no interpretive methods foresworn. The central premise in this commentary series is that doctrine provides structure and cogency to scriptural interpretation. We trust in this premise with the hope that the Nicene tradition can guide us, however imperfectly, diversely, and haltingly, toward a reading of scripture in which the right keys open the right doors.

R. R. Reno

AUTHOR'S PREFACE

When the Bible speaks of a time of peace and comity, of fair and equal receipt of God's blessings, it uses this language: "In that day everyone will sit, each under their own vine and fig tree, and none shall make them afraid" (Mic. 4:4). The bulk of the writing of this commentary was done literally under vine and fig tree in a rented cottage in the village of Les Baux, in the Provence region of France, renown for olive oil, figs, and wine. I was fortunate to have a summer research break from teaching at Wycliffe College, enabling me to write and walk and think and pray in relatively undisturbed fashion. This commentary is dedicated to my wife, Elizabeth, in thanksgiving for her companionship and love. We will long have pleasant memories of our little orangerie cottage in the olive grove "La Serre."

I also want to thank those parishioners at the Church of the Incarnation in Dallas, Texas, who read Paul's letter to the Colossians with me during lunchtimes in 2011. I was invited to give the Gross Lectures at Valparaiso University in 2010, and this gave me the opportunity to think in depth about Paul's use of the scriptures, especially for those newcomers in Christ for whom they were new wineskins exploding with fresh meaning. Thank you, George Heider and Gilbert Meilander and your fine colleagues at Valparaiso. David Trobisch read initial drafts of portions of the commentary and offered wise counsel and support. I mention with gratitude Don Collett and Mark Gignilliat, who received email attachments from France and commented in helpful ways on what I was trying to do. Jonathan Reck offered good editing and bibliographic assistance at key points. Errors in judgment and expression are of course my own, under my own professional vine and fig tree.

I want to acknowledge the hard work of Brazos editors Rusty Reno and Ephraim Radner, in working through the first written drafts. Thanks to Dave Nelson and Lisa Ann Cockrel for their editorial help in the latter stages as well. Rusty probably had no business inviting an Old Testament scholar to pretend he was a theologian writing a commentary, consistent with that discipline in its modern guise, on a letter in the New Testament. All the same, I like to imagine my grasp of the Old Testament and its rhythms as placing me closely alongside Paul himself, in ways that the New Testament guild or theologians properly speaking come at it less directly. In any event, the idea of throwing off the usual patterns of commentary design is one I resonate with. I hope this volume is a fruitful contribution to the series and a commentary that opens up some fresh angles of vision for those who read it and use it. Writing it did that for me.

Feast of the Epiphany, 2014

ABBREVIATIONS

Biblical Translations

BZAW	Beihefte zur Zeitschrift für die alttestamentliche Wissenschaft
ESV	English Standard Version
KJV	King James Version
NA^{27}	*Nestle-Aland Novum Testamentum Graece*, edited by B. Aland et al., 27th edition (Stuttgart: Deutsche Bibelgesellschaft, 1993)
NET	The NET Bible (New English Translation)
NIV	New International Version
NJB	New Jerusalem Bible
NKJV	New King James Version
NRSV	New Revised Standard Version
RSV	Revised Standard Version
TNIV	Today's New International Version

Biblical Books

Acts	Acts	Eccl.	Ecclesiastes	Hag.	Haggai
Amos	Amos	Eph.	Ephesians	Heb.	Hebrews
1 Chr.	1 Chronicles	Esth.	Esther	Hos.	Hosea
2 Chr.	2 Chronicles	Exod.	Exodus	Isa.	Isaiah
Col.	Colossians	Ezek.	Ezekiel	Jas.	James
1 Cor.	1 Corinthians	Ezra	Ezra	Jer.	Jeremiah
2 Cor.	2 Corinthians	Gal.	Galatians	Job	Job
Dan.	Daniel	Gen.	Genesis	Joel	Joel
Deut.	Deuteronomy	Hab.	Habakkuk	John	John

1 John	1 John	Mark	Mark	Rev.	Revelation
2 John	2 John	Matt.	Matthew	Rom.	Romans
3 John	3 John	Mic.	Micah	Ruth	Ruth
Jonah	Jonah	Nah.	Nahum	1 Sam.	1 Samuel
Josh.	Joshua	Neh.	Nehemiah	2 Sam.	2 Samuel
Jude	Jude	Num.	Numbers	Song	Song of Songs
Judg.	Judges	Obad.	Obadiah	1 Thess.	1 Thessalonians
1 Kgs.	1 Kings	1 Pet.	1 Peter	2 Thess.	2 Thessalonians
2 Kgs.	2 Kings	2 Pet.	2 Peter	1 Tim.	1 Timothy
Lam.	Lamentations	Phil.	Philippians	2 Tim.	2 Timothy
Lev.	Leviticus	Phlm.	Philemon	Titus	Titus
Luke	Luke	Prov.	Proverbs	Zech.	Zechariah
Mal.	Malachi	Ps.	Psalms	Zeph.	Zephaniah

INTRODUCTORY MATTERS

What Is an Introduction to a Single Letter of Paul?

The modern commentary belongs to a genre in which certain conventional matters can be expected to be treated. This includes what appears in the introductory section preceding the commentary proper. The present commentary operates with three general presuppositions that impact those expectations.

The first is that the Bible exists in relationship to a community (the people of Israel, the church through time). This means that it maintains its own literary integrity but that this integrity is received into the life of the church in time in the form of preaching, catechesis, exposition, paraphrase, and commentary. The "history of interpretation" represented by this reception is not confined to either a premodern context or a modern one said to be an improvement on or replacement for it (or a postmodern one renegotiating them both). Practically speaking, this means that, while a certain kind of (especially historical) commentary tradition may be more familiar to us (positively or negatively), the Bible's reception history is not to be confined to the last two hundred years but must be evenly evaluated, in terms of what it as a phenomenon communicates, across a longer period of time. This is a function of the Bible's living character. It means that certain questions raised to a particular acuteness in one age, due to cultural realities under God's providence, do not match the questions and answers given at an earlier age, even as the same witness is sounding forth. The positive side of this is that the questions of one age, including our own, sometimes need to be changed, once they have had their day and the limits of their probing and concerns have been exhausted or borne their wonted fruit. What can be discovered, furthermore, is that by examining an earlier period in the lived life of the Bible's reception, the proper proportion of what we seek to know can be corrected or reappraised. The amnesia of the present age can be overcome or ameliorated, and a wider set of concerns reidentified as worthy of our attention.

The second and related presupposition is that what we mean today by the word "historical" is not self-evident but requires probing. Given the character of the material we are seeking to interpret—sacred literature of a certain character—historical questions are immediately and ineluctably hermeneutical questions. What is meant by "the original" (whether an authorial intention, or first audience, or an early "setting in life") has a historical dimension to be sure, but equally may this be said of developmental/medial and final periods of a text's life: in the form of a single letter (in the case of Paul), a letter in association with other letters, or of the Pauline letters in the New Testament canon or indeed of that canon in relation to the scriptures of Israel or Old Testament with a two-testament Christian scripture.[1]

The final presupposition flows from this as well. Paul's letters come to us in a given canonical form. That form foregrounds certain things and lets other things fall out of specific focus or priority. It is possible to regard the canonical presentation as empty of significance, as necessitating a certain kind of recasting, or as a cataract on the "real truth of the matter." But this commentary will take the view that the canonical presentation has its own kind of significance that requires attention and care to evaluate properly. The canonical presentation guards against imbalances emerging at periods in the history of interpretation, when certain questions have been hyperextended or no longer gain interest or lose their capacity for resolution or assent. The canonical presentation offers a commentary on how history and God's abiding voice are inextricably related. It seeks to maintain a balance in what is worthy of comment and what is less decisive.

With these three presuppositions in place, inevitably what we might mean by an "introduction" to Colossians is also affected. The Brazos Theological Commentary on the Bible offers no strong replacement model here, in the form of a single new template. What the present commentary on Colossians seeks to do is rehearse some of the classically modern themes one expects to appear in a commentary introduction, now with an eye toward recasting them in the light of the presuppositions we are seeking to honor and uphold in the commentary as such. This commentary assumes that the usual genre of "introduction" is fairly well known or, more surely, that it is readily available for consultation. Sometimes the introductory sections of an individual letter of Paul can be almost as long as the commentary proper. Under discussion are things like (1) Asia Minor at the time of Paul, (2) authorship (did Paul write this letter?), (3) the character and structure of the letter, (4) the date and place of writing, (5) distinctive theological emphases and themes, (6) the relationship with other letters of Paul, and the list goes on.

It is my judgment that the reader of the present commentary will find answers to these questions either in the present introduction or in the commentary itself. What I wish to do here is survey the modern questions from the standpoint of

---

1. Consult my *The Character of Christian Scripture: The Significance of a Two-Testament Bible* (Grand Rapids: Baker Academic, 2011) for a fuller account and examples.

the contribution that I believe is best secured when the presuppositions of our approach are observed. I begin by asking what it means for an individual commentator to select one letter of Paul for commentary, given that the letters of Paul come to us in a fairly stable and standardized collection order. What has this meant in the modern period and how might one undertake a single commentary project mindful of the letter-collection dimension as a factor in the history of interpretation and as part of how the church received, heard, and proclaimed "the canonical Paul"? I then turn to a series of topics typically treated as introductory but handled here in the light of canonical factors as well as the earlier history of interpretation: (1) the question of the *setting* as the material itself presents this (Colossians and the other prison letters); (2) the *occasion* for Paul's writing as such and in the wider canonical presentation; (3) Paul's *use of scripture* (to be called in time the Old Testament) and the implications for his own epistle writing as itself a kind of emerging *graphē*; and (4) letter composition and the question of *Paul as author*. The final introductory section explains the appeal to the term "canonical" for the approach adopted and also the format, translation, bibliographical, and structural matters.

Colossians in the Pauline Letter Collection: The Proper Implications to be Drawn Regarding a Commentary on a Single Letter

In the history of interpretation, anomalous would be, not an Old Testament interpreter commenting on a New Testament book, but any interpreters confining themselves to commentary within a single Testament, much less leaving theological construction to others coming after. The Brazos Theological Commentary on the Bible seeks to listen to—if not also restore—an older set of assumptions and learn from the church's long history of hearing God's voice in a two-testament Christian scripture.

What *would* be anomalous would be choosing to write on a single letter of Paul, to the exclusion of the others (including the writings of the New Testament in their entirety). There are exceptions, of course, but they are notable for being such.[2] The effect of this can be stated negatively and positively.

Positively, greater focus has been given to the individuality of the letter and concern with matters such as (1) authorship, (2) setting, (3) date, (4) distinctive features, (5) relation to other letters, and so forth. The negative effects flow

2. Martin Bucer produced a special commentary on Ephesians, as did John Davenant on Colossians (*An Exposition of the Epistle of St. Paul to the Colossians* [Cambridge, 1627; repr. Edinburgh: Banner of Truth, 2005]). Part of the reason for this belongs to Reformation controversies and the desire to focus attention on their possible resolution through specific, detailed exegetical treatments. In the modern period, Colossians (because short) can be grouped with Philemon (so Dunn 1996 and Moo 2008) or with the "prison correspondence" (Ephesians, Philippians, Colossians, Philemon). I will discuss the implications of these subgroupings below.

from this as well—including a focus on such matters arguably in disproportion to their significance for interpretation. So by contrast, a quick look at the attention given to these matters in the history of interpretation shows that they are generally worthy of discussion (though, e.g., the commentary of Thomas Aquinas says virtually nothing on these topics), though chiefly to establish a basic working conception. The main task is interpretation of the message of the letter and its application, with allowance for whether the locus of commentating is desk (Theodoret, Erasmus), pulpit (Chrysostom, Calvin), lectern (Luther), monastic homily (Jerome), and so forth. The wide agreement on Pauline authorship and the assumption of the equally wide setting (Roman imprisonment)[3] mean not a lot of attention is given to the history-of-religion or where an individual letter is to be situated in context, on a timeline purporting to show the historical sequence of letters, now standardized in New Testament introductions. I will have more to say about that below when it comes to the "Colossian heresy" and how the older history of interpretation proportionalized attention to this within the cumulative task of interpretation.

Two matters conspire at this point. Because interpreters typically handle the entire corpus of Paul's letters (including Hebrews and the Pastorals) as the task to be undertaken and because they simply assume that Paul authored them, their instincts are deeply integrative.[4] That is, they tend toward seeing synthesis, and they major in theological cross-reference. And this is true not just of Paul's letters as interpreting each other, but also as they are interpreted together with the Old Testament writings and the rest of the New Testament. Thomas Aquinas is typical on this score, especially in his creative ranging across the Testaments in order to draw out theological significance (2006). One may note as well that his is not a study of how Paul uses the Old Testament, but is a study of how God uses the inspired scriptures as a whole, as a pluriform set of witnesses, to inform and enhance and interpret one another. Much of the modern preoccupation with particularity—whatever its strengths—has meant a forfeit or even disqualification of reading the letters in the light of one another.[5] Indeed, the very idea of Colossians being non-Pauline turns on the assumption that something is so distinctive in the letter it must be accounted for by saying it is discontinuous in sufficiently serious ways. Ours is not here a question of historicity (did Paul in fact author Colossians, or Ephesians?) but is rather an observation about the naturalness of a more integrative reading when these questions have not been

3. The Marcionite Prologue of Colossians and the somewhat ambiguous view of Erasmus, in favor of an Ephesian imprisonment, notwithstanding.

4. Hebrews is its own problem; and there are some exceptions regarding other letters of course. See Trobisch 1994: 45–46. The special case of Hebrews is discussed in Seitz, *Character of Christian Scripture*, 115–35.

5. Of course the letters are compared and contrasted. But this work is undertaken so as to put them in proper historical sequence and pursue questions of authorship and development of thought (history-of-religion).

foregrounded, due to the existence of a literary collection that orients them toward one another as a totality. To produce a single commentary on the letter to the Colossians, then, could raise in its wake all the sorts of issues this commentary will seek to move beyond in a constructive way. So mention of the assignment and its possible limitations or expectations needs to be registered up front. This is a commentary on a single letter attributed to Paul (Colossians), but it will seek to read the letter without the modern assumptions attending single-letter commentary, where a certain species of particularity and independence is prized as the goal of interpretation.

The same comment could be made about the assignment of individual books of the Old Testament (the Minor Prophets come to mind) to individual writers of commentary and the implications—maybe even unintended—of that. Commentary by Theodoret of Cyr or John Calvin handles the Minor Prophets as a whole in the same way the letters of Paul are handled: as individual writings subsisting in an ordered canonical collection. Exceptions to this practice would have seemed odd. I leave to the side the idea that it is better or more natural to distribute the books among separate commentators who will write on only one book for a series that will then include them all as authors of individual, specialized treatments. This is the modern practice, and it has been carried over into a new theological commentary series that nevertheless intends to seek newer and older horizons at the same time. It would be difficult, if not impossible, to read and integrate an older history of interpretation in the work to follow without acknowledging the wide gulf separating its assumptions about the Pauline letter collection and those of modernity, where individual treatments of individual letters by individual commentators have become the norm.[6]

Where we do find comprehensive treatments of the Old and New Testament writings, undertaken by an individual author, these have migrated in the modern period from the genre of "commentary" into what is called "introduction." This genre is suited to a particular curriculum need and setting, such as arose after the Reformation, especially in the German university context and its eventual derivatives. The genre is also invested in the set of questions regarding author, setting, sequence, distinctive features, and so forth mentioned above, for the purpose of achieving a larger, developmental picture. Introduction is also a discussion of the state of the academic discourse as "introductions" have pursued this: who has argued for what view and how they have come to the conclusions they have, with an evaluation and fresh (it is hoped) proposal. Raymond Brown's careful contribution is a good example. In the case of Colossians he will canvas the views on a topic like "Pauline authorship" and give the pros and cons and indicate where the scholarly consensus is.[7] In cases like Colossians where the views are divided,

---

6. Compare the popular treatments of William Barclay ("The Daily Bible Study Series") and N. T. Wright ("The New Testament for Everyone").

7. R. E. Brown, *An Introduction to the New Testament* (New York: Doubleday, 1997). He writes: "At the present moment about 60 percent of critical scholarship holds that Paul did not write the letter"

he will give his own view, but then be sure to say how the discipline is, at the moment of his writing, leaning.

My point here is not to dispute Brown's conclusions, but rather to note the changed climate of evaluation. If 99 percent of the church's earlier position on author and setting was uncontroversially "Paul in Roman imprisonment," this will play no role in his discussion of the aggregated consensus. Again, the question is not whether an earlier consensus lines up with what now goes with discussion of these matters, as essential to historical inquiry popularized since the nineteenth century; it most certainly does not. At issue, rather, is what the earlier position meant when it asserted such things and then went about the business of writing commentary. It is a relatively easy thing to omit notice of the earlier consensus on the grounds that it was not asking the same sorts of historical questions and so is irrelevant to the modern discipline of New Testament studies and its conclusions. But it is a different thing to fail to ask why the earlier commentators *moved briskly by such questions* in favor of what they regarded was a more obvious fact: Paul as the author of a collection of letters *whose interpretation required coordination and theological integration*. For it is not true that they were poor readers of the original or translated languages or could not see divergence or development of thought by comparing one letter with another. Rather, they accounted for this in other ways. In this they were constrained by the assumption that the canonical portrayal was itself a given and so was deeply ingredient in the task of interpretation itself. Thirteen letters are attributed to Paul.[8] They are not in obvious chronological order, so other indexes must be in play. Rather than seek for this kind of historical contextualizing (rearranging the letters according to a proper order), they allowed the canonical form to order the way they approached the interpretation of single letters and the whole.

It is difficult today to speak of "the canonical Paul" without hearing that as a way to smuggle in answers to questions about authenticity, in turn foreclosing on matters of differentiation and particularity in the name of harmony and apologetics. But that thirteen letters circulate under a Pauline egis of some kind does not tell us exactly why that is so, in precise historical and sociological terms. Speculations there are and they rush in to close the gap. Theories of pseudepigraphy are to hand, available by careful comparison to other literature of the time. Other factors are claimed to be relevant (the process of dictation, the role of the secretary in editing, collaboration with colleagues, development of thought, adaptation for the audience anticipated by Paul or others, Paul's own editing, and so forth). But the letters do not foreground these explanations and instead claim the authority of Paul without telling us just how that is so. The letter collection is "the church's guide for reading Paul" as one interpreter puts it (Childs 2008). This rubric covers

---

(610); and "I am treating it in the deuteroPauline section of this *Introduction* because that is how most critical scholars now treat it" (617).

8. With Hebrews the count is fourteen, but its status has always been viewed as requiring special evaluation.

over a host of questions made central by historical-critical method, not so as to sidestep them, but to indicate that speculation undertaken according to a certain kind of historical method can go only so far. At some point the canonical portrayal sits there before us and requests that we take it seriously as a factor in interpretation, however we might explain that in more precise historical terms (having to do with origins and development and stabilization). It is at this point that the difference between the earlier history of interpretation and the present age is so stark. What was previously taken as a given and, as such, offering hermeneutical guidance in a low-flying sense, has in the modern period become a matter of high seriousness. The canonical portrayal is held to be empty of significance, and so significance of a very different kind is to be sought. What in turn drives the business of modern interpretation is its pursuit of questions that are difficult to answer in the nature of the case because the canonical portrayal is frankly of a different order of presentation.

A certain species of modern historical analysis can, however, also identify limiting factors to historical questions too narrowly framed. Three examples are illustrative. On the issue of authorship, one modern author, having canvassed the matter in the thorough way now expected in modern commentary, concludes in this way:

> At all events, whatever the precise circumstances of its composition, Colossians strongly suggests that the distinctions between a Paul who himself changed in style and developed in theology, a Paul who allowed someone else to interpret his thought and concerns, and a Pauline disciple writing shortly after Paul's death but seeking to be faithful to what he perceived would be the master's thought and concerns envisaged in the letter become of *uncertain and diminishing significance*. (Dunn 1996: 39, emphasis added)

This judgment is made on historical grounds, not on theological or canonical ones. Yet here is where the overlap is unavoidable. So while Dunn believes Timothy to be the author of the letter, under loose supervision by Paul, the theory will not dislodge his use of the name "Paul" when he speaks of the true author of the letter and also when reflexively he attributes the message he comments on to the apostle.

On the problem of individual uniqueness in modern historical questing, in the context of the individual letters of Paul, another historically alert commentator points to certain basic limitations in this line of inquiry:

> It turns out, for example, that the differences are not large between Paul himself writing this letter, Paul writing with the aid of secretary, Paul authorizing an associate to write it, and the letter being composed by a knowledgeable imitator or pupil of Paul. Perhaps with our intense concern to demarcate "Paul" from "non-Paul" we are working with an artificial or anachronistic notion of individual uniqueness: was Paul completely different from his contemporaries and associates, or did he

typically work with others, influencing them and being influenced by them? Have we created a Paul of utter uniqueness in line with the peculiarly modern cult of the individual? (Barclay 2004: 35)

The history of interpretation is a helpful reminder that the canonical presentation need not be handled in a manner in which certain questions of individuality and uniqueness overshadow the basic contours provided by a collection of writings attributed to a single individual. Barclay writes as a historian careful to observe when a species of historical questing may run up against problems of its own making given the literature and its presentation in the form we receive it.

The third example also does not invoke the term "canonical" and the approach related to it, when it comes to precision in identifying the problems Paul is addressing in the letter, as they relate to the church at Colossae. But the same limitations noted by a canonical reading for a species of modern historical analysis are assessed hermeneutically by the author in a way that is congenial with such an approach, also in the context of a modern commentary concerned with historical context. The following quotation prefaces the discussion of the false teaching at Colossae as scholars seek to clarify this:

> What exactly the false teachers were saying can be determined only by analyzing the nature of Paul's response to them against the background of what we know generally about the first-century world of Colossae. But this process is a very inexact and uncertain one. Paul naturally presupposes that the Colossians know what the false teachers were saying, and so he only alludes to their teaching in making his points. And these allusions involve some of the most debated exegetical points in the letter. Moreover, it is sometimes difficult to know when Paul is describing what the false teachers were saying and when he is characterizing their teaching in his own terms.[9] And, finally, we do not know nearly as much as we would like about the Colossians' own "world." What we do know about it suggests that it was very complex, with many religious, philosophical, and cultural movements jostling for attention. (Moo 2008: 49)

And so Moo continues:

> All of this makes it extraordinarily difficult to pin down the exact teaching Paul opposes in Colossians and explains why scholars come to so many different conclusions about it. Indeed, we are not convinced that the letter provides enough information for us to be even reasonably sure about the identification of the false teaching." As Lincoln puts it, "Although the prescription for cure comes across reasonably clearly to the present-day reader of Colossians, the ailment defies a really detailed

9. The same problems dog interpretation of the critique of idolatry and idol construction in Isa. 40–55. In the sociology of knowledge this is the tension between emic and etic description. Are the descriptions the prophet gives accurate ones, or are they broad-brush, intended by contrast to bring out the character of the God of Israel?

diagnosis on his part."[10] Such an uncertain conclusion is disappointing in some respects but is, in another respect, hermeneutically fruitful. For it means that we can apply Paul's teaching in the letter to a wide variety of historical and contemporary movements that share the general contours of the false teaching. Our inability to pin down the false teaching does not mean that we cannot describe some of its basic tenets. (Moo 2008: 49)

This comment tracks well not only with the implications of canonical interpretation in respect of historical contextualizing, but also suggests that the final form of the letter, as it now exists (where the solution precedes the problem: cure before diagnosis) properly belongs to the interpretative intention of the letter—whatever we might say about success in bringing precision to the false teaching Paul is addressing (from afar and secondhand).

Here one can spot something of a similar caution operating, for different reasons, in the earlier history of interpretation. After all, the letter is meant to address us, one commentator will conclude, as he faces into the complexity of reconstructing the heresy in its original situation (is it Jewish, philosophical, a hybrid, etc.).[11] Calvin handles the matter in his own way, prefacing his brief discussion (he thinks of a form of Platonized Judaism) with a familiar line, in which he has in view the principle of parsimony and clarity he seeks to honor: "As, however, it is not my intention to refute the opinions of others, I shall simply state what appears to me to be the truth, and what may be inferred by sound reasoning" (1996: 133). In consequence his "front matter" is vastly overshadowed by the exegesis and interpretation of the letter itself. The same is true of interpreters as different as Chrysostom, Ambrosiaster, Theodoret, Augustine, Pelagius, Thomas Aquinas, Erasmus, and others. Typically a very short preface or "argument" (drawn in some cases from the superscriptions and subscriptions of the textual tradition) is provided before the more extensive and more significant commentary, paraphrase, homily, or *ennarratio* is set forth. Almost reflexively coordinated with the parsimony of what is given by the canonical portrayal, as measured against historical-critical interests and emphases, interpreters are content with Paul as author and Roman imprisonment as setting, and a basic statement of the problem he appears to be addressing, before moving to the task at hand: interpretation of one of Paul's letters in the context of them all, of the New Testament more generally, and of the Old Testament as Christian scripture.

10. Lincoln 2000:561. We will see below the candid acknowledgment of Wayne Meeks about how earlier questions he had posed about the specific details of the controversy simply proved incapable of final resolution.

11. That the letter can be read profitably by another church is taken by Ambrosiaster as hermeneutically significant. Commenting on 4:16 he writes: "Since the apostle's instructions were universally applicable and his letters written for the benefit of everyone, he directed that this letter should also be read to the Laodiceans so that they might learn from it what they should be doing. He also wanted the Colossians to read their letter, for the same reason" (quoted in Bray 2009: 100).

"Remember My Fetters": Imprisonment in Canon, History, and Theology

Paul's imprisonment is mentioned specifically in several letters (Eph. 3:1; 4:1; 6:20; Phil. 1:13–14; 4:22; Col. 4:3, 10, 18; Phlm. 9; cf. 1 Cor. 15:32; 2 Cor. 1:5–10; 11:23). Colossians is but one of these. The modern commentary in endeavoring to provide the historical setting of the letters will invariably give account of which prison Paul was writing from, discussing the various options, and concluding in favor of one of these. Acts tells us Paul was in prison (very briefly) in Philippi, for two years in Caesarea (after his transfer from Jerusalem by Roman authorities), and of course under house arrest in Rome. In addition, Paul speaks of the experience of imprisonment in 2 Corinthians, and some believe this argues for an Ephesus period of confinement. So the serious candidates have been the last three of these locations, with consideration given to how long it might take to travel from one place to another, the alleged date of the letters in relation to one another, Paul's announced intentions, the overlap of persons named and how to account for them and their movements, and so forth. Some hold that Philippians and Colossians were written from an otherwise unknown incarceration in Ephesus; others that they come from Rome; Caesarea is also a proposed candidate.[12] Philemon and Ephesians are subject to similar analysis. These four letters all mention Paul's imprisonment as a fact unto itself and as the subject of the apostle's own reflections and exhortations.

The general opinion of the earlier tradition tends toward a uniform Roman setting for Ephesians, Philippians, and Colossians, letters that are also in canonical order and grouping (at the end of the collection, the short letter to Philemon is also considered Paul's composition from Roman prison; the overlap of named associates with Colossians is obvious). Yet Colossians was held by Erasmus as having been written in Ephesus, and the tradition is reflected in earlier textual subscriptions (e.g., in the 1388 Wycliffe Bible).[13] An Ephesian imprisonment for

---

12. Representing the Caesarean imprisonment for the composition of Colossians are B. Reicke, W. G. Kümmel, E. Lohmeyer, and J. A. T. Robinson; for the Ephesian imprisonment are the Marcionite Prologue, R. P. Martin, and D. L. Duncan; for the Roman imprisonment are F. F. Bruce, C. F. D. Moule, and D. J. Moo. Dunn 1996: 39–41 inclines toward Rome but accepts Ephesus as a possibility. Lohse 1971: 167 denies Pauline authorship and so favors a late date, which makes the prison idea less historical and more thematic: "In post-Pauline times this situation was generalized, and the Apostle was represented as constantly suffering." Wright 1986: 39 argues for the Ephesian imprisonment for both Colossians and Philemon and the earlier date this requires (52–55), in favor of Paul as author. Barth and Blanke 1994: 126–34 favor the traditional view.

13. "Colossians are also Laodiceans. These are of Asia, and they had been deceived by false apostles. The apostle himself came not to them, but he brings them again to correction by epistle, for they had heard the word of Archippus that had underfonged the ministry into them. Therefore the apostle, now bound, wrote to them from Ephesus by Tychicus the deacon and Onesimus the acolyte" (*The Wycliffe New Testament [1388]*, ed. W. R. Cooper [London: British Library, 2002], 337). Erasmus reproduces this view but then goes on to adjust it: "In our arguments [here he means the Latin arguments found in the Vulgate], Onesimus is added to Tychicus as a colleague [as in the Wycliffe New Testament], just as

the authoring of the letter to the Colossians is another scholarly view, as we have seen, though the reason for the Latin subscription reference to Ephesus is odd and in any event is not explained.[14]

As is well known, the letters of Paul come to us in the manuscript tradition as a collection of letters.[15] The remarkable standardization of the order (Hebrews alone migrates, and the explanations for that are not hard to come by) is noted in recent studies.[16] Trobisch controversially argues that Paul was himself responsible for the editing of the first books (Romans, 1–2 Corinthians, Galatians). He and others notice the obvious fact that the letters are in descending order by length (not breaking up paired letters), and Trobisch speaks of the codex as partly responsible for this (gauging the length of the material to be copied and coordinating the quire of the codex being no simple thing, it is wiser to get the longer works in first so that they not be broken up).

There is one curious exception to this descending order, however. The letter to the Ephesians is longer than its predecessor (Galatians) by over nine hundred characters, yet the copyists never confuse the order of Colossians and its predecessor (Philippians), though it is only about one hundred characters shorter. This suggests to Trobisch a conclusion congenial with his larger theory: that Ephesians and the letters to follow (which are in descending order) are a secondary extension after Paul's death to enlarge his original collection, which had concluded with Galatians. It also raises for him the possibility of aspects of a view (now widely rejected) held by Goodspeed-Knox (see Trobisch 1994: 101n22), that Ephesians was a cover letter composed as a distillate of circulating Pauline letters, intended for multiple audiences. Always hard to explain was why the letter is never first in any list (the lists are remarkable for their uniformity).[17] Though Trobisch speaks of this only in a footnote, the point he allows is that, on his theory, Ephesians would indeed be the first letter of a (nine-letter) extension of the original Pauline letter collection (Romans, 1–2 Corinthians, Galatians), now ending with the Pastorals (and Hebrews).

Paul attests in chapter four; while the Greek subscriptions affirm that it was sent from the city of Rome, certainly it was from Rome that he sent back Onesimus who he had begotten for Christ when he was in chains in that place" (*Collected Works of Erasmus*, ed. R. D. Sider [Toronto: University of Toronto Press, 2009], 43.396). My conjecture is that Erasmus in fact leans toward the Roman setting after all, prefaced by the remark regarding the Latin textual tradition.

14. For other superscriptions and a brief discussion of the peculiarity of the one for 1 Corinthians, see Trobisch 1994: 44–45.

15. The New Testament writings circulate in the manuscript tradition in four groupings: Gospels, Pauline letters (with Hebrews), Acts and General Epistles, and Revelation. This is the order of the Wycliffe Bible of 1388 (which includes as well the letter to the Laodiceans).

16. See Harry Y. Gamble, *Books and Readers in the Early Church: A History of Early Christian Texts* (New Haven: Yale University Press, 1995); and Childs 2008: 5.

17. See Markus Barth, *Ephesians 1–3*, Anchor Bible 34 (New York: Doubleday, 1974), 40; and John Muddiman, *The Epistle to the Ephesians*, Black's New Testament Commentary (Peabody, MA: Hendrickson, 2001), 13, for example.

Introductory Matters

Another possibility is that Ephesians finds its place after Galatians because this allows the theme of imprisonment, missing from Galatians, to be associated with the letters next to follow, where it is prominent. The letters of Paul have indeed been arranged according to descending order. Ephesians has been shifted one place so that it can be read together with Philippians and Colossians. Philemon is simply too short to defy the order principle and has its own logic of location following the letters to Timothy and Titus. First and Second Thessalonians follow naturally after Colossians according to this principle, and then the Pastorals in descending order of length.

If the canonical order is significant for this reason, it may mean that the exact determination of the place of imprisonment (is it Rome, or Ephesus, or Caesarea?) as the original location of the letter's dictation is less decisive. That is, what is crucial is the theological significance of Paul's imprisonment and less our ability to determine the original location, a determination that must rely on a correct account of the proper historical order of the letters' composition, and thus a dismissal of significance in the canonical presentation as such. The canonical presentation may well favor the Roman imprisonment over a more oblique Ephesian or Caesarean one, considered strictly historically. My own view is that the traditional position of Ephesians, Philippians, and Colossians as written by Paul in Rome is the one suggested by the presentation of the letters themselves, given what they choose to share with us.

Returning then to the earlier history of interpretation, note the way Chrysostom discusses the imprisonment setting and its significance, as he moves from letter to letter. Concerning Ephesians: "He wrote the Epistle from Rome, and, as he informs us, in bonds" (2004: 49). Regarding Philippians: "But when he wrote to them, it happened that he was in bonds. Therefore he says, 'So that my bonds became manifest in Christ in the whole pretorium,' calling the palace of Nero the pretorium" (2004: 181).[18] A sort of crescendo is then reached when Chrysostom comes to Colossians and summarizes:

> Holy indeed are all the Epistles of Paul: but some advantage have those that he sent after he was in bonds: those, for instance, to the Ephesians and Philemon: that to Timothy, that to the Philippians, and the one before us: for this also was sent when he was a prisoner, since he writes in it thus: "for which I am also in bonds: that I may make it manifest as I ought to speak." (Col. iv.3, 4.) ... And it is evident from hence: that in the Epistle to Philemon he says "Being such an one as Paul the aged" (ver. 9), and makes request for Onesimus; but in this he sends Onesimus himself, as he says, "With Onesimus the faithful and beloved brother"

18. That modern scholars today speak of the pretorium as more of a group than a place ("the pretorium guard") does not answer the question of location. Gordon Fee strongly defends the pretorium guard as "the emperor's own elite troops stationed in Rome" rejecting alternatives in Ephesus or Caesarea; *Paul's Letter to the Philippians*, New International Commentary on the New Testament (Grand Rapids: Eerdmans, 1995), 35.

30

(Col. iv.9). . . . Wherefore also he boldly says in this Epistle, "from the hope of the gospel that you heard, which was preached in all creation under heaven" (Col. i.23). For it had now been preached a long time. I think then that the Epistle to Timothy was written after this; and when he was now come to the very end of his life. (Chrysostom 2004: 257)

He then continues, answering the question he had posed:

But why do I say that these Epistles have some advantage over the rest in this respect, because he writes while in bonds? As if a champion were to write in the midst of carnage and victory; so also in truth did he. For himself too was aware that this was a great thing, for writing to Philemon he saith, "Whom I have begotten in my bonds" (ver. 10). And this he said, that we be not dispirited when in adversity, but even rejoice. At this place was Philemon with these (Colossians). (Chrysostom 2004: 257)

Chrysostom, observing the canonical presentation and the suggestions it makes for interpretation, notes several important things. First is the theme of imprisonment associating Ephesians, Philippians, and Colossians, augmented by Philemon. Second is the way the presentation unfolds into theological interpretation. The bondage gives evidence of the lavish grace of God, enabling Paul to "raise trophies" and, by so doing, to encourage and exhort others. And lastly, he sees the aged Paul in his bonds and in his seniority nevertheless raising up the next generation, by the ministry of his letter writing and by his final personal actions, with Timothy and with Onesimus.

The canonical form brokers basic historical information but at the service of theological significance, as Chrysostom offers his homily: now in the place of the apostle, following carefully his legacy of personal and literary witness. It is time to consider what I call the occasion of the letter's construction, within the ministry of the apostle, taking my cue from the canonical presentation and the apprehension of it by a commentator like Chrysostom.

Why Did Paul Compose a Letter to the Colossians?

An answer frequently given is that Epaphras asked him to do so.

This is of course far too simple an answer but certainly aspects of it are correct. The "beloved fellow servant" is mentioned very early in the letter (1:7), and the same man "who is one of yourselves" sends greetings through Paul at the close (4:12). Colossae is an insignificant city in the Lycus Valley of Asia Minor, compared with Ephesus (the third largest city in the Roman Empire) and even the more excellent Laodicea just eight miles away. Paul had never visited the city (2:1) though he was present in Ephesus some eighty miles away for a period of three years, preaching and teaching.[19] Epaphras brought the gospel to the church (1:7), and in the context of the letter he is the one who informed Paul about their faith, which he calls "your love in the Spirit" (1:8).

As I have already mentioned, Paul's exhortations in 2:8–23 imply that he has learned from Epaphras of issues in the Colossian (and Laodicean; see 4:16) context that give him concern. But the letter does not begin with this set of issues and instead moves from thanksgiving (1:3–8) to assurances of intercession (1:9–14) to a description of the supremacy of Christ (1:15–23) and indeed to rejoicing over their "firmness of faith" (1:24–2:7)—before he sets forth his address to these concerns.

In that sense, the letter to the Colossians is not unlike other letters of Paul, written to correct and shepherd a flock, yet one he does not have firsthand knowledge of and has never visited. Unlike Romans, it is not an extended treatise or epideixis, and it does speak to specific issues of local concern. The letter to the Romans, like Colossians, also addresses an audience Paul knows about only secondhand, but one that he will in fact eventually visit (Acts 28:16–30).[20] Such a reality appears now more wistful in the case of Colossians, probably due to the uncertain fate of Paul in Rome (Phlm. 22).

The Occasion of Paul's Writing

It is here that the second major consideration for the occasion of Paul's writing must be mentioned. To recap, Colossians is written to a church Paul has never visited. It discusses a set of problems Paul has heard about secondhand. It does not begin with this concern but instead on a more personal note. It is a letter that can be read by another one close by with profit. It has been argued that the letter to the Ephesians—which is so close in language and content as to be regarded by many as developed on the basis of Colossians—was likewise addressed not to one specific congregation only, but to the churches throughout the region.[21]

19. Theodoret (2001: 84) believes Paul had actually visited Colossae, though his view is unusual and is not shared by his Antiochene colleague Chrysostom.

20. Most believe Romans was written from Corinth. That Acts ends with Paul in Rome and is then followed by Romans closes the gap in some sense (at least in the orders where Acts precedes the Pauline Epistles) by reversing the chronological order. The preaching Paul is shown to undertake in Rome at the end of Acts finds an exemplar in Romans. The concerns Paul articulated at the close of the letter also proved to be true (15:22–33). See L. E. Keck's comments in *Romans*, Abingdon Biblical Commentary (Nashville: Abingdon, 2005), 21. For the majority of the orders, Acts introduces the General Epistles. There is evidence of Acts positioned after the Gospels and before the Pauline corpus in the Marcionite fragment, Irenaeus, Tertullian, and Origen. See the brief discussion in Childs 2008: 225–26.

21. This is a view widely held, and not just for those who find persuasive the Goodspeed-Knox idea of Ephesians as a distillate of other Pauline letters written to introduce them. Theodore of Mopsuestia held the view that it was actually written by Paul *before* he visited there, a curiosity demanded by what he saw as its lack of concrete details regarding the Ephesian church (where Paul was active for three years). See the discussion in Theodoret 2001: 31–32. He rejects this view in a lengthy introduction.

The occasion for writing, in the light of these several factors, cannot be the specifics of a problem Paul is concerned about and solely that. In this letter Paul is speaking about himself and about the way he is coming to understand his apostolic office, in the light of changed and probably unforeseen circumstances, over against the ministry he is depicted as undertaking in Acts. Note the following distinctives:

1. Paul is "we"—joined chiefly by Timothy but also by Epaphras and all those named in 4:7–17. His ministry is a joint one. It is one that began with the work of others and grows independently of him (1:1–8).

2. Paul's ministry is prayer and intercession, and he calls attention to this because he wants the church at Colossae—which he never visited and did not plant—to understand the significance of this form of his apostleship alongside the vocation he can be seen, for example, to exercise in Acts. It is a ministry of exertion and labor with its own character (Col. 1:9–14; 2:1–7).

3. Paul's ministry is one of mature theological clarification before it is one of problem address. The similarity with (the more extended) Ephesian discourse is obvious, especially in Col. 1:15–20. Before we hear of angels and elemental spirits and the challenges they represent and that Paul addresses, we hear of Christ and his all-embracing reign.

4. Paul is writing a letter whose occasion is borne of his own self-reflection and a new understanding of his apostleship in Christ, the result of prayer and companionship in prison, in the later years of his life. The main opening units of the letter make clear that this occasion is every bit as important as the specifics of the church situation in Colossae, as this has been related to Paul by Epaphras. The gospel is spreading in ways Paul could never have anticipated, independently of him. He is in bonds. The gospel is unhindered. Indeed it spreads because of this.[22]

Given this reality being borne in on him, Paul has occasion to consider the way God has been at work in him quite apart from his own early intentions and plans, as God vouchsafed them to him—both as reported in Acts and in the specifics of letters considered to be earlier, where Paul addresses congregations he has himself planted or visited. He speaks of a mystery whose final purpose is now becoming clear, and by that he means the way God was intending always,

---

22. Chrysostom, Melanchthon, and Calvin all note the rhetorical effect of beginning the letter in this way and so put this down as flattering the audience before Paul brings up the serious matters he deals with in Col. 2. But is this the real point of the opening units of the letter? Erasmus likewise offers a paraphrase of the letter in which matters to be dealt with in Col. 2 are explicitly referred to here and there in the movement of 1:1–2:8, thus anticipating and giving prominence to the occasional specifics Paul will address in 2:9–23. This is not to take seriously the content and intention of the material as it takes its place in the canonical shape of the letter.

by the cross of Christ, to address those outside the covenants, placing them in the end on a footing with its own logic alongside that of the covenant people of address and promise (1:26–27; cf. Rom. 11:25–36; Eph. 3:1–13). But he does not speak of this as an independent revelation or theological datum, worthy as it is on those terms of expression and proclamation. He speaks of this, rather, in direct connection to his own "divine office" (Col. 1:25) "given to me for you." This divine office is tied up with the mystery of dual citizenship, in God's hidden and revealed plans, but it also has to do *with a fresh revelation of the character of his own vocation, now being borne in him in Christ.* This explains why, before he says a thing about the specifics of the Colossian situation, he speaks of thanksgiving (1:3–8), petition and intercession (1:9–14), the protological Christ (a truth likewise only now being made clear, though there at the beginning; 1:15–20), and a transfer from estrangement (1:21–23) to an "inheritance of the saints in the light" (1:12). Paul is here speaking of a ministry given to him, part of a much larger plan entailing "every creature under heaven" (1:23).

It is at this point that Paul—in an audacious manner—puts his finger on an understanding of his vocation that has been borne in him and that explains why his apostleship of prayer, mutual thanksgiving, new revelation, and sacramental disclosure takes the form it does, as its own kind of mystery revealed. I have noted the theme of imprisonment associating the letters placed side by side (Ephesians, Philippians, Colossians) and Paul's commendation of his circumstances as worthy of remembrance and reflection. I believe this is also a strong reason for Paul's writing to the Colossians and helps explain why the letter unfolds as it does. Paul is giving explanation for an apostleship that exists now differently from how he had exercised that previously, as church planter and shepherd. Paul wants the Colossians to know that this vocation is continuous with his previous role, though he is now bound up and geographically limited in prison. Unlike Philippians, where Paul is also in prison and writing from a distance, Paul had no personal contact with the church in Colossae. For different reasons, the "letter to the churches who are also faithful in Christ Jesus" (Eph. 1:1) is written without comment on the specifics Paul might be concerned to address in that church and instead takes the form of a long theological treatise.[23] It too mentions Paul's imprisonment in connection with the mystery of God's intention vis-à-vis the Gentiles (3:1–13), and this is one of the passages notable for its close relationship to Colossians.

So in my view Colossians brings to a crescendo—alongside the features noted by Chrysostom—Paul's mature theological reflections on his vocation as an apostle, given the context of imprisonment and affliction. He writes in Col. 1:24: "Now I rejoice in the sufferings for your sake, and in my flesh I complete what is lacking: in Christ's afflictions for the sake of his body, that is, the church."

---

23. Was the letter always meant to address multiple churches? See the discussion of Nils A. Dahl, *Studies in Paul: Theology for the Early Christian Mission* (Eugene OR: Wipf & Stock, 2002).

The interpretation of the verse—given its prominence in the history of interpretation and the possibility of misinterpretation—will be the topic of the commentary at its proper place. For now, let it simply be said that Paul has come to understand there to be an ongoing work in respect of proclaiming the gospel—to Jew and Gentile, in the light of the mystery hidden and revealed—that is Christ's extended and intentional work, accomplished on the cross and now working its way through to completion "to every creature under heaven, and of which I, Paul, became a minister" (1:23). In Paul's personal apostleship, there is a sharing of Christ's afflictions, as the body is related to the head. Nothing is lacking in Christ's earthly afflictions—the passage does not refer of course to Christ's work of reconciliation on the cross—save the shared work of proclaiming his finished work, which entails a kindred affliction, ongoing, for the risen and exalted Lord and for his body the church.[24]

This is a message Paul wants to share with the Colossians because it explains that his absence and his imprisonment are precisely in accordance with God's plans for his apostleship in relation to them and, rather than hindering the spread of the gospel, insure its fulfillment. One can see the relation between the work of the cross—the radical emptying that brings about the once-for-all fulfillment—and Paul's own prison dying (and experience of affliction; 2 Cor. 11:13–33), and between them both and the manifold Old Testament types (Jonah, Ezekiel, the Suffering Servant, Jeremiah, the Davidic voice of the Psalms, Moses). Paul does not begin with an effort to exhort them in respect of challenges specific to their Colossian experience of false teachers, because he wants them first to understand the character of the apostleship he has come to see is deeply intrinsic to it and to the gospel he wishes to proclaim. He is not rhetorically easing them into a position where they can hear a stern word of correction and warning, but is proclaiming a gospel in which his identity and vocation are now explicable in the light of Christ's own ongoing work as risen Lord of the church.

Colossians, Ephesians, and the Beginnings of a Collection Concept

Since at least the 1872 monograph of H. J. Holtzman, who sought to clarify the relationship of Colossians and Ephesians, great effort has been expended more precisely to define the patterns of dependence that might explain the overlaps between the two letters (as well as Philemon's relationship to Colossians), if not also account for the changed style and syntax of them both.[25] That the evidence

24. For a thorough discussion of the history of interpretation, see John Reumann, "Colossians 1:24 ('What Is Lacking in the Afflictions of Christ'): History of Exegesis and Ecumenical Advance," *Currents in Theology and Mission* 17 (1990): 454–61.

25. "The author of Ephesians not only first imitated an original Colossians, but subsequently interpolated Colossians with material from Ephesians" (Childs 1984: 317). Compare the modern treatment of Muddiman, who holds that Ephesians is a later edition of a genuine letter, intended to remain faithful to Paul but also edited to direct his teaching toward later circumstances (*Epistle to the*

has been used to argue for discontinuity and continuity both, and the lack of anything like a firm consensus regarding authorship forthcoming after generations of labor, means that the canonical portrayal simply does not yield the kind of data necessary for scholarly resolution at this level.

Brevard Childs makes an important observation about the canonical shape of the letter to the Ephesians with implications for Colossians as well. He notes the textual evidence that allows for the view (held in antiquity as well as more recently) that the letter once addressed more than one church (Eph. 1:1), and was only secondarily related (in some way) to a specifically Ephesian congregation (i.e., some believe this interpolation refers to where the letter landed and was treasured, in one case, and not to whom it was specifically addressed by the author). He sees the force for an argument for post-Pauline composition, but concludes the canon does not allow us to decide for this categorically. Elements of continuity exist alongside alleged discontinuity:

> What distinguishes the Ephesian letter from the great majority of Pauline letters is that the canonical intention to shape the original letter in such a way as to render it accessible to later generations of believers did not take place on the redactional level. The textual expansion in 1.1 ["to the saints who are *at Ephesus and* faithful"] only confirms this basic point. Rather, it is reflected in the primary level of the composition, which is to say, that it derives from the author's own intention. The concern to address a new generation of Christians, unknown to Paul, is a small step removed from a growing consciousness of the role of the canon which performed a similar function. The point to be made is that the grounds for the subsequent canonical process extend back into the actual compositional level of the New Testament literature itself. (Childs 1984: 326)

A similar point was made about the note with which Colossians concludes, which speaks of a transfer of letters. Long ago Ambrosiaster commented on 4:16: "Since the apostle's instructions were universally applicable and written for the benefit of everyone, he directed that this letter should also be read to the Laodiceans so that they might learn from it what they should be doing. He also wanted the Colossians to read their letter, for the same reason" (quoted in Bray 2009: 100).

The commendation of Paul's apostolic office and the clarification of it to the Colossians can find association with what we read in the other "captivity letters" even as it makes its own very particular contribution. What Childs says about Ephesians, and what he and others indicate about the character of Colossians, is true about them both in conjunction. That is, the "compositional level" of the New Testament literature, to which Childs refers above in respect of a single letter, is a shared feature in the case of a different letter (Colossians), and the Pastoral

Ephesians, 20–24). He believes the parallels with Colossians are too varying to think primarily of a letter composed on the basis of it.

Epistles will represent a yet further example of such broadening. Is it possible to decide at what moment we are speaking of "the compositional level" and what he calls a "consciousness of canon," on the one hand, and when we are speaking of something like the effect of association when more than one letter is under consideration on the other hand?

The point I wish to make is that comparative studies of language, syntax, and themes take us only so far and may not be able to resolve the matter (of relationship and dependence) given what the canon shares with us when it comes to the literary form of individual letters. What seems clear is that both Colossians and Ephesians—for similar and for different reasons—represent efforts to speak more broadly than an account of them focused only on "the Colossian heresy" or the "Ephesian situation" would allow. Something else is going on. That both letters participate in this move toward shared meaning—the churches in Asia Minor, in the case of Ephesians, or the way Paul's apostolic office is larger than an individual church context, or concerns Paul may have about concrete challenges to be faced in a congregation, as with Colossians—may well suggest that canonical shaping is extending beyond individual letters and has to do with the phenomenon of an emerging collection as such.[26] So in addition to compositional level and canon we might need an intermediate conception as well. It is not that far a cry from "have this letter read at that church" to "please read Colossians and Ephesians and other letters in the light of one another," for that is a kindred idea, congenial with what we might mean by an author's intention historically determined.

The point for present purposes is that when it comes to the distinctive theme of Paul's afflictions, as Colossians sets this out, it is hard to isolate interpretation of this from what is said elsewhere about Paul's experience of imprisonment and the character of his apostolic office. This is not a matter of determining dependence or noting thematic similarities between books, but flows from the notion of wider intention in the scope of a single writing, especially when one can see this happening in more than one letter at the same time. To simply discuss the phenomenon in terms of "Paul" or "non-Paul" shifts the question to matters of historicality, which on the one hand cannot be resolved and which furthermore may not deal with the hermeneutical challenge of the canonical reality before us.

The historical Paul and the canonical Paul simply cannot be easily extricated, and this may go back into the compositional and associative levels of his letters both. Paul has become aware that his letter writing is a form of apostolic ministry with its own integrity and afterlife, especially in the form of letters in emerging collective association. This is evidenced in the compositional level of more than

26. E. J. Goodspeed (*The Meaning of Ephesians* [Chicago: University of Chicago Press, 1933]) thinks in terms of letters that were scattered and needed to be gathered up (and of the concern for a Paul fading from view). But the idea of sharing (so Colossians) and of a general epistle like Ephesians intended for more than one church points instead to a concern for preservation possibly at work in the very act of conceiving and composing a letter.

one letter, and in my view is manifested in Colossians by virtue of its final literary form, where concern for the specific challenges in a congregation is registered through the lens of reflections on the apostolic office in the broadest sense. Philemon speaks of Paul as both aged and a prisoner. What flows from that reality is precisely the sort of reflection on his apostolic office we see in Colossians.

Paul's Letters and the Scriptures of Israel

There is much interest at present by New Testament specialists in understanding Paul's use of the Old Testament. Paul's use of the Old Testament differs from book to book, and studies of Paul as Old Testament interpreter may choose to focus on a single letter or, in the case of wider studies, will operate under the strictures that one must determine which of the Pauline letters are authentic and then limit the investigation to those letters.

Colossians offers a special challenge because the Old Testament does not appear in the letter in the familiar form of a formula citation ("as Isaiah said" or "so it is written"). What we have are allusions or echoes.[27] Why does this happen? Is it to do with the audience addressed? Is it a sign of the non-Pauline character of the letter? In this section I address the questions in the light of my concern to understand the implications of the letter collection form.

But it is important to understand that the influence of the Old Testament ranges more widely than a study of citations may typically appreciate. I leave aside for a moment the more specific question of where such studies are headed theologically and hermeneutically. Does one seek to understand Paul's use of the Old Testament because in some sense it is materially normative for Christian use of the Old Testament in the church today, that is, the historical precision in understanding this phenomenon is at the service of hermeneutical imitation? The church should imitate Paul's exegetical freedom with respect to the Old Testament, and that freedom extends to appropriation of the New Testament as well.[28] Or, alternatively, the church imitates the exegesis of Paul and is in some sense hedged about by the proper appreciation of how he goes about his work in this regard.[29] This is only one way to think about the role of the Old Testament as Christian scripture when it comes to the letters of Paul in the New Testament canon. Before moving to a discussion along these lines (i.e., the material appearance of the Old Testament in Colossians and what to make of that), I will start with reflection at a different level. This is because the influence of the Old Testament is not to be restricted to this material use only or what we might understand to be Paul's

27. Beetham uses the term (indebted to Richard Hays's earlier study) in the title of his 2008 monograph.

28. Andrew Lincoln, "Hebrews and Biblical Theology," in *Out of Egypt: Biblical Theology and Biblical Interpretation*, ed. C. Bartholomew (Grand Rapids: Zondervan, 2004), 313–38.

29. This is closer to the position of Richard Hays in *Echoes of Scripture in the Letters of Paul* (New Haven: Yale University Press, 1989).

human intentions as exegete and thinker, as exposed by a study of his citations or allusions. If the history of interpretation of the Pauline corpus shows us anything, it is that a modern inquiry into the techniques by which Paul handles the scriptures of Israel would represent a limitation in respect of what is judged to be significant about the horizon these scriptures continue to have in the Christian church, now in possession of a two-testament canon.

The Thirteen-Letter Collection and the Book of the Twelve

Leaving aside the Pastoral Epistles—letters written not to churches but to individuals (Timothy, Titus, Philemon)—the small letter to the Colossians is third from the end in the sequence of the letter collection, followed by 1–2 Thessalonians.[30] That is, Colossians is the third smallest "church letter." It is but four chapters, or about the length of the compact Old Testament books of Ruth or Jonah.

In the Old Testament a long narrative (historical) section sits astride the prophetic genre books (the three major and twelve minor prophets), called by scholars the Deuteronomistic History whose concluding books are 1–2 Kings. The point of contact between this historical chronicle and the prophetic books is most obvious in the superscriptions of the prophetic books: six of the Minor Prophets are correlated with the reigns of specific kings, accounts of which are supplied by the Deuteronomistic Historian: "The word of the LORD that came to Hosea son of Beeri, in the days of Uzziah, Jotham, Ahaz, and Hezekiah, kings of Judah, and in the days of Jeroboam son of Joash, king of Israel" is how the superscription of the first of the twelve Minor Prophets reads; and similar chronological notices, typically less full, now stand at the head of the books of Amos, Micah, Zephaniah, and the postexilic prophets Haggai and Zechariah. Other than that, the individual (Minor) prophets play no actual role in the literary unfolding of the history itself. Only Jonah is mentioned (briefly, at 2 Kgs. 14:25). The (Major) prophet Isaiah is mentioned in 2 Kgs. 18–20 (the text itself is very close to Isa. 36–39), and Jeremiah is argued to have been edited by the same hands that gave final form to the History itself.

In the New Testament, the narrative (historical) chronicle of Acts likewise provides a loose interpretative framework for the thirteen letters of Paul. The points of contact are greater yet also different in kind. In Acts the letter writing of Paul is never mentioned. Several communities for which we now have Pauline letters are, however, mentioned and Paul's missionary contact with them described. In consequence, it is usually thought helpful to have some sense of Paul's missionary journeys in mind when reading the letters of Paul. The Philippian, Thessalonian, Corinthian, and Ephesian correspondence can be associated with what we know about Paul's actual activity in Acts (in that order in Acts 16:11–20:38), and indeed

---

30. The letter to Philemon is written as well to Apphia and Archippus and "the church in your house" (Phlm. 1–2).

most modern accounts of Paul's letters (and theology) assume we must get the letters in the correct historical sequence if we are properly to interpret and understand them; here Acts is brought into service.[31] The same has been held with regard to the twelve Minor Prophets.

Romans, the longest of Paul's letters and so in first place, picks up where Acts leaves off (with Paul in the Rome he had said he hoped to visit at the end of the letter to the Romans, written on his second missionary journey, according to most correlations, from Corinth; see Acts 18 and the mention of the Jews from Rome, Aquila and Priscilla). The author of Acts, Luke, is also likely the "Luke the physician" who has joined Paul in prison, according to Col. 4:14 (cf. Phlm. 24).[32] The final chapters of Acts end with the first-person-plural "we" (from 16:10 to the end), and that seems a natural way to think as well about Paul and Luke in fellowship at the close of Colossians, if not also at the beginning (Col. 1:3–14).[33] Aristarchus, one of Paul's Jewish brothers also in prison with him (4:10), is mentioned briefly in Acts 19:29 and 27:2, in the nearer sea approach of Paul and Luke to Rome (from Malta). And of course Timothy is Paul's close companion in Acts (16:1). He is certainly to be thought of as integral to Paul's "we" address at the opening of Colossians ("we always thank God"; Col. 1:3). The letter to the Colossians is sent from Paul and Timothy (cf. 1–2 Thessalonians to follow; 2 Corinthians and Philippians earlier).

Similar to the relationship between the twelve Minor Prophets and the history recorded in Kings, the book of Acts and the Pauline letter collection have not come to us in a form originating in, or headed toward, a concern for tidy correlations at every point.[34] The respective books have their own integrity and their

31. As we have seen, the letters to the Ephesians and to the Philippians are written from a later context of prison, most likely in Rome. The letter to the Ephesians is probably intended to be read in a number of different churches, and it lacks any mention of specifics in the Ephesian church, such as we have in detail in Acts—unusual given the length of time Paul spent there. To account for this oddity, Theodore held the position that it was written before Paul arrived. This was clearly an effort to account for the absence of details, which in the modern period is handled differently by recourse to critical theory (Ephesians is a later, non-Pauline letter).

32. Oddly enough, Calvin contests this (1996: 230), believing that the appellation "the Physician" intends to distinguish him from "the Evangelist." He also holds the curious view that Onesimus (4:9) is not the slave of Philemon (1996: 227). This is the incipient "historical-critical" Calvin, in my view.

33. This may also be one reason why what is likely the earliest order (Acts introducing the General Epistles) can also be joined in time by the one familiar in modern English printed Bibles (Acts before Romans and the letters of Paul). See the discussion of Childs 2008: 225–26; compare Trobisch 1994: 9–10.

34. "The canonical collectors sought to preserve both the Pauline letters and the book of Acts. By so doing they established a context for the reading of Acts which was different from that of the original author of Acts who composed his book without recourse to the Pauline letters. Secondly, the literary effect of this new context is clear, regardless of whether or not the church fathers gave explicit formulation of its role. Because Acts offers a narrative of Paul's ministry with fixed chronological and geographical sequence, it provided the framework into which Paul's letters which lacked a sequence were fitted. This traditional use of Acts as the interpretive guide to the Pauline letters has been assumed by the church because of the canonical collection and not challenged until the rise of the critical method discovered tension between the materials" (Childs 1984: 239).

own literary history. Paul never visited Colossae, and so nothing can be gleaned in any specific way about it from Acts. Colossians makes clear that what Paul knows about the church there he knows from Epaphras (1:7; 4:12) and perhaps from Archippus (4:17). Philemon also belongs to the church at Colossae, and Archippus is mentioned again in that letter as a member of the church "in your house" (Phlm. 2). Onesimus is "one of yourselves" Col. 4:9 tells us, and together with the letter carrier Tychicus, Paul says at the close of the letter, "they will tell you everything that has taken place here."

The thirteen-letter collection of Paul and the prophetic collection of the Twelve can be fruitfully compared. There is no evidence that the former was given a template in the latter in any specific sense. Rather, kindred concerns for guarding the specificity of the occasion of prophetic and apostolic activity, but also shaping a written testimony for future generations, are what overlay the development of both collections.

In both instances, a concern for chronology and orderly historical sequence is not the main issue at work in the collections.[35] The books and the letters can of course be placed in this kind of order, with the aid of history and of Acts and based upon internal arguments. This tracks well with the prophetic and apostolic material having emerged from specific historical occasions.[36] But the canonical form has not sought to make this the main feature for their interpretation. In the case of the Twelve, undated witnesses (from arguably later historical contexts) have been placed next to the dated ones (these are in a general historical sequence, leaving aside the arguments for the earlier date of Amos as against Hosea). The effect is not to generate concern for locating these undated witnesses in the same periods of their dated neighbors, though this has often been the assumed reason for their location (Jerome held this view; others demurred). Rather, their placement is thematic, and the occasion for this is theological, concerned to release a former prophetic word into a new future of address.

That the thirteen-letter collection moves from longer to shorter witnesses points to a different logic of arrangement. That does not prevent features emerging that indicate intentional shaping. The prologue to Romans, it is argued, functions to introduce not just that individual witness, but serves as an appropriate summarizing

35. Chrysostom comments on order in the Pauline letters and in the Twelve, in the introduction ("The Argument") to his *Homilies on Paul's Epistle to Romans* (thanks to Robert Kashow for this citation): "And that to the Galatians seems to me to be before that to the Romans. But if they have a different order in the Bibles, that is nothing wonderful, since the Twelve Prophets, though not exceeding one another in order of time, but standing at great intervals from one another, are in the arrangement of the Bible placed in succession. Thus Haggai and Zachariah and the Messenger prophesied after Ezekiel and Daniel, and long after Jonah and Zephaniah and all the rest. Yet they are nevertheless joined with all those from whom they stand so far off in time." Chrysostom's comment about the Minor Prophets is not entirely clear, but he seems to be noting that Ezekiel should appear in sequence before the final three Minor Prophets, but finds his place elsewhere. Other than that, he believes the Twelve are in historical succession, though separated by "great intervals."

36. Standard introductions usually place the letters and the prophets in historical order and understand this to be necessary for proper interpretation. See my discussion in *Prophecy and Hermeneutics* (Grand Rapids: Baker Academic, 2007).

entry for the collection proper.[37] I also note above the mislocation of Ephesians and seek explanation for this in the concern to place the prison letters next to one another, with the associating refrain "remember my bonds" in Col. 4:8 (so also Chrysostom 2004: 49, 181, 257). It is difficult not to see in the conclusion of the collection a significant transition, from Paul to the next generation that will carry on after him (Timothy and Titus). The Paul of Philemon is both prisoner for Christ and the aged apostle who has given birth to Onesimus in baptism.

As with the Twelve, the historical specificity of the Pauline letters is never subsumed into an abstract theological system, but retains all its rooted significance, as the real Paul confronts real problems and real hopes in real communities. The ordering from longer to shorter is clearly a mechanical feature that has emerged from the context of a secondary organization, with its own constraints. But this has not prevented the collection serving as "the church's guide for reading Paul"—a guide whose achievement is to relate to future generations the concrete witness of the historical Paul, but that has seen in the man and his letters a consciousness deeply rooted in the historical specifics themselves, that Paul's achievement is God's achievement in him. This means that history serves the purpose of transparency to God's use of Paul and cannot be isolated as theologically or objectively significant in its own register. To declare some letters (1) much later and (2) at distinct odds with the pure teaching of Paul is to undo the historical specificity of the letter collection as its own achievement, in the name of another species of history (i.e., the non-Pauline letters are capitulations to this or that later social force).

As with the book of the Twelve, the later witnesses are theologically integral to the earlier proclamations, because the one God is inspiring the former and latter things under his own providential ordering of time. In the Pauline letter collection, the temporal span is of course far more compressed, and the letters are all associated with a single inspired witness. But the effect is the same. The present letter collection guards the historical specificity (as Acts in the New Testament and 1–2 Kings in the Old Testament speak of that), but also allows for development and movement. These are the consequence of changed circumstances in the churches addressed, as well as the march of time as Paul himself experiences this, as the one untimely called and untimely superintended both. He will come to understand that his final vocation, prisoner in chains, slave for Christ, is to give thanks for the spread of the gospel apart from his own efforts and to place into the hands of the next generation a testimony that God bequeathed to him through the scriptures and bequeathed in him, in the legacy of his letters. Second Peter concludes on precisely this note, as the logic of Paul the letter writer is grasped in all its significance: "And count the forbearance of the Lord as salvation. So also our brother Paul wrote to you according to the wisdom given to him, speaking of

---

37. See Childs 2008: 66; and Robert Wall, "Romans 1:1–15: An Introduction to the Pauline Corpus of the New Testament," in *The New Testament as Canon*, ed. Robert Wall and E. E. Lemcio, Journal for the Study of the New Testament Supplement 76 (Sheffield: Sheffield Academic, 1992), 142–60.

this as he does *in all his letters.* There are some things in them hard to understand, which the ignorant and unstable twist to their own destruction, *as they do the other scriptures*" (2 Pet. 3:15–16, emphasis added).

In the Pauline letter collection, it is one and the same Paul who speaks to specific communities a specific gospel word of address and who releases his letters to new purpose under God's providential care. One cannot pull these two Pauls apart without destroying the historical integrity of the letters themselves as they maintain this balance, going back to Paul himself. Peter speaks of "all his letters" and relates them reflexively to the inherited scriptural testimony, the Old Testament. In time it will be not just the "twisting" to different purpose but also the selection and truncation of the letters that causes misunderstanding and destruction (as Peter puts it); so, e.g., Marcion's "Paul." Reading Paul by focusing on individual letters to the isolation of others is precisely what the canonical form seeks to guard against. This can be done in the name of historical precision, or by application of a theory of what must be non-Pauline, or because of theological preference, even under the congenial rubric of "canon within a canon." The canonical form, by contrast, seeks to attach Paul's authorizing significance evenly across the thirteen books and resists various theories of developmentalism, pristine origins, or special theological privilege.

Influence of the Scriptures of Israel and the New Testament as Canon

This brings us to a second matter of equal importance, when one thinks of the role of the Old Testament and Paul's letter legacy. I have mentioned already the interest by New Testament specialists in Paul's use of the Old Testament. In Colossians, we have an additional challenge because the book does not show a Paul using scripture by means of formal citation. Instead, the Old Testament makes its force felt through allusions. Two recent studies seek to give precision to this, with the number and character of allusions set forth and evaluated.[38] So, for example, Paul speaks of the gospel "bearing fruit and growing" (1:6), and this is taken to be an echo of Gen. 1:28. The unhindered spread of the gospel is happening under the authority of the image of the invisible God (Col. 1:15), the new Adam. Beetham finds ten such echoes in the letter to the Colossians, from across the Old Testament; his doctoral supervisor, Greg Beale, detected and argued for seventeen; and Barth and Blanke, Hubner, Fee, and others have their own enumerations (see Beetham 2008: 6–7 for full discussion on these scholars).

In addition to such listings and their evaluation is a related set of questions. Why does Paul adopt this manner of citation when elsewhere he is more explicit? Does this lean in the direction of arguing against genuine Pauline authorship? Beetham, for his part, sees in the avoidance of formula citation an indication that Paul wants Christ to be taken by the Colossians as the true Torah; Torah itself, he

---

38. Beetham 2008; and G. K. Beale, "Colossians," in *Commentary on the New Testament Use of the Old Testament,* ed. G. K. Beale and D. A. Carson (Grand Rapids: Baker Academic, 2007), 841–70.

wants the Colossians to conclude, is a "faithful, if incomplete, source of revelation and wisdom" (2008: 262).

Further questions arise. Scholarly studies can detect these echoes, but how many would have been picked up by Paul's actual audience in Colossae?[39] This question touches on a larger area of debate, namely, audience competence and its significance for understanding an authorial intention and purpose. Must Paul cite scripture (or allude to it) only in accordance with what he knows or presumes about the competence of his audience? Does Paul write letters like Romans, Ephesians, or Colossians—more literary than private letters—with only a single audience in view, or rather is his assumption of a wider currency and application? In my view this question is tied up with the actual phenomenon of scripture citation and allusion, both. I will deal with the question of the appearance and significance of individual allusions in the commentary proper. At issue here is the more general question of the status of the Old Testament as scripture.

Beetham thinks that the avoidance of formula citation by Paul indicates significance in a transfer of authority from Torah to Christ, which Paul has come to see. At the same time, on the question of audience competence, he otherwise draws the conclusion that Paul commends scripture at the close of the letter (3:16) precisely because he assumes that, whatever audience he addresses, he expects that they will study the scriptures in the course of their becoming mature in Christ. The allusions he registers in the letter, their own sustained encounter with scripture will in time reveal. In the context of regular worship and the hearing of scripture, the church at Colossae would become competent inhabitants of the symbolic universe of scripture, as Beetham puts it. He concludes his speculations in this way: "It is also possible that Paul wrote with especially the functionally literate in view, some of whom would certainly have held leadership roles in the churches, and expected of them to teach and explain his message to the rest of the congregation, including its Old Testament foundations" (2008: 257).

The question I pose is whether this evaluation is far too restricted by a view of strict "authorial conscious intention" at a number of levels. Paul alludes to scripture. This is an intentional matter: on its own face and because, so it is argued, of a wish to avoid formula citation. Paul then also commends scripture and assumes the congregation and/or its leadership will so learn, teach, and instruct that allusions will be grasped for their significance. This particular view also makes Paul the center of attention vis-à-vis the scriptures, whose importance lies in the area of foundations for understanding his thought and purpose, communicated through his letter. The scriptures' eventual significance turns on their resourcefulness for filling out Paul's original communicative intention in an individual letter to a church who reads it.

There is of course another way of speaking about this, which is centered less on "Paul the author" and more on "Paul the authored." On this account, Paul is

39. Christopher D. Stanley, *Arguing with Scripture: The Rhetoric of Quotations in the Letters of Paul* (New York: T&T Clark, 2004), esp. chap. 3.

less self-conscious of the allusions he is making. The scriptures are projecting their horizon as a consequence of his deep educational internalization of them, now being heard in the apostolic cause of speaking forth Christ and explicating his eternal significance as they bore and bear witness to this mystery. The dots cannot be neatly connected. The portions of scripture alluded to cannot be mapped on a tidy exegetical grid, but indicate an allusive penetration of his thought and argument. Scripture is grasping Paul in this, and not the other way around. The use of allusion (and not formula citation) is not a signal of lesser importance or a transfer of authority from written Torah to christological wisdom, for its own sake or measured against a different practice to be noted elsewhere (the formula citations in Romans), now leaving the Old Testament to serve as foundations of something else. No, the scriptures are declaring their own christological purpose, and they are doing so in a way that Paul may only partly comprehend but not fully track or encompass. That we can see them now through careful study, moreover, is a sign of our own present knowledge of these scriptural texts, much as Beetham reasonably speculated that churches in time would enter the symbolical universe of the Old Testament because Paul himself so expected.

In this sense, then, we are not so much imitating the exegetical practices of Paul as we are allowing the scriptures to speak their word over and alongside his own efforts. Paul does commend the scriptures to his audience, and Peter will be bold to commend Paul's letters alongside them (2 Pet. 3:15–16). The way, then, that the scriptures will function is not as foundations but as declarative of mysteries they genuinely guard in their own literal sense, which are coming to light in ways Paul cannot himself fully grasp, but only be grasped by. The scriptures of Israel, the Christian Old Testament, will be heard in the church as reading Paul and clarifying his apostolic word. It is not difficult to assume that Paul expected that this would be so, as the "oracles of God entrusted to the Jews" (Rom. 3:2) would become entrusted to a wider circle: following the dominical example of Easter day, now being opened more widely to a particular Christian hearing and instructing, for which Paul serves as a central apostolic example. (For a creative presentation of how Paul the Jewish Christian and the now largely Gentile church orient themselves around both scripture and the gospel, see the appendix.)

The Mechanics of Letter Composition and the Question of Pauline Authorship

The Witness of the Old Testament and Authorial Inspiration

The prophets of Israel were public speakers, and so the path that leads from this inspired activity to the legacy of written texts, now bearing their names, is in large measure hidden from view. In the texts they have left us we get glimpses only, a signal certainly that the important thing is the word vouchsafed and preserved and not the means by which that has happened. Jeremiah had a secretary. Isaiah had disciples. Elijah and other prophets had schools within which they worked and saw to the transitions called forth by God, from one generation to the next. Ezekiel "swallowed a scroll"—a metaphor perhaps for more direct involvement by the prophet in the compositional achievement of prophetic witness. Some argue that works like Isa. 40–55 were composed more on the order of extended discourse than brief prophetic utterance, but whether that amounts to a literary shift is the stuff of speculation only. The later prophetic books (Haggai, Zechariah, Malachi) do appear more literary in character, perhaps the function of a new understanding of the prophetic office. And one very important aspect of this—probably not sufficiently noted—is the emergence of a prior literary record. Postexilic prophecy becomes prophecy in relationship to a written record. A classical period has emerged. Prophecy does not die out as a live phenomenon but is internally transformed, coexisting with an "agony of influence" from prophecy as it went forth in the past and continues to sound forth in the context of ongoing, yet now very different, prophetic address. As Zechariah the latter prophet puts it, "Your fathers, where are they, and the prophets, do they live forever? But my words and my statutes, which I commanded my servants the prophets, did they not overtake your fathers?" (1:5–6). And again, "Were not these the words that the LORD proclaimed by the former prophets?" (7:7), followed by a precise summation of that former speech, now addressing a new generation (7:8–14). The book of Zechariah can be read as a reestablishment of prophecy given the realities of postexilic life (kingship, prophecy, priesthood all sundered or brought under severe judgment in the destruction of Jerusalem and exile), by means of dream visions and by the ability to reconnect with what prophecy had been, as this exists via the medium of a growing scriptural witness ("words and statutes" being collections in association with the prophets and Moses).

Where does Paul the apostle fit within such a conception? Like Amos, he is a voice wrested by God to a particular vocation, untimely born. Like Ezekiel, he has "swallowed a scroll," by means of an education whose purpose was the internalization of God's prior speech as found in the Law and the Prophets. Like Zechariah, he faces into that same scriptural legacy as an undoubted authority from the past, but with a word still to speak enlivened by God's vocation given him as inspired apostle. He is one of the Twelve, Judas's true replacement, as Barth (*Church Dogmatics* 2/2: 478–506) provocatively states: an inspired voice among a choir of apostolic voices, typologically figured in the Twelve Prophets, and now fulfilled in the presentation of Acts, the Pauline letter collection, and the General Epistles of the New Testament.

Like the prophets, Paul's vocation was not the literary production of books. He dictated his letters to secretaries, and their names and personal attestation have been preserved (e.g., Rom. 16:22). How did he go about the business of internal organization of his thoughts and anticipated speech and address? How did he call up the scriptural references? What is the relationship between the final form of a letter as we now have it, where he has signed off in his own large-lettered hand (1 Cor. 16:21; Gal. 6:11; Col. 4:18; 2 Thess. 3:17), and previous stages of dictation and editing and reconception? We can trace out answers to these questions by comparison with letters from antiquity and what we can know about that process, including even speculation about letter collections and how they became such. But in many ways, not unlike with the prophetic books, we will not know all we might like to know because the predominating concern was with the message itself and not descriptions of the process; these come to us as intriguing incidentals. We must also be prepared to accept that there might be something *sui generis* about the forms of composition held to be at the base of New Testament proclamation. Paul's letter collection is entitled to be both like and unlike what we might find in the letters of Seneca. And this is not least because of the influence and overshadowing prophetic authority of the scriptures of Israel, under whose shadow these letters find form. The New Testament is "accorded testimony," and in that sense it finds a modest exemplar in the prophetic writings themselves. The book of the prophet Isaiah is a testimony of "former and latter things." The latter things are what they are in relationship to a prior divine word, and that must be grasped before what is truly new can make its force felt. The postexilic prophets also find their logic and their warrant in relationship to "former prophecy."

Paul as Author of Letters

As we have seen, much hard labor has gone into the business of determining which letters were authored by Paul and which ones were not. This project has been tied up with the individualization of the letters. Even the tendency to comment on only a single letter is a relatively recent development, as the tradition typically interpreted the letters as a group. Initially this may have had less to do with an intuition about a single selected letter being more decisive than the others, though certainly the idea of a "canon within a canon" bespeaks an instinct toward prioritization on some principle other than the canonical presentation. Bucer was well known as an Ephesian commentator and was invited by Thomas Cranmer to lecture at Cambridge and prepare material for what he planned would be a collaborative project, unifying the Reformation churches around a fresh Latin translation together with commentary. Other single-commentary compositions arguably took place because of certain central theological themes the author felt needed to be pressed inside a newly conflicted ecclesial situation.

In the modern period, the individualization came as part of the industry of historical-critical evaluation. The books needed to be placed in their "proper" sequence. Critical was a determination of setting, provenance, and distinctive theological contribution. Part and parcel of this method of proceeding was a determination of authenticity based upon an account of the development of Paul's thought and the place where it appeared certain letters had moved into discontinuous territory. This could be accounted for by theories of pseudepigraphy, which might well dismiss the idea of fraud or radical disjuncture, as these sometimes accompanied the judgment of *antilegomena*. Partly to their credit, such conclusions at least reminded us that authorship as meant in the antique world and in our own are very different conceptions.

As we have seen, the quest for the human author in the case of Old Testament prophetic books (and elsewhere) was always held in sharp contrast with modern conceptions due to the oral and public character of prophetic speech. The path to written legacy was not obvious or straightforward. How was Moses thought to be the "author" of the Pentateuch and what was meant by that traditional conception? How is Isaiah the "author" of the sixty-six-chapter work now associated with him? How does the book of the Twelve go back to individuals but also represent an authorship greater than the sum of its parts?

In addition, in the later period, as a classical conception of prophecy emerged in connection with an emerging canonical witness, to be a prophetic author was also to relate to and in some sense defer to a prophetic legacy with which any new prophecy was to be in accordance. Newer forms of inspired writing also emerge at this period, some of them from circles associated with the wisdom tradition. Wisdom becomes what one author called "a hermeneutical construct," that is, by means of specific editorial handling of the tradition, the wise are those who understand how an ancient word overtakes and addresses a new generation and, more importantly, how this happens when the authoritative tradition has aggregated.[40] Now the questions for the wise to answer and learn from have to do with seeing proper associations across a developing written witness. How does the Psalter relate to the life of David recorded in the history? How does the first book of the Twelve serve as a lens on the collection as a whole? Does the book to follow (Joel) press for an individualized reading, or is its sense to be grasped in connection with how it appropriates and relates to the first witness (Hosea)? How did a word from Isaiah continue to accomplish God's purpose: an authorization that led to extended prophetic address after his lifetime, but consistent with and drawn from the original inspiration given to him? His word is what it is to his own generation, but it contains the seeds of God's accomplishing address for a later day.

Much about the process of extended inspiration is hidden from view and can be reconstructed (modestly and tentatively) only on the basis of close reading and on the assumption that "the prophet Isaiah wrote the book of Isaiah" does not adequately capture what the sixty-six-chapter book means when it declares itself the vision the prophet saw (1:1). The term "pseudepigraphy" does not sufficiently clarify what is going on and what is at stake, precisely when it comes to the inspiration and the manner of authoring we call "divine."

When it comes to the letters of Paul we are on seemingly firmer and also different ground. The movement from author to written letter is more temporally compressed, more capable of explication, and more direct. But other factors intrude that have their Old Testament analogies. Paul is not an isolated figure but exists in

40. Gerald T. Sheppard, *Wisdom as a Hermeneutical Construct: A Study in the Sapientalizing of the Old Testament* (BZAW 151; Berlin: de Gruyter, 1980).

relationship to a wider apostolic movement. Paul is a writer of letters to specific congregations, but he is also one who stands under scriptural authority, in Christ, and who seeks to hear that former word delivering up a sense consistent with its own deliverance in time, while yielding also an extended sense due to the conviction that Christ or the Spirit was inspiring the first witness toward a final end. The many and varied ways the scriptures make their force felt across the letters mean that this authoritative horizon would lose its character if made the focus of a study of only a single letter or a focus on an individual witness apart from the wider collection.

Here it is that a declaration of some letters as non-Pauline must run up against what is arguably too thin an account of authorship to begin with (Barclay 2004: 35). The letter collection proceeds on the basis that Paul stands behind the total inspired witness, and to do this it merely declares him its originating force without distinguishing different forms of that. His name appears at the top of every letter, if not also at the close. Why is it that distinctives appear in the letters (in language, syntax, content) that seem to be good evidence of some other intruding force? Answers are given on the basis of development of thought, changed circumstances, collaboration, and other factors. Undeniable is Paul's being, especially later in his apostolic life, a man among other men (and women), in a way different from what we see of his companionship in Acts. If the epilogues of the letters are not taken to be efforts to give historical color to a later secondary composition, Ephesians, Colossians, and Philemon show a Paul in a setting where his thinking must invariably be affected by the presence of others and also his own reflections on the history of his apostolic life up to that point in time. Could it be otherwise?

Of course, we cannot know why Paul's thought and forms of expression appear to change, and we can note this only within the compass of the canonical presentation that allows his name to stand over the whole. Has Timothy begun to work more closely alongside? Philippians, Colossians, and 1 Thessalonians all mention him en route to the letters to Timothy proper, which follow. Colossians reflexively uses the "we" form in thanksgiving at its opening (compare the first-person singular in Phil. 1:3 and the plural "we" in Colossians and 1 Thess. 1:2 and 2 Thess. 1:3). Colossians closes with a veritable "seminar room" setting, with such luminaries as Mark, Luke, Jesus called Justus, Epaphras, and Aristarchus (latterly travel companion with Paul and Luke, as Acts reports it)—all companions of the apostle. Just as statements written by more than one person look different than ones with a single author, even though one person must do the final authoring, can we be sure that an account of Paul as author is sufficiently tuned to the realities of the day, and how apostolic witness in accordance with the scriptures takes its form, such that we can refer to it now as part of the inspired work of Paul in a final letter collection? Here the challenge is not to make Paul measure up to what we mean by "author," but instead to concede that we must go to school again when it comes to understanding inspiration in the context of a scriptural horizon (Old Testament) and an apostolic testimony (New Testament), which in the nature of the case seeks a common point of origin in the one Holy Spirit of inspired address.

Paul stands alone as canonical author of the thirteen letters, and how that is so is less prominent in the presentation than that is so. To introduce an alternative understanding in the name of modern conceptions is to fail to accept the limitations of modern inquiry into what is a scriptural convention.

In the appendix, I seek to bring together the conclusions of this opening section in the form of a first-person account. This resembles in some ways the "paraphrase" genre in Erasmus's work. His is a representation of Paul's letter with expanded first-person supplementation, and the rhetorical effect is notable upon even a brief reading. But I did not generate it for this purpose. I was struck at how certain economical accounts of introduction to the letter to the Colossians often served the purpose better of allowing the historical Paul to step forward, with all the allowances that must be made for how secure a portrayal it was. Paul is clearly a personality in his letters and in Acts, and the autobiographical exists alongside the substantive theological. This opening section has hopefully shown why this is unavoidably so, when it comes to apostolic witness from the maturing, imprisoned Paul. This is part and parcel of the letter collection's canonical unfolding.

I do not, however, intend the paraphrase to present itself as history after the modern example. It is more in the form of a "historylike" account, to borrow a phrase from Hans Frei.[41] As such it is a heurism, intended as a lens or overture, by which one may enter the commentary proper. For this reason I introduce the notion of Paul as an actual letter *writer*, when strictly speaking it is doubtful that such a vocation was ever his in the manner I tease out. This is to give indication that I mean the portrayal of Paul to be a heurism, and not some sort of competition or displacing exercise with respect to the letter collection itself, and Colossians as one integral part of it. I intend this only as a way to give proportion to the reality of Paul as a person, as the letter collection allows us a glimpse. I hope it summarizes the findings of this more formal introduction in a readable, congenial way. That will better serve the purpose of introducing the commentary proper, where he appears in all his specificity and all his vocational humility. It is placed in the appendix so that those who wish to move directly to the presentation of Colossians in the form of commentary may do so.

A Final Word about the General Approach to Reading Colossians

At points along the way in composing this commentary I have been tempted to refer to the approach adopted in respect of Colossians "canonical." The term "canonical"—whatever its technical, semantic, or practical limitations—is likely now fated to a context of misapprehension or caricature. A "canonical reading" is either a genre mistake or a piety masking illegitimate ("unhistorical" in our present parlance) interpretation. A canonical reading is a holistic reading that eschews

41. Hans Frei, *The Eclipse of Biblical Narrative* (New Haven: Yale University Press, 1970).

matters of historical background, favoring the final form and leaning toward, even if unintentionally, a hermeneutics of reader-response and kindred objections.

But of course a canonical reading as adopted specifically by Childs is a resolutely unpostmodern reading, and when it comes to the letters of Paul, the business of properly associating a single letter with the achievement of the letter collection forbids anything like holistic reading (Childs 1984 and 2008). Minimally, a canonical reading should mean something basically proper like paying attention to the text's final form in its totality and also not preempting the historical character of the text's coming-to-be. The balance will prove to be the real issue.

Or—another complaint often lodged—a canonical reading is some degenerative form of theological reading. In Barclay's 2004 survey of the modern interpretation of Colossians—and with attention to the postmodern challenge—almost reflexively he lumps what he calls a theological reading (whatever that might mean) with a literary ("unhistorical") reading. But he must quickly concede, and does, that no theological reading is exempted from having to attend closely to what is said and the historical implications of that (see the discussion on authorship in the introduction). Such readings could take the form of situating Paul within his own corpus or seeking to understand what his audience might hear in the theological realm of Paul's address. Either reading is at once theological and historical.

It seems to me that what captures the concern of a canonical reading, if the term may be indulged for a moment, has to do with the proper proportion between what is said as an act of intentional communication and the circumstances said to be generating it. Both are historical data. The one exists in time and calls up terms and contexts relevant to historical precision-making. The latter is a speculation based upon what the text says. A canonical approach seeks to assure that these rhyme and that the speculations about the circumstances generating the material are in proper proportion to what the text actually highlights and prioritizes in its final total form, or in "the way the words go." So, to say that Epaphras has had a falling out with the Colossian community would require much more in the explicit unfolding of what Paul says than appears in the final text, and as I show below, other explanations better conform to the actual words. Or, to say Timothy cowrote Colossians is fine as speculation, but it cannot be called historical as over against something canonical. Rather, it is a speculation based upon various bits of evidence, none of them in the form of the letter saying "Timothy cowrote the letter." This would be the proper canonical representation of such an idea. If that were the case, we would conclude that the canonical text gave proportion to this historical claim. In my view this is simply not so. The point here is that a canonical reading tries to pay attention to what is not said by a text and to conclude this lack of plain deliverance is significant. Proper proportion must be weighted to what is said. There is nothing especially theological or holistic or unhistorical in such an approach. The text is honored for what it chooses to communicate in the form it chooses to say that, and historical judgments are kept in proportion to this reality.

When it comes, then, to reflection on the character of Colossians within a letter collection, great care must be taken to understand where and how significance in this broader realm lies. Barclay again is helpful here. He speaks of the unavoidable reality that everyone must create a portrait of Paul by the very act of seeking to retrieve one from the material sitting before us in thirteen letters. Surely this is right. Is there something called a canonical portrait of Paul given by his letters?[42] Yes, in the sense that taking the letters as a whole and asking what sort of Paul is being communicated by them in their totality is possible. What is difficult to know is how this kind of endeavor is historical on the terms of the present meaning of the word. One can read the Pastorals and by various means of historical comparison argue they are not by Paul but represent some effort to speak in his name at a later date and under circumstances not his own. What one in turn does with such a conclusion is another matter, but it does mean that the Paul created in this portrait has no coloring from these three letters. A similar thing can be said of a method that would exclude Colossians or Ephesians as non-Pauline.

Childs in his work on the Pauline letters seeks to work around certain constraints implicit in this sort of approach. So, he can conclude that arguments for the non-Pauline, or later, character of certain letters make a sort of sense, while remaining agnostic about claims as to their actual character and intention (he does not find the comparisons with ancient pseudepigraphical writings compelling, for example). But his concern, after noting this, is to ask what kind of Paul the letter collection, in the form we have it, has sought to give us. In this manner has he just avoided the historical question by a clever sleight of hand? Does the word "historical" refer to the subsequent decisions as to how to present Paul and so these are not seeking to lodge a claim for ostensive reference at the same level of canonical significance? How was it possible for later hands to extend Paul's portrayal in letters that so clearly depict him as their author, without making an inappropriate transfer historically? If they did this, should we? These are the questions that might be posed if one seeks to understand how a canonical approach is a historical approach but with a wider lens on history and reception history.[43]

In this context I am going to content myself with not writing on the Pastorals, as in my view they represent the most serious challenge as to how we face this kind of question. I believe Childs is on the right track by seeking signs of organic

---

42. For simplicity's sake, we can leave the presentation of Hebrews (which does not foreground a Pauline character as author) and Acts (which does give us a clear "Paul" portrait) to the side. They do illustrate, however, the challenge. See Seitz, *Character of Christian Scripture*.

43. A similar set of considerations emerges in the discussion of the modern scholarly conception "Luke-Acts," which conception does not appear as hermeneutically or materially significant in the earliest commentary references. Is the conceptuality of "Luke-Acts" historical, and the one that has Acts introduce the General Epistles nonhistorical? Or is one forced to posit a moment in time that is historical in which the former conceptuality is in place, even as we have no record of it in the earliest history of reception? What kind of history is it that only with difficulty links up with the earliest reception history? See A. F. Gregory and C. K. Rowe, eds., *Rethinking the Unity and Reception of Luke and Acts* (Columbia: University of South Carolina Press, 2010), 74–81; and Childs 2008: 219–36.

extension, and not ones glued on after the fact and made to say something either un-Pauline or something of an altogether different purpose at a period when he was gone from the scene and his concerns were no longer logically extendable to subsequent churchly adjudication.[44] The single statue of Nebuchadnezzar's dream as seen by Daniel (Dan. 2:31–35) had ten toes (2:41–43), did it not? The two main sections of Daniel do not represent subsequent layers of *vaticinia ex eventu*, but organic extensions based upon the conviction that the original visions had more to say than was constrained within the "historical" context of Dan. 1–6.[45] So too, one might think of the relationship of the Pastorals vis-à-vis the so-called *homologomena*. But again, I am not forming a strong opinion about how one should assess the Pastorals in the context of the letter collection. I agree with Childs that something like a broader approach to the question of historicity must be entertained when it comes to the interpretation of Paul in the canonical-historical portrayal. And if that is so in the case of the Pastorals it is even more so in the case of Colossians and Ephesians, both of which have been held by reputable scholars as Pauline on the grounds one typically, in the modern period, engages the question.

In this commentary I will defend the view that a strong argument for non-Pauline authorship or for pseudepigraphical composition cannot be sustained. I believe that far easier explanations lie close to hand. I hold that the distinctive circumstances of Paul's authorial location explain how and why his diction and his perspective look like they do. He is observing, through the testimony of Epaphras, the vibrant growth and spreading of the gospel independently of his own efforts or expectation. The Colossian church is non-Jewish in character and therefore will need to hear the patterns and themes and truths of the scriptures Paul treasures in a distinctive idiom tailored to their reception among them. Because the growth of the church is happening in dramatic ways and because the Gentile composition of this congregation is forefront in his mind, themes like the mystery hidden and revealed, via the extensional senses of the one scriptural witness, are prominent.

I will explain at appropriate points why a certain kind of inquiry into allusions and echoes of scriptures in Colossians will misfire if the question is whether those addressed are in a position to pick up on them, or why Paul "avoids" direct quotations in the form we find them elsewhere.[46] I believe a better answer is available for how and why Paul proceeds as he does.

A brief word, then, about the way the commentary will be undertaken.

Translation. The English translation is in bold so the reader can know where we are in the text of Colossians. The translation is my own. The only thing I try to do consistently is maintain the same word order as the Greek, when that does

---

44. This becomes relevant in the commentary, for example, on the "household code" in 3:18–4:1.

45. See Brevard S. Childs, *Introduction to the Old Testament as Scripture* (Philadelphia: Fortress, 1979), 614–18.

46. See Beetham's discussion about a subsequent "biblical literacy" Paul in time would expect of a Gentile congregation (2008: 255–57). I do not agree with the conception of Paul "avoiding" direct citation and of explaining this as having to do with "Christ replacing Torah" (2008: 262).

not create an idiosyncratic rendering in translation. I also try to comment on no more than one verse at a time. At points in the commentary I will speak more in the way of summary introduction to verses where such a treatment is called for.

Units/text division. I believe the letter as a whole gives indication that Paul was thinking in terms of a sustained discourse. Like any composer, he moves from topic to topic, and one can sense beginnings and endings and transitions of various description. But on the whole I am convinced there is a coherence to the units when taken in relationship to one another. I will introduce subdivisions in the chapters and give explanation for the logic of these. But it will also be true that strong divisions, going back to form-critically determined discrete units, are not often in evidence. This should be obvious as one reads along, and it does not require further elaboration here. I mention it only as a matter of format in the context of this Series.

Selection of commentaries. Brazos Theological Commentary on the Bible is intended to avoid digging a fresh scholarly ditch (*ein wissenschaftliche Grabe*). That said, I have read widely in modern and ancient commentary and know what kinds of issues predominate in both. What has been given most attention has often happened appropriately. That said, it will always be the case that certain kinds of issues (e.g., the diachronic or genetic coming-to-be of the text in its final form is a good example in the modern period: how the "hymn to Christ" looked in its "pristine form" and how it has been augmented; how the "household codes" of antiquity have been adapted in Hellenistic Judaism) are given a length of treatment in the commentaries that does not necessitate another rehearsal here. One can easily consult the literature to see how the discussion has gone. The present commentary will give indication that these are areas for further consideration by those so inclined, and it will offer its own view. But it will not unroll the nineteenth/twentieth-century discussion in detail and show that it knows it well. I am a biblical scholar trained in historical-critical method, and I know this kind of analysis better than I know certain phases of the history of interpretation. But I endeavor to give proper proportion to the scholarly discussion in its more recent phases so as to allow a theological reading to emerge from the canonical text before us.

Paul as the subject of verbs. I believe it is appropriate to refer to "Paul" as the creative mind at work in the letter to the Colossians. I will therefore allow him to be the subject of the verbs in my commentary on his letter. But equally, I believe there are no genuinely suitable alternatives for this. For those who believe Paul had considerable help from Timothy, or that the latter was the real composer/dictator of the letter, the avoidance of "Paul" *simpliciter* as author is not easily accomplished, practically speaking, when it comes to line-by-line commentary.[47]

---

47. Dunn is a good example here. He believes Timothy is in some measure the author of the letter and that this is the implication of 1:1. Yet he also describes the practical limitations of setting this forth: "We may, for example, envisage Paul outlining his main concerns to a secretary (Timothy) who was familiar with the broad pattern of Paul's letter writing and being content to leave it to the secretary to formulate the letter with a fair degree of license, perhaps under the conditions of his imprisonment at that point able

For those who prefer to think of a pseudepigrapher or a "project of the Pauline circle," a generic "the author" is the expediency required; or, one can speak of the purpose of the letter in general terms and avoid reference to its author entirely (so, e.g., Kiley 1986 and Lincoln 2000: 553–669). The text is the subject of the verb.

In some ways Lincoln also puts his finger on the issue, though perhaps inadvertently, when he concludes his introduction to the letter with these sentences:

> Although the following commentary is written from the perspective that the letter is to be dated sometime after Paul's death and that the interpretation of 1:24–2:5 and 4:7–16 is to be linked to the device of pseudonymity, this is a matter still under dispute. For those who disagree with such a stance on authorship, all that is necessary in most of what follows, is, of course, to make the mental substitution of "Paul" or "Timothy" or both for "the writer." (Lincoln 2000: 583)

A theological commentary on the canonical scriptures would need to be able to defend a view of biblical texts whereby it falls to readers to make mental substitutions of various kinds so as to have the letter to the Colossians conform to their own wishes in respect of authorship. I believe here one sees the deeply practical reality that inhabits the claims of the biblical text and of commentary on the same. A text has an author of some description. If on every occasion one must make mental substitutions of some kind in order to clarify the author and subject of verbs in the letter to the Colossians, it is nevertheless the case that the matter is not open ended. A choice must be made in some way (Paul, Paul/Timothy, post-Pauline project, the writer). I believe it is true to the account the letter to the Colossians makes of itself that we make the author neither anonymous ("the writer") nor a cipher for a theory nor even Timothy acting with Paul's imprimatur (however we imagine that). In the case of Colossians, I also believe there are far fewer problems with simply using the word "Paul" than the alternatives. The reader of our day and age, and one who consults this commentary, will know that these matters have been debated in the modern period. That is simply presupposed as a "reader reality" and a threshold fact. But the practical reality remains that a name must be given for the subject of verbs in this letter. "Paul" is beset with fewer problems at this basic level. Moreover, to do this leaves open the connection of Colossians to other letters in the thirteen-letter collection. And it attaches the present commentary to the long history of interpretation where

---

only to add the briefest of personal conclusions (see on 4:18). If so, we should perhaps more accurately describe the theology of Colossians as the theology of Timothy, or, more accurately still, the theology of Paul as interpreted by Timothy. On the other hand, if Timothy did indeed write for Paul at Paul's behest, but also with Paul's approval of what was in the event written (prior to adding 4:18), then we have to call the letter 'Pauline' in the full sense of the word, and the distinction between 'Pauline' and 'post-Pauline' as applied to Colossians becomes relatively unimportant" (1996: 38). That is a lot of words to conclude that the use of Paul without scare quotes is an appropriate way to speak of the letter's author. Eduard Schweizer holds a similar view and faces a similar challenge; "Kolosserbrief—weder paulinisch noch nachpaulinisch?" in *Neues Testament und Christologie im Werden* (Göttingen: Vandenhoeck & Ruprecht, 1982), 150–63.

economy on matters of authorship meant that attention was given over to other more important matters of interpretation and application.

Paul and scripture. My commentary gives special attention to Paul's scriptures and the role they play in his letter to the Colossians. The commentary will speak for itself on this matter. Only one thing to note here. When Paul speaks of these scriptures he has not of course attended a modern introductory course where three Isaiahs, the separate authorship of Gen. 1:1–2:4a and 2:4b–3:24, or even the significance of the exile are major topics on the syllabus. This means that at times we must retrain ourselves, who have attended these courses, to try to consider how the scriptures of Israel are making their force felt at the time Paul is communicating them. Also, and fundamentally, it will be emphasized below that Paul's relation to these scriptures is of a specific sort having to do with his own DNA as a particular Jew, now seeing these scriptures from the standpoint of one cross. Those he is speaking to do not share his scriptural DNA, but this means only that his achievement will consist of making their literal and extensional senses heard from the standpoint of a single cross and Lord, who is opening up these senses as a genuine bequest from their single, literal, stable presentation.

Excurses. Interwoven in the commentary proper the reader will find a series of Excurses. These are intended to amplify on some aspect of exegesis that ranges more broadly than the specific text under discussion. They also allow for a more sustained look at some contested area of interpretation. Finally, they permit a perspectival concern to come better into focus, or so it is hoped. As such they can be skipped for one turning to the commentary for help in one narrower part of the letter to the Colossians only. I have tried to write the commentary as a single sustained argument, in which certain key themes receive sustained attention and guide the interpretation of individual sections. That is consistent with my view of Paul's own intention in this short letter.

A final personal note, upon having completed the commentary writing on Colossians. My hope has been that because the "oracles of God entrusted to the Jews" are central to my own training and my own understanding of the character of Christian scripture, I might be in a position to stand closer to Paul—even in my own Gentile DNA—than many commentators working at present in a field of biblical studies where two divisions of labor have opened up, spawning in turn innumerable subspecies of study. I am not a New Testament scholar at work in an academic shop set up in the modern academy. I am also not an Old Testament/Hebrew Bible scholar who believes that a "historical sense" can set aside canonical and theological considerations. These aspects are so deeply ingrained in what the scriptures are and how they make their sense as to be inextricable, and indeed the center of what makes them what they are as such under God. This will likely inform the commentary to follow in particular and significant ways—not least because I believe they also give an accurate (historical, canonical, theological) account of how Paul is working in the letter to the Colossians.

FORMAL INTRODUCTION
AND SALUTATIONS

(1:1–2)

1:1 Paul, apostle of Christ Jesus by the will of God, and Brother Timothy—By the convention of his day, so begins the letter dictated by Paul. The letter concludes by convention as well, with Paul signing off on what he has constructed: "I Paul write this greeting with my own hand" (4:18; cf. 1 Cor. 16:21). The conclusion to 2 Thessalonians adds to this same phrase, "This is the mark in every letter of mine; it is the way I write"; and the conclusion of Galatians explains that the script of Paul is different from that of a trained secretary: "See with what large letters I am writing to you with my own hand." The letter to the Romans kindly lets us see the secretary himself, who in the case of Romans offers his own greetings: "I Tertius, the writer of this letter, greet you in the Lord." Occasionally, Paul will use the opportunity to add some additional notes of his own, matters that come to him after the dictation itself (1 Cor. 16:22–24).[1] In Colossians this is the ever so brief: "Remember my fetters" and "Grace be with you" (4:18).[2]

Ancient authorship is characterized in ways that compare with modern notions but also depart from them, when it comes to inspired biblical writings. Two factors at least bear underscoring. Examples from the prophetic books of the scriptures Paul inherits and internalizes are helpful for comparison with his own compositions. Prophets were speakers, not writers. How their speech made it into written form is nowhere the subject of detailed or explicit treatment, and what we have

1. Trobisch (1994: 98) playfully signs off with his own cursive script and with further notes to the reader in his own hand.
2. See Eadie 1856: 302–3, where the publisher opts for a different font to capture the signing-off aspect.

are only incidental glimpses, provided in the context of other matters. Prophets had disciples who "bound up the testimony." Baruch was Jeremiah's "secretary." Ezekiel swallowed a scroll, and so perhaps initiated a longer style of discourse that may have involved his own compositional role. Isaiah 40–55 reads like an extended dramatic accomplishment, though how exactly it came to form we do not know.

To be inspired by God is to be given a word intelligible and divinely spoken to a generation confronted by God's agent in time. It is also to be given a word for the ages, one that accomplishes what God intends beyond the comprehension of the human agent himself. So the psalmist speaks of David but also of David's greater Son, at one and the same time. We may call this either prophecy or figural presentation, and the degree of comprehension of the "latter thing" to which it corresponds will vary, often in ways our own efforts to understand the human agent's intentions cannot penetrate.[3] That is what makes it a divine word. Isaiah speaks a word that is concrete and specific and as such closes ears—and also one that will sound again beyond his own time and place (Isa. 43:8).

Paul stands in this tradition. In addition, he has this same scriptural word and inheritance shedding a particular kind of light on his place in God's time, as a minister of the gospel that is now being proclaimed to every creature under heaven (Col. 1:23). One sees Paul in Colossians in a specific kind of apostleship. Like Isaiah, he speaks to a people he knows, whose temporal frame of reference he shares, even as he has accepted the call to preach the gospel to a people not his own. The ironic legacy of Ezekiel has come about after all: "Not to a people of harsh speech do I send you . . . they would listen" (Ezek. 3:6).

But this congregation Paul has never visited. He did not preach to them. He does not intend to visit them in the future, so far as the letter itself speaks of it (cf. Phlm. 22). The word of the gospel has borne fruit of its own, and its capability to do that is itself a matter of rejoicing for Paul in his own communication to this church (Col. 1:3–6). It is as though the word that addressed him has now asserted its own independence, in the same way Isaiah's received and transmitted word has gone on to speak again of its own accord, as former and latter horizons of God's intention come into coordination. Though Paul will not refer to it in these terms, this is also the reason what he now says he can ask to be heard beyond the limitations of the Colossian congregation as such, in Laodicea (4:16). Paul is striving for them (2:1–2) in the selfsame context of his striving and praying for the congregation I have come to associate this letter with, the epistle "to the Colossians."[4] God's inspired word to prophet and apostle is directed to one specific place and time but precisely in such a way that it can sound forth more broadly and reach out to enclose us as well, who overhear and hear.

---

3. See the extended discussion of *theoria* by Bradley Nassif, ed., *New Perspectives on Historical Theology: Essays in Memory of John Meyendorf* (Grand Rapids/Cambridge: Eerdmans, 1996), 343–77.

4. For an amplification of the view that the "Letter from Laodicea" (Col. 4:16) is most likely a reference to the Letter now referred to in the canonical collection as "Ephesians," see also the appendix. This view has been widely held in modern and earlier times.

The second feature of divine inspiration is more difficult to grasp given the high priority we place, in the modern West, on the individual. Here it is that liberal and conservative provocations often meet themselves in paradoxical ways. The former seeks out the original and the discrete, on the grounds that temporal proximity must be wrested from the canonical form. There is a "real Paul" somewhere behind the text, and we must get at him by means of excavation. He is discrete and his ideas must be sufficiently unchanging for the logic of his extraction to operate. But above all, he is an individual, a specific genius of inspired thought, if we search to uncover and set forth the precise limits of that, behind the canonical form.

The conservative version of this quest has the very same view of the propriety of the individual, but argues in the same context of questing that the canonical form points in very precise terms toward the "real Paul" of temporal specificity. On occasion one can see the efforts made to alter the terms of the discussion. After all, Paul had a secretary,[5] and who knows what effect this may have on how we understand what we are looking for in our search for Paul the individual (in terms of style, diction, sentence structure, content, theological nuance). Or, Paul is affected in what he says in Colossians as an individual composition by his association with others (Timothy or the many named individuals of the final chapter). Or, Paul is imprisoned and so has adopted a new style given the specifics of that setting. All of these efforts to adjust what we are looking for acknowledge that what any inspired author says or intends must be coordinated with the range of influences operative given the wider social location. An overly individual portrait of Paul may believe it has isolated the true genius of his inspiration, by liberal or conservative methods of extraction, and in so doing has protected his apostleship. But what does the actual canonical form seek to convey?

The letter collection does not transmit introductory or concluding rubrics in anything like a stereotyped form. Again, the comparison with the superscriptions of prophetic books is revealing, for they do not follow any fixed pattern across the fifteen witnesses we have. The first letter of the collection, Romans, appears to have a superscription that with its fuller form could function to introduce the collection as a whole (Rom. 1:1–6). What about the reference to colleagues in the letters? There is no clear pattern here: Sosthenes appears in 1 Corinthians; Timothy in 2 Corinthians in the precise same wording as in Colossians; Galatians and Ephesians mention no colleagues; Philippians mentions Timothy but now in a different manner: "Paul and Timothy, servants of Jesus Christ"; following Colossians, Timothy appears in 1–2 Thessalonians, now joined by Silvanus.

It is difficult on the basis of this to see any explicit claim for Timothy as an actor in the compositional process of Colossians (compare, e.g., Dunn 1996: 35–39). If the canonical form is claiming anything, it may be the simple fact of Paul as joined by fellow Christians in the context of what he has to say. Paul is a Christian among Christians. In his vocation as inspired apostle, latterly called, he

---

5. Schweizer, "Kolosserbrief—weder paulinisch noch nachpaulinisch?"

is always a Christian among Christians. He speaks out of that context. "We thank God" (1:3). "We have heard" (1:4). Epaphras "our beloved brother" (1:7). "He has made known to us" (1:8). "We have not ceased to pray for you all" (1:9). "He has delivered us" (1:13). Colossians could lay claim to being a letter that foregrounds the associative character of Paul's Christian walk more than any other. Hence the emphasis on the church as within God's eternal purpose (1:18). Hence the emphasis on suffering, in Christ, on behalf of others (1:24). Hence the close association of Colossian Christians and those in neighboring Laodicea and Hieropolis (2:1; 4:13–15). That the gospel has been preached and is growing independently of his individual efforts fits perfectly alongside this associative emphasis. Epaphras, Tychicus, Onesimus—each in his own way, but also corporately—are "letters from Christ delivered by us, written not with ink but with the Spirit of the living God . . . on tablets of human hearts," as Paul will state it in another place (2 Cor. 3:3). Epaphras is "our beloved fellow servant" who brought the gospel to the Lycus Valley churches and who "is one of you," but who now remains with Paul as a fellow prisoner. Tychicus will bear the letter, but he will also bear the news of Paul and his fellow Christians, in all its rich forms.[6] Onesimus will bear the message of incorporation into Christ's body and with that a new form of servant living.

Paul writes to the congregations in this setting, then, and with him is Brother Timothy. What do they hear when they hear Paul speak through this inspired medium, when they hear the letter read aloud and mention of Timothy is made? They hear that Paul is a Christian among Christian brothers. As the letter is read, further along Timothy is joined by Epaphras, the Laodiceans, then a final roll call of circumcised and uncircumcised brothers (and sisters), and Archippus in their own midst, who is charged to complete his ministry (4:7–17). These are all "authors" of the gospel of Jesus Christ as it is communicated by the apostle Paul. And if they were fortunate enough in time to have the entire letter collection, as shortly churches indeed will, they might also draw the conclusion that mention of Timothy points not to Christian association only but temporal extension more critically, as Paul's associates become the bearers of his gospel proclamation to a next generation. The brother will become the son, the next generation (1 Tim. 1:2), in the same way Isaiah's children will bear witness to him and to God's word in its accomplishing march through time (Isa. 8) or Baruch will give testimony of God's word by Jeremiah. Timothy is himself surrounded by faithful preceding generations (2 Tim. 1:5). And the final letter of the collection (Philemon) will reprise the names given in Colossians, reminding of God's faithfulness in surrounding Paul with witnesses and fellow Christians right to the end. The wistful hope that he might be with them for a visit lingers in the air, in the way Jeremiah saw into a future that would be beyond his own days. That the letters are not in chronological order, but by descending length, means only that such a manner of deliverance

6. Probably a third of the letter communicates matters of concern the letter itself does not expressly convey in its own letter of address.

was not deemed significant enough to preserve. As it stands, the letter collection allows certain conclusions to be drawn in a most general way. Colossians stands out as making the Christian fellowship Paul enjoys, including his imprisonment and afflictions for Christ, a critical aspect of the letter's communication.[7]

One further aspect of the letter's communicative purpose I have not mentioned. The imprisonment motif—if I might speak of it that way to avoid an immediate quest for "which prison and when?"—is obvious in Philippians, Colossians, Timothy, and Philemon. If we ask what the canonical form is seeking to communicate, it certainly is not the provision of details suitable for precise adjudication—is it Caesarea, Ephesus, or Rome? The traditional view (Rome) flows from reliance on the canonical form as a primary witness. If precision at the level we might now wish is not the intention of the form, then what purpose is being served? Surely it is to emphasize the afflictions Paul undergoes for the sake of the gospel, on behalf of the church, and its relation to Christ's work once-for-all on the cross and continuing in his body. I mentioned the wistful reference—because we come to know it did not transpire—of a guest room being kept at the ready for Paul (Phlm. 22). In my view the understanding of authorship the letter endeavors to convey is one that depicts Paul with the shadow over his own physically active,

---

7. Wayne Meeks refers to how the Colossians are to come to know what Paul means to communicate, in ways beyond the regulatory or instructional aspects of the apostle's proclamation. Yet he falls prey to a residual kind of historicizing, even as he seeks to move beyond it and its limitations for setting forth the real point of Colossians (which he concedes could not be grasped by focusing on false teaching). He still asserts that the letter is not Paul's but is the creative work of an emissary using Paul's name. In her response to Meeks, Eleonore Stump focuses on this limitation, exposing how difficult it would be to hold up Paul as a model along the lines of Christian fellowship and obedient emulation, if, as Meeks holds, the letter was transmitted by witnesses who knew Paul had not actually written it and yet were passing it off as authentic, with Paul himself as its author. Meeks sits easy to the received view of Colossians as non-Pauline (as the modern historical argument tracks), but adverts sufficiently to it that Stump could charge that this was a deceptive practice undercutting Meeks's larger argument. The point here is not to determine who is right or wrong about Pauline authorship in the narrow context of the Meeks-Stump exchange, but rather to argue the way the discussion proceeds is simply too narrow and does not track well with the claims the letter itself makes. Barclay (2004: 33), Barth and Blanke (1994), and Ben Witherington (*The Letters to Philemon, the Colossians, and the Ephesians: A Socio-Rhetorical Commentary on the Captivity Epistles* [Grand Rapids: Eerdmans, 2007], 100–103), among modern authors, have their own forms of this concern. Moreover, the appeal to pseudepigraphy does not actually match very well what we know about the genre of that category as compared with Colossians. The long epilogue (4:7–18) would have to be judged a ploy, carefully drawn up on the basis of the list of names in Philemon available to a later author. If the city of Colossae, moreover, was destroyed by earthquake around AD 62, the reason for writing to a nonchurch at a later period would be to have a different audience reach certain obviously false conclusions about its authenticity. It is better on the whole to ask what the implications of the letter itself are for authorization and inspiration, given the form of the letter and the position it will in time be given in a letter collection. To separate history from reception history is to misunderstand what history is in its antique form. In my view authorship began to carry a kind of extra freight in the modern period without proper proportion to the literature being evaluated. Colossians is a first-person-plural letter, with all that means. Paul is himself being written by the gospel he proclaims. The Meeks and Stump essays are in Eleonore Stump and Thomas P. Flint, eds., *Hermes and Athena: Biblical Exegesis and Philosophical Theology* (Notre Dame, IN: University of Notre Dame Press, 1993), 37–58 and 59–70.

missionary ministry drawing longer. He speaks to a church he has not started and will not visit. His apostleship is being transformed into one of prayer, striving, affliction, and pending death ("remember my fetters"). And alongside this comes the awareness that the gospel will bear fruit not just where he did not directly set down his plow, in Colossae or Hieropolis or Laodicea, *but where he never will*. That will be for Timothy, and all his name represents to undertake as Paul mentions him in the opening verse of this letter and of others. Paul as a Christian among Christians will pass that ministry to others. As the letter ends we hear: "Say to Archippus, 'See that you fulfill the ministry that you have received from the Lord.'" Followed by: "Remember my fetters." And the very brief final four words: **Grace be with you.**

1:2 to the Colossians, saints and faithful brothers in Christ: grace to you and peace from God our Father—The emphasis noted above, on the first-person-plural orientation of the letter, is clearly maintained here. Timothy "the brother" (1:1) who joins Paul as he writes has his counterparts in "the brothers" in Colossae, who have faith in Christ. The God who willed Paul's vocation (1:1) is the "our Father" from whom flow all grace and peace. Note the strong emphasis in Romans, 1 Corinthians, Galatians, and Philippians on the first-person singularity of Paul. The contrast with Colossians (and Ephesians) is clear. Further, Paul the called and Timothy the brother may not be all that is meant by the "we" of the opening section to follow, as Paul may be speaking on behalf of his community more generally.[8] Lightfoot notes: "In the letters to the Philippians and to Philemon, the presence of Timothy is forgotten at once (see Phil. 1:1). In this letter, the plural is maintained throughout the thanksgiving (verses 3, 4, 7, 8, 9)" (1997: 62).

I agree that nothing too much should be read into the opening reference to "will of God" as if a countervailing view is being put to the side. The mood of the opening verses is one of thanksgiving. Calvin and Melanchthon speak of a kind of flattery intended to give Paul a good purchase on his audience, but that is nowhere clearly signaled in the letter of the text.[9] Paul is reflexively thankful. Equally, the "saints and faithful brothers" should not be taken as implying a differentiation later to unfold in the rhetoric of the letter ("you who are set apart and who have faith in Christ, and not the others").[10] The letter does not give us enough evidence for this kind of further stipulation. All that is being asserted is that Paul and his community are joined with the brothers in Colossae in the one grace and peace that flows from "our Father." To make the concern of Paul chiefly with a specific religious challenge is to miss the significance of the form of the letter. Those issues (religious conflict or false teaching) are not foregrounded

8. Moo 2008: 75–76 discusses the issue with customary thoroughness: "we" could be authorial; "we" could be Paul and Timothy only. If authorial, why not everywhere then in Paul's letters? The position taken here is that "we" means Paul, Timothy, and those associates with him whose greetings he later sends, especially Epaphras, "one of yourselves" (4:12).

9. P. Melanchthon, *Paul's Letter to the Colossians*, trans D. C. Parker (Sheffield: Almond, 1989).

10. Lightfoot 1997: 62: "In this way he obliquely hints at the defection."

as the reason for Paul's writing, but emerge later in the context of positive commendations.[11] What the letter says about Epaphras is that the Colossians learned from him, heard and understood the grace of God in truth (1:7). What did he make known? That they were under threat by false teaching? Not according to these opening words. "He made known to us your love in the Spirit" (1:8) is the way the next section concludes.

It is important to allow the letter to guide our interpretation according to the way it has been constructed to unfold and be heard. If a "mirror-reading" approach is difficult in Romans or Galatians, it is extremely strained in Colossians or Ephesians. We know only what Paul chooses to tell us in the form he does. What we learn in the next section is that Paul and his community have learned about developments in Colossae through a visitor to them, Epaphras. What he indicates as of first importance in that regard has an integrity of its own and is not the occasion for teasing out a religious context of false teaching of a specific kind and making that the main agenda of Paul in writing. When Lincoln perceptively writes: "Although the prescription for cure comes across reasonably clearly to the present-day reader of Colossians, the ailment defies a really detailed diagnosis on his part" (2000: 561), he has still in my view not got the matter quite right. The "ailment" as well as "the prescription for cure" are both secondary to the letter's primary intention, which is grasped by hewing as closely as possible to what is written and viewing that in comparison with other kindred Pauline witnesses. The alternative is to judge the opening reflexive thanksgiving as a form of rhetorical strategy before Paul "gets down to work" or as incidental to an otherwise consistent interest in writing letters to address specific problems. This in turn forces all the letters of Paul into a single anticipated mode that a survey of them all does not justify. Romans and Ephesians come especially to mind here, both being letters than most likely seek a wider reading that one community or its special issues would exhaust.

Excursus: "By the Will of God"

Several distinctive theological issues are raised by Paul's language for God, here at the outset of the letter to the Colossians and throughout this and the other epistolary witnesses. But these (literally) theological issues cannot be treated as simple conceptual

11. Moo speculates: "Epaphras's reason for making this trip to visit Paul was almost certainly that he wanted to enlist the apostle's help in dealing with a dangerous yet slippery variation on the Christian gospel that had arisen in the community" (2008: 27). The problem is that the letter never says this and Paul does not so speak of his relationship to Epaphras in this way. Moo continues: "Epaphras, we may assume, has journeyed all the way to Rome just to present his mentor, the apostle Paul, with the problem and to enlist his help in responding to it" (2008: 47). Again, the letter nowhere says this. Nothing prevents the view that Epaphras sought Paul out for the same reason Onesiphorus did according to 2 Tim. 1:16: "he was not ashamed of my chains," or he sought me out for basic fellowship in Christ. That need not have any other purpose.

loci to be described and fleshed out as if they were universals in some generalized sense. What Paul says of God he says from within the conceptual DNA provided by his immersion in "the oracles of God entrusted to the Jews" (Rom. 3:2). To be who he is, claimed by God for a particular willed mission, is to be seized by the God who has made himself known from within a particular revelatory compass. But at the same time that specific compass is being broken open for a new readership, brought near by the work of Christ in one cross (Eph. 2:11–14). To be included in that new and final act of God is to be issued a particular kind of library card, one that Paul has had, has used, has worn through use, but that is also for him proving to be more than he had imagined in terms of its scope and range. Paul does not start with a general word for God and then sees how this maps out in his scriptures, more present or true here, less so there, available for dogmatic description in terms of attributes, characteristics, and such like. God is the willed "I am who I am" who in covenantal relationship has made himself known in a specific, personal, desisting, forebearing, and judging way with a chosen people (Exod. 34:6–7). He has allowed himself to be referred to by means of a generic word ("God"), one that can resonate beyond the covenantal relationship and that indeed can have its own very different semantic range in that generic potential ("God" or "gods" in Hebrew ʾelohim). But the personal name (YHWH) bespeaks a specific personal covenantal relationship with the judging and forebearing "I am with you."

Of course "the name above every name" has been given to the One who obediently submitted himself to our mortal frame and who died that all sins might be forgiven and new life granted for all, Jew and Gentile. In consequence of that, every knee will bow, and the name above every name will now be parsed Father, Son, and Holy Spirit as Jew and Gentile are brought near by the one cross (Phil. 2:9–11, based on Isa. 45:23).[12] But Paul is aware of all the transfer means. How can this transfer and the new life it bespeaks be made known abroad to those who exist outside the covenants, those who were promised to be included and who, when they would in time read the old scriptures, would discover that it was addressing them in its own distinctive way? As Luther puts it, it is as though being invited to the reading of a will of someone you never knew and learning that, astonishingly, you had a portion of the inheritance after all, by virtue of an act of beneficence by the owner's son.[13]

In order to speak of the issue of theological language properly, we need to think a bit further about Paul's audience. Every missionary has a particular account that guides his or her life journey, and it is not an account that exists in generic terms, but revealed and highly personal ones, themselves going back to the call of Abraham and

12. David S. Yeago, "The New Testament and Nicene Dogma: A Contribution to the Recovery of Theological Exegesis," *Pro Ecclesia* 3 (1994): 152–64; and Bauckham 1999: 52–53.

13. "For the New Testament is nothing more than a revelation of the Old. Just as one receives a sealed letter which is not to be opened until after the writer's death. So the Old Testament is the will and testament of Christ, which he has opened after his death and read and everywhere proclaimed through the gospel" (Luther's Sermon on John 1:1–14, "Third Christmas Day [or the Principal Christmas Service]," in *The Complete Sermons of Martin Luther*, ed. and trans. J. N. Lenker et al. (Grand Rapids: Baker, 1983), 1/1–2: 174.

the work of one cross. How to make that account comprehensible without sacrific-
ing the particular and personal, the willed act of God in Christ: this is the challenge
of all Christian witness. Paul cannot jump out of his scriptural skin, but those same
scriptures announce to him they are competent to be heard in Christ by others. Only
by understanding this exchange and transfer, this negotiation of one specific frame
of reference into another, can we really speak of theology in its precise meaning. God
is a personal and willing God, with a name, a history of relationship, and knowing him
and his name is to be transferred to a new realm of existence: the bringing near of
Gentiles. This is true in specific form as one reads the life of God with a people in "the
oracles of God entrusted to the Jews" even as an outsider to that story. But having
been brought near by Christ, the first story of transfer—the call of Israel—is redolent
of a second story—the adoption of outsiders—and now encloses under older names
("holy ones") former and latter citizens both ("saints"). That language flexibility—specific
and extensional—lies at the heart of the gospel's proclamation as fully and eternally
"in accordance with the scriptures."

What follows is a single example, on Paul and the scriptures, dealing with the material that follows in the first chapter of this letter. To understand what the theological
language of Paul means, and how it means what it means, requires some sense of how
the scriptures' older and specific horizon is extending itself. It does this, moreover,
without in any way diminishing the particularized speech and action of God in the
old covenants, and indeed shows them to be casting a shadow that is before and after
Christ, for Israel the church, called as was and is Israel.

Paul participates in his own particular account of God's willed work, as imparted
to him via "the oracles of God entrusted to the Jews." Yet he is using that particular
account with those who do not know its details, and so in Colossians he has an extensional version of it he has crafted to his purpose. That is, it is not a matter of avoiding
specific textual quotations due to being in a different (chiefly Gentile) frame of reference—hence no formula citations, specified allusions, and so forth in the letter to the
Colossians.[14] Rather, we may assume Paul has learned very well how to negotiate the
transfer from his own "elected" place as an Israelite into the world he has been called
to convert to Christ. Indeed, he speaks clearly of being situated in the midst of these
delineated groupings in his final greetings (those of the circumcision and those not
of the circumcision). Paul has now had a long career of preaching and teaching, and
this has involved proving Christ from the single holy scriptures before his own people,
addressing proselytes, and speaking to Gentiles (e.g., Acts 17), each context of which

14. Beetham's 2008 monograph examines the evidence for allusions in Colossians. Why does Paul
not provide explicit references as elsewhere? The audience is assumed to be primarily non-Jewish, on the
one hand, and Paul wants to insist that the place given to Torah in creation is now held by Christ, on the
other. Not citing the scriptures in direct ways helps serve this purpose. The view held here is that Paul
is simply an effective missionary who thinks himself into another frame of reference in a way that, over
time, he has become adept at. He is not avoiding reference to the scriptures, and it is not a matter of his
being unconscious of what he is alluding to. Rather, the story of Israel is so his own that he draws on it
consistently with its own extensional potential.

has its own instructional integrity and challenge, each provided with some measure of symmetry and overlap by virtue of there being one cross.

In Col. 1 Paul uses the language of bearing fruit and multiplying, and it has been argued convincingly that here we touch upon the conceptuality of Gen. 1. Others argue against this, as is the usual way in such matters.[15] Some look for explicit recycling of precise phrases and collocations as the Septuagint brokers these so as to make the case more effectively; or to the contrary. In my view the matter requires a looser and not a more restrictive panel against which to pose the question.[16] The language of bearing fruit and multiplying of course does not exist on its own in the Old Testament, but plays out against the effects of sin and disobedience recorded in Gen. 1–11, whose resolution is provided in the promises to Abraham. By means of him, all the nations of the world will be blessed, by this willed calling of him by God in a particular time and space. In part the promise to Abraham is fulfilled, according to Exod. 1. Israel is fruitful and multiplies—to such an extent a hostile "nation" ("Pharaoh who knows not Joseph") plots execution where there had once indeed been blessing in Egypt, for Israel and the nations.

God rescues his people. He gives the law. He provides a deliverer in Moses and in Joshua. He transfers his saints to a promised land, in spite of a generation's rebellion and death in the wilderness. Moses suffers that God's people may be freed and remain his people. He is afflicted on their behalf, asking that his own name be written out of the book of life, and he dies in the wilderness, seeing the promised land—the inheritance promised to Abraham and the ancestors—only from afar. When the promise is again threatened in the period of the prophets, it is renewed and extended afresh, with exile in figural place of wilderness.

This is the basic creedal life of Israel, and it even finds rehearsal in something like that form at various points in the Old Testament, as noted by Gerhard von Rad, and made to serve a prominent reconstruction associated with his name (e.g., Deut. 26:5–11).[17]

When then we hear the language "bearing fruit and growing" the force of its expression as such, and the context from which it emerges, is strengthened when alongside it we hear of the deuteronomic concern for increase of knowledge across the generations (Deut. 6:20–25), of leading a worthy life in the promised land, of giving proper thanks to the Father, of sharing in an inheritance, and of a transfer from a realm of wilderness darkness to a new kingdom. The sacrificed Moses and the deliverer Joshua have become the beloved Son, and the kingdom is one where sin is finally and everlastingly dealt

15. J. Ernst, *Die Briefe an die Philipper, an Philemon, an die Kolosser, an die Epheser*, Regensburger Neues Testament (Regensburg: Pustet, 1974), 158; and Moo 2008: 88n31.

16. Moo in particular is anxious to find precise wording being repeated from the Septuagint, and without this he does not like associations being made. One can see how profligate associative readings could become, but in this instance his method is overweaned insofar as it attends to words in isolation (2008: 103; especially his n94, where he looks for more references to the words for "rescue" and "redeem" in Exodus and finds the verbs insufficiently attested). Moreover, one need not be forced to choose between wilderness and exile, as in the scriptures they are already types. Isaiah's promised land is a redeemed Zion.

17. Gerhard von Rad, *The Problem of the Hexateuch and Other Essays* (New York: McGraw-Hill, 1966), 1–78.

with and put away. The deliverer who makes the promises of Genesis happen is a new Adam, in the eternal image of God, and the being fruitful and multiplying are being accomplished obediently by him. Those who now comprise the saints are those insinuated into a new covenant by divine action, those joining the saints of old, and giving the term a new extensional meaning. The promises to Abraham, which originated in an act of election of a particular people, are made to serve a wider, national purpose. For this, Paul uses the language of "the whole world," which is neither rhetorical exaggeration nor what such a world might look like to him given his Michelin map with its antique limits. It is the language of divinely willed promise. What the scriptures of Israel said to him in their specific detailed promise, he has creatively addressed the Colossians with. Those of the Old Covenant, should they be among the churches in the Lycus Valley, could nod their heads and see the allusions, while those outside the covenants of God, now being called saints with them, can hear the language in its own logical, now exalted register. And in time, as they become mature in Christ, the scriptures of Israel will be opened up to this purposeful apprehension as Paul brokers it on their behalf, and a new extensional significance will also be grasped. So Paul is concerned before he says farewell to exhort the Christians in Colossae to let the word of Christ dwell richly with them: "Teach and admonish each other in all wisdom, and sing psalms and hymns and spiritual songs."

Saints and faithful brothers—Paul makes clear that what he has to say, and who he is concerned for more generally, is directed to the churches of Colossae, Laodicea, and Hieropolis. The letter opens with a focus on the Colossian church with the language "saints and faithful brethren in Christ [*hagios kai pistois adelphois en kristō*] at Colossae." Later (1:12), in speaking of Christ's work of qualification, of rescue, and of transfer, he also speaks of "sharing in the inheritance of the saints in light [*tō hagiōn en tō phōti*]."[18] The phrase is subtle enough to have occasioned discussion, and other renderings of the syntax are proposed. On my view the reference to light is given to contrast with "the dominion of darkness" as this appears in the next verse, where the transference idea is completed.

It is unlikely that with the opening language Paul is speaking of two distinct groups, saints and faithful brothers. However "and" is to be construed, the sense is not "saints" over here and "faithful brothers in Christ" over there, but rather, along the lines of "friends, Romans, countrymen" or "saints, faithful brothers in Christ." When the term "saints" appears in connection with the language of sharing an inheritance "of the saints in light," and a transfer is being accomplished, many have taken the word "inheritance" as triggered by the larger figural background of the Old Testament story. If that is so, and it fits the larger picture described above, the image is not far from the one I have been referring to, whose home is in Eph. 2:11–13: "Therefore remember that at one time you Gentiles in the flesh

---

18. Compare Eph. 1:18: "the hope to which he has called you, what are the riches of his glorious inheritance in the saints [*tis ho ploutos tēs doxēs tēs klēronomias autou en tois hagiois*]."

... were at that time separated from Christ, alienated from the commonwealth of Israel, and strangers to the covenants of promise, having no hope and without God in the world. But now in Christ Jesus you who were far off have been brought near in the blood of Christ."

Paul continues by describing how the union has been accomplished, not by two different (one for willful disobedience and one for estrangement and darkness) but by a single cross. In Ephesians this argument has its own integrity and does not rely in the same way on an unfolding "history of redemption background" (from creation to Abraham to exodus to promised land) such as we sense operating in Colossians in Paul's creative extension for "the saints and faithful brothers in Christ" in 1:3–14. I find it unlikely that Paul addresses two distinctive groups with this opening language (those who are saints and those who are faithful brothers brought near), as this is simply too explicit a delineation to ask the language to bear. We would need a clearer syntactical marker and follow-up in the flow of the address itself.

It is worth noting the textual variant at 1:12 is relevant to this discussion of transfer from a dominion of darkness and being "qualified to share in an inheritance of the saints in light." If the variant "he has qualified *you*" (which has wide support) were adopted, it would perhaps emphasize that Paul is distinguishing between his own state of affairs—as is made clear in Ephesians—and that of Gentiles. Obviously when Paul makes this a point of emphasis in Ephesians he is not imagining two different works of Christ, one for himself and God's people and one for Gentiles, but is rather underscoring what the one cross has done for a particular fulfillment of God's purposes, stretching back to Genesis foundations. One reason for maintaining the reading "he has qualified *us*" is that the first-person plural is a feature of these opening verses in their entirety, as I have emphasized, and because the next sentences read, without textual variation: "He has delivered *us* from the dominion of darkness and transferred *us* to the kingdom of his Son, in whom *we* have redemption, the forgiveness of sins." Here the genius of Paul's logic is made clear. The one story of redemption inherited from the scriptures Paul first-person pluralizes. The inheritance of the saints is figurally given in the entrance to the promised land, beyond the desert of disobedience. The sojourners in the midst accompanied Israel, and faithful Gentiles would play their critical roles (Caleb, Rahab, Ruth), if however always in the supporting parts. When God spoke of a new and renewed Zion (Isa. 54), after the punishment of a different wilderness in exile—a place of chaos and darkness with its own character—those bringing gifts from afar were representatives of the nations. Not the plunder of Egypt this time, but freewill offerings, even from those, so to speak, of "Caesar's own household"—Persian kings drawing from the treasuries of Ecbatana (Ezra 9).

The "holy ones" of God certainly are those called by God in every generation who bear faithful witness to him, but the term arises from its particular place in the story of God with his people as vouchsafed to Paul. It is simply that now the term's extensional meaning is paramount in Paul's mind. Included in the transfer from the kingdom of darkness, included in the qualification for an inheritance of the saints in light, because of the one cross, Paul will highlight no distinction. The word "saints" ranges alongside "saints and faithful brothers" to mean those brought near from the nations, but also, because Paul sees the one story to have its one fulfillment, a common first-person plurality requiring no further conjugating. The scriptures have made their one story a story of one cross's accomplishment for "all the saints."

Somewhat in the spirit of how Ephesians handles this, and for its own rhetorical reasons in Colossians, it is important to note that Paul can emphasize a distinction corresponding to the fate of the Gentiles. So in 1:21–23 the individual first-person Paul can speak to the "you all" he is addressing as "estranged and hostile in mind, doing evil deeds"—a reference that applies to the Gentile condition fairly specifically. But this follows the logic of the movement of Colossians in its full form. Here, at this juncture, Paul is moving toward a specific account of his suffering "for your sake," and this necessitates a shift in horizon, whereby his individual *hyper hymōn* role, alongside the once-for-all redemptive work of Christ, is to the fore (1:24–29). Paul's ministry of affliction on "your behalf" ranges alongside his role as teacher ("to make the word of God fully known") and complements that. Here again we find reference to "the saints" (1:26). The saints are the privileged recipients of an unveiled mystery, having to do with God's revelation to the Gentiles, that is, "Christ in you, the hope of glory." Paul uses the scriptures' extensional sense to relay this mystery, which was imbedded in the literal sense of God's prior word, but could be grasped only by the generation whose eyes were unveiled to see it, given the finished work of Christ. The saints are the first-person plurality God has made possible by this selfsame work.

Grace and peace to you from God the Father—For Paul, the "name above every name" (YHWH) has found proper reference through a gloss in Greek translation, *kyrios* ("the LORD"). How and why this practice emerged within the bosom of Israel we do not know and are unlikely ever properly to know in detail.[19] Perhaps concern with honoring the third commandment came into specific view as Israel found itself "among the nations." Perhaps the practice arose as sacred texts emerged, not from an oral speech origin of proclamation to Israel, but as written compositions that in turn enabled such conventions to be used, identified, and respected (e.g., YHWH *'adonai* in Isaiah and Ezekiel) in the way a written text allows, thereby providing cues for public reading.

The emphasis on "the name" is so frequent in the Old Testament as to threaten to become a cliché or to lose its significance for outsiders. Indeed, it is hard to imagine what use of the proper name of God within the covenantal life actually bespoke. Exodus 3 and kindred texts give us glimpses: to know God is to know his name, and to know his name is to experience his judging and forebearing life

19. Do we see the beginnings of this in later prophetic texts where *'adonai* appears next to the tetragrammaton? Does a diaspora context require special concern for the name (Exod. 20:7)?

with his elected people. The name YHWH is not a hypostasis as in time wisdom might qualify to be called, or the word of God, or the Spirit of God. YHWH ("the LORD") is the Triune God in the form of an acoustic icon.[20] But what that might mean is now overshadowed by the properly triune name as spoken in faith in the church. "Baptize them in the name of the Father and the Son and the Holy Spirit." Israel's Psalms say, "In Judah God is known" and "he has not made his name known to any other nation. Alleluia." So when Christians recite the psalms and say, "Blessed be the name of the LORD / the maker of heaven and earth," that LORD/YHWH finds particular reference in the now Christian gloss, "Glory be to the Father and to the Son and to the Holy Ghost, as it was in the beginning, is now and ever shall be, world without end. Amen."[21]

Paul addresses the saints and faithful brethren, a first-person plurality that includes himself and also the particularities of his theological DNA. Paul is not himself "estranged and darkened of mind" but rather possesses the mystery-bearing "oracles of God entrusted to the Jews." These oracles declare "in Judah God is known" even as God is always hiding himself by his own gracious act as ingredient in "I am who I am" and "the LORD compassionate and merciful" (Exod. 34), and even as he is always more fully to be known. How does Paul communicate to those being brought near and those for whom his ministry—the divine office—is to make God fully known (Col. 1:25)? Can he simply speak the name of Christ and point to the cross? Yes and no, because both require their deep accordance with what has been revealed to be made known, as what it means to comprehend Christ and his cross.

So Paul opens his address to the Colossians with the horizon potentially most inclusive horizon. Paul is "an apostle of Jesus Christ," and he is this "by the will of God." The God of Israel is a jealous God, which means above all that he is a God with a will. By that will he created the heavens and the earth, called Abraham, delivered Israel, gave a revelation of his will, gave an inheritance. And called Paul into that will and work by the address of his Son. So Paul's first theological word to the saints and faithful brethren is "Grace and peace to you from God the Father." "Grace" is the equivalent of "greetings" as any Colossian would hear that, and "peace" is the "shalom" of Paul's more familiar "hello." These are now joined into one as they come from one Father. He is "our Father," and so the address continues the first-person plurality as it explains that God is "Father" because he has a Son, Jesus Christ, and he is "our Father" because "the Lord Jesus Christ" is "our Lord." Paul is not doing complex mathematics here, but he is also not making any errors as he moves through the declension of "the LORD is our God, the LORD alone" (Deut. 6:4 and Mark 12:29) to "the will of God" to "God our Father" to "God, the Father of our Lord Jesus Christ." The one LORD (YHWH, *kyrios*) who is God

20. The phrase appears in William Propp, *Exodus*, Anchor Bible 2 (Garden City: Doubleday, 1999), 272.

21. Most recently, Christopher Seitz, "The Trinity in the Old Testament," in *The Oxford Handbook of the Trinity*, ed. G. Emory and M. Levering (Oxford: Oxford University Press, 2011), 28–40.

alone, includes within his own eternal life (this to be more fully explored below; 1:15–20) the Son Jesus Christ, who is "our Lord" (*kyrios*). The saints and faithful brethren are who they are because they have been included in this history of redemption, and Paul departs not one iota from the theological DNA that is his particular willed destiny as he understands a first-person plurality now brought within its saving address. "Grace and peace to you from God the Father: God, the Father of our Lord Jesus Christ" is the trinitarian confession enabled by the Spirit, in its particular biblical idiom, embracing Jew and Gentile in the fulfillment of God's will and purpose as set forth in the mystery of his revelation.[22]

---

22. For further reading, Yeago, "New Testament and Nicene Dogma"; Christopher Seitz, *Figured Out: Typology and Providence in Christian Scripture* (Louisville: John Knox, 2001), 131–44, 177–90; and Bauckham 1999.

PAUL AND ASSOCIATES
GIVE THANKS

(1:3–8)

1:3 we thank God, the Father of our Lord Jesus Christ, always, whenever we pray for you—For what reason might it be proper to give thanks for others, except as we have firsthand experience of them? So, in the opening verses of Philippians Paul gives personal thanks for his remembrance of these fellow Christians (1:3). Paul is thankful for a partnership he has experienced with them and continues to maintain (3:2). He holds them in his heart, even as he is away from them and in prison (1:7). Paul would be happy to depart and be with the Lord but he would miss out in marking their progress and joy in the faith (1:25). Paul acknowledges the hope he has shortly to return and visit them personally (2:24). The intimacy and tenderness of this exchange are well known and fitting given the knowledge Paul has of the Philippian congregation based upon his experience with them.

The Thessalonian correspondence is similar in its grounding of Paul's thankfulness (1 Thess. 1:2–10). Paul speaks of his remembrance of their "faith and labor of love and steadfastness in hope" (1:3). They became actual imitators of Paul and as such examples to others, whose faith was thereby nourished. The firsthand character of Paul's fellowship with them he likens to nursing (2:7), and the sharing of his very self as a father with children. As in Philippians, Paul has had expectation of revisiting them, but has had to dispatch Timothy in his place. The report Timothy has brought brings only thanksgiving and the hope that he will soon see them face to face (3:10).

When we come to Colossians the situation is altogether different. Paul has no firsthand experience of this church. What he learns from Epaphras (1:7), as with Timothy in Thessalonians, heartens him, but Paul has had no role in proclaiming the gospel in their church or in raising up Epaphras in this role of "faithful

minister." He never speaks of visiting them, or of the hope of this. He acknowledges that the faith among them for which he gives thanks was the consequence
of another's labor and not his own.

It is important to keep the distinctive character of Paul's thankfulness in this
letter in mind, and the signal position his account has in the letter's unfolding.
Colossians 1:3–8 forms one continuous sentence, and the awkward syntax of this
run-on style is one of the reasons many argue for a different hand than Paul's at
work. But arguments from style must contend with the different circumstances
within which declarations are being made, and Colossians offers a distinctive
context for Paul's thankfulness over against the other epistolary witnesses. Like
Romans and Ephesians, Paul is addressing a church whose faith has arisen independently of his own efforts. Indeed, Eph. 1:15 ("for this reason, because I have heard
of your faith in the Lord and your love for all the saints") is phrased in terms so
close to that of Col. 1:4 it presents one of those places where people argue Ephesians is the first commentary on Colossians, or vice versa, or some amalgam of both
views. Paul is witnessing a church being born before his eyes and without his usual
missionary exertions, for which in Thessalonians and Philippians he gives robust
thanks in respect of fruitfulness. My point in emphasizing this is that one must
contend with the possibility that this development was not foreseen by Paul in
these terms. Something is happening in consequence of activity he did not initiate
or oversee or even hope for from afar. His ministry is now a ministry of ardent
praying, alongside letter writing and a fellowship of encouragement and concern
and mutual reflection (4:7–18).[1] Even the mention of the role of Epaphras comes
at the end of the long sentence unit and not at the beginning. The faith Paul gives
thanks for is "your faith," and it has spilled into acts of love and of hope.

The sentence reads in something like this way, picking up from the initial
thanks and then proceeding as follows: **We thank God whenever we pray for
you: having heard of your faith in Christ Jesus and the love that you have for
all the saints, our thanksgiving being grounded, in the hope laid up for you
in heaven, which you (also) heard before in the word of truth, the gospel that
has come to you, just as in all the world it is bearing fruit and growing—so
also among yourselves, from the day you heard and understood the grace of
God in truth learning it in this way from Epaphras our beloved fellow servant
who is faithful on our behalf, the servant of Christ, and he has made known
to us your love in the Spirit.**

Before I turn to the implications of this form of expression, I need to broaden
the lens to capture something of the context assumed by the letter, and how this
is specifically a factor in the way Paul now addresses the church far away in the

---

1. On *peri hymōn proseuchomenoi* Eadie comments thus: "The apostle prayed for them—such was his
interest in them, and sympathy with them, that he bore their names on his heart to the throne of grace. Nor
could such an 'effectual fervent prayer of a righteous man' be without its rich results. The suppliant in his
far off prison was like the prophet on Carmel, and as he prayed, the 'little cloud' might be descried, which,
as it gradually filled and darkened the horizon, brought with it the 'sound of abundance of rain'" (1856: 7).

Lycus Valley of Asia Minor. Then I can better reflect on why the syntax appears to pile up subordinate clauses whose relation to one another seems overextended.[2]

Excursus: Prison Apostleship and Fellowship

The modern commentary tradition provides ample discussion of Paul's journeys and particularly his time in Asia Minor, and I will not rehearse that here. Theodoret's view that Paul visited the Lycus Valley and had personal contact with the church of Colossae is virtually a lone view in the tradition and has rarely been defended in modern commentary; the plain sense of so much of the letter makes clear that Paul has had no firsthand contact with the churches in Colossae, Hieroplis, or Laodicea. If Acts is to be trusted for its geographical presentations, it stands to reason that Paul's three-year stay in Ephesus might well have resulted in conversions to the Christian faith of men like Epaphras. He is a native of Colossae according to Col. 4:12. Philemon and Onesimus also hail from the Lycus Valley. The larger towns of Hieropolis and Laodicea are sufficiently nearby for them to merit mention in the same context as Paul's address to the church at Colossae. Was this city destroyed by earthquake in AD 61–62, as intimated by ancient sources, and to such an extent that the date of the letter must reasonably be set prior to this time (or shown to be written to a fictional city for other purposes at a later time)? I have no fixed method to determine this, as much effort has been expended all the same. The letter simply stands before us: as dictated by Paul, in association with Epaphras and Onesimus, who have joined him in his imprisonment. Paul knows what he knows about the churches of this section of Asia Minor not by having traveled there (as the main roads go, it would have been a difficult journey from Ephesus, and Acts mentions nothing about it in its travelogue references, which would have been easy enough to do) but by the accounts of his associates (Phil. 4:14 speaks of "partnering" with Paul) and from his general knowledge of the area more broadly.

It is argued that Roman imprisonment makes difficult sense given the distance from Colossae and the assumption that a runaway slave and a man like Epaphras would not easily make the trip or be expected to return so. But this is far from clear. The journey is by boat and not overland. It is far easier to join the tradition and assume that the common reference to imprisonment in Philippians, Colossians, and Philemon is Roman. In my view that is the canonical-historical intention, and it makes far better sense than inferring an unknown Ephesian or Caesarean context; the reasons to oppose these reconstructions are widely available.

Why would people visit Paul? To help share his jail time, some hold. To bring him monetary and other support, so Philippians declares. To seek out the apostle of renown and honor him with prayers and fellowship, must also be considered. Paul himself refers to these visits as personal in character, having to do with supporting him in whatever way they or he consider encouraging. If the incidental reference in 2 Tim. 1:16–18 is not to be judged false (due to theories about the Pastorals' non-Pauline character),

2. Moo 2008: 81 has a helpful illustration of the subordinations (he terms them "digressions").

Paul's visitor Onesiphorus eagerly sought him out. Paul speaks of those who share his troubles and of gifts sent to him by personal emissary in Phil. 4:14–18, from one Epaphroditus. Most hold that this name, whose shortened form is Epaphras, refers to a different individual than our church planter in Colossians and Philemon. All the same we get some idea of prison visitation in specific respect of him earlier in the letter. He is called the Philippians' messenger and minister to Paul's need (Phil. 2:25), and Paul also refers to him in his own context as "brother and fellow worker and fellow soldier." By some means—it would be intriguing to know how, if not by well-traveled lines of communication—the church who sent him has learned that he was gravely ill, "risking his life to complete your service to me" (2:30). Paul is sending him back to the church so that they may receive him with joy as restored to health.

In Colossians the reasons for Epaphras's visit to Paul are never given, so it makes little sense to highlight these via speculation, as is frequently done. If the main reason for his visiting is to speak of problems he is having and ask Paul's support to combat false teaching, as many hold, it is odd that the references to him sound very much like he has no intention of returning (so Lightfoot 1997: 30; Moo 2008: 27). In 4:12 Paul conveys his greetings from afar. Epaphras is described as a man of striving prayer on behalf of them. Paul bears witness that "he has worked hard for you and for those in Laodicea and in Hieropolis" (4:13), and there is no suggestion of any pending return. The letter is being sent via Tychicus and Onesimus, not Epaphras.[3] Instead he is ranged alongside the many others who are in fellowship with Paul and who for various reasons send their greetings along with him, who Paul refers to with the preeminent title of "servant of Christ." Greetings are given to the church at the house of Nympha, and letters are to be exchanged. None of this implicates Epaphras as exercising any future role in any way. Even more final sounding is the farewell from the letter to Philemon, where Epaphras again appears and is called "fellow prisoner," listed first among the "fellow workers" (Phlm. 23–24).

It is argued that references to Epaphras in this way are such as to argue he has had a falling out with the church in Colossae, and that is why no suggestion of his return is being made.[4] Paul is siding with him against his detractors and opponents. But this simply reads too much into the meager accounting we have. It relies on the implication that the matter is too sensitive to refer to except obliquely. The better course is to accept Paul's thanksgiving for the church at Colossae at face value, as well as his reference to Epaphras as the source of their learning of faith in Christ Jesus without implication of special pleading on his behalf. More importantly, when 4:13 speaks of Epaphras as constant in striving prayer on behalf of the church he has departed to

---

3. Moo writes of Epaphras's visit to Paul: "He had traveled to where Paul was in prison 'for the sake of the gospel,' and had, apparently, even joined Paul in his imprisonment (in Phlm. 23 Paul calls him a 'fellow prisoner')" (2008: 27). Moo provides no corroboration for his next assertion: "He was not able, then, to travel back to Colossae with the letter Paul writes, so Paul commissions Tychicus to do the job instead" (2008: 27). Was he "unable"? The letter does not tell us this. Epaphras appears congenially and thankfully alongside the apostle, with no appearance of "let or hindrance."

4. See Wall, "Romans 1:1–15"; and the counterarguments of Moo 2008: 344.

be with Paul, he mirrors Paul's own vocation on behalf of them (especially 2:1). It has become a vocation with its own integrity. He and Paul share it, "absent in body yet with you in Spirit" (2:5) as fellow prisoners. Indeed, one could argue that a general rubric under which to lodge "the intention of Colossians" is found in the context of Paul's own remarks about Epaphras's ministry of prayer and hard work: "That you may stand mature and fully assured in Christ" (4:12). Paul uses the same language of his own ministry on their behalf in 1:28 (*teleton/teletoi*). When he speaks with some gravity about stewardship of his office "that we may present each man mature in Christ," it would be wrong to move too quickly over the first-person plural. Paul and Epaphras (and Timothy and others) share a vocation on behalf of a church whose maturity is their concern, even as they are not present, and indeed *precisely because they are not*.[5]

New occasions teach new duties. Paul's imprisonment has its own sacramental efficacy and providential intention. Having seen eliminated a particular kind of first-person singular role of missionary travel, teaching, arguing from scripture, and proclamation, Paul's apostleship has broken forth into a new mode of partnership for Christ that has its own intention in God's mysterious purpose. Paul has been given insight to see and accept that. Colossians is the letter that makes this transition clearer than others we possess. This also explains something of the change in style and content this letter displays. As Barclay economically puts it: "But if the topic of the conversation differs, we cannot insist that Paul always use the same language!" (2004: 29). The topic of the conversation is different because Paul's apostolic vocation is now being exercised under the constrains of "remember my fetters" but also under the equally unbridled fellowship of prayer and companionship in affliction and encouragement in Christ. When therefore we hear the opening "we" thanksgiving that sets the tone for this letter, Paul is not chiefly thankful, as in Philippians, that a church he knows is maturing

5. In Kiley's study of the pseudepigraphical Paul in Colossians, he is forced, as others who hold this view, to think through what the purpose of the letter then might be. Did the letter emerge from the rubble after an earthquake destroyed the town? Or was it written to a destroyed town so as to effect a more universal message not limited to one place, and if so, what was it? This would enable the letter to be exchanged, a theme that Kiley wants to highlight and that is otherwise congenial with my own nonpseudepigraphical reading. What is intriguing is the very oblique purpose that emerges from his conception: "On the simplest level, the presentation of Epaphras in the letter may allow us to say that, in some sense, Col serves as a letter of recommendation for Epaphras" (1986: 103). Following C. L. Mitton (*Ephesians* [London: Oliphants, 1976], 29), Kiley holds that Colossians "is Paul's message for today" intended to "portray the universal and timeless aspects of Paul's teaching" (Kiley 1986: 106). P. W. Meyer ("Pauline Theology: A Proposal for a Pause in Its Pursuit," in *Pauline Theology*, ed. E. E. Johnson and D. M. Hay [Atlanta: Scholars Press, 1997], 4.140–60) speaks of the difficulty with prohibiting Paul from having his own changes in view as he writes each letter afresh. So what evidence is there from the letter itself that Epaphras will return to Colossae accompanied by a recommendation in the form of the letter? All we learn from Colossians is that its bearer to the church in the Lycus Valley is Tychicus. I suppose the letter could serve to warrant his ministry if we had a better picture of his anticipated role than the letter in fact gives us. Certainly the letter does envision a particular exhortation in respect of Archippus (4:17). But it is clearly Paul's exhortation. The letter speaks for itself and recommends itself. It is a "letter of recommendation for Epaphras" (Kiley 1986: 106) only in the sense that he is one of them and serves as a shining example for them.

in Christ and that one day he may visit them again. Nor is he thankful that a church he raised up has thought enough of him to remember him with a sustaining gift and with a personal emissary who he will soon return to them after a bout of grave illness. In Colossians the thanksgiving is for the church having received the gospel from one who is now with Paul and who with him is fast in prayer on their behalf, as a vocation unto itself. It will be by this means that he will exercise his ministry in fellowship with others and by this means also accomplish his vocation of bringing them to maturity in Christ. His letter will give instruction both through its content and also through its report of what is happening in the context of Paul's present life. Meeks was right to speak of different models of instruction, in this case, including not only the teaching first imparted by Epaphras or imparted via Paul's epistle exhortation in the hands of emissaries, but also as focused on himself as in a fellowship of prayer and encourage-ment on their behalf, no longer a matter of firsthand exchange.[6]

1:4 having heard of your faith in Christ Jesus and the love that you have for all the saints—Thus begins the long sentence running from 1:3 through 1:8, to be further developed in 1:9–14.[7] Why such compounding? To say it is a different author is not to answer that question, but to move it around. My "in the letter answer" is that the coming of the gospel to the Colossians was in such a manner that Paul is correlating that independent action with what he knows to be so in his own frame of reference, and so is assuring them of its authenticity. In addition, the independence is not fully without human agency: Epaphras is from whom they learned "the grace of God in truth." But before he registers that, he wishes to assert a symmetry between the way the gospel has come to the Colossians, to himself (as such and as verifier), and indeed to all the world. This accounts for the piling up effect that now is in evidence in 1:3–8, and that therefore requires careful attention as to proper translation.

In 1:4, to start off, Paul and those for whom he speaks give thanks always because the Colossians' faith in Christ and the love for all the saints that results from that have become known to them. Paul leads with this statement, rather than reference to their teacher and his agency in their reception of the truth of the gospel. This is consistent with the idea shortly to be set forth that "the word of truth, the gospel" is making itself known in all of the world (1:6). It is prospering according to God's command, given in similar form in Gen. 1.

The sentence continues: **our thanksgiving being grounded, in the hope laid up for you in heaven**. Here we encounter the first significant interpretative prob-lem created by the syntax of Paul's complex declaration of thanks (necessitating my parenthetical interpretation). Some hold that "hope" should be part of a familiar triad (faith, love, hope) and that what is being said (via a lapidary *dia* in Greek)

---

6. See Meeks's essay in *Hermes and Athena: Biblical Exegesis and Philosophical Theology*, ed. Eleonore Stump and Thomas P. Flint (Notre Dame, IN: University of Notre Dame Press, 1993), 37–58.

7. Note the repetitions of 1:6 and 1:9 ("heard"); 1:3 and 1:12 ("thank"); 1:3 and 1:9 ("always"; "not stopped"); 1:3 and 1:9 ("pray"); 1:6 and 1:10 ("bearing fruit"; "growing").

is that the Colossians' faith and love is in consequence their reliance on the hope that is now laid up for them in heaven. This is of course its own interpretation, and a more neutral way of translating would simply leave the matter up to the reader to decide ("because we have heard of your faith . . . because of the hope"). TNIV and NIV are more specific in making the faith and hope of 1:4 based on the hope of 1:5: "The faith and love that spring from the hope."

1:5 I prefer the arguments of Eadie and others that Paul is here giving thanks because of the hope he is convinced, in consequence of the faith and love manifested by them, is laid up for them.[8] Further, he is clarifying his acknowledgment that they themselves heard of this hope when they received the gospel independently of his own labor. Hence 1:5's finale: **That you (also) heard before in the word of truth, the gospel**. This makes the best sense of the compound syntax. It also avoids what became a theological debate traceable to the alternative translation, namely, that the faith and love of Christians is generated primarily on the basis of an account laid up in heaven, itself constituting "hope." Instead, the achievement of Paul in this expression is to coordinate what he knows to be the result of their faith in Christ and love for the saints—hope is laid up for them in heaven—and what he believes confidently they also heard on this score when the gospel, the word of truth, came to them. What he testifies to, in thanksgiving, is what he also confirms was the way the gospel came to them "before."

1:6 The independent coming of the gospel is the theme of the following verse as well, where the scale on Paul's map is revealed: **That has come to you, just as in all the world it is bearing fruit and growing**. Paul's argument is that what he knows to be the case, as apostle of prayer from afar, namely, that hope is stored up for the Colossians in heaven by virtue of their faith and love, is consistent with the message that first came to them in the word of truth, the gospel. And moreover, this selfsame reality is marching fully into all of the world. He will show us the scale on his map a second time in 1:23 when he writes: "I have become a minister of the gospel that you heard, *which has been preached to every creature under heaven*."

1:7–8 I discussed above the framework out of which Paul is working. He has not sat down with his Bible and mapped out a one-to-one reconfiguration of the story of Genesis through Joshua, now in a key that Gentiles can hear, in a way that might satisfy us doing the same thing from the Gentile side of the equation, armed with a Septuagint and his text and thus tracking him closely. In more general terms he uses the story he lives in and extends its sense-making in the light of Christ's work of redemption, for which that of Abraham and Moses and Joshua is a deeply

8. Eadie offers this interpretation in a paraphrase: "'Having heard of your faith in Christ Jesus, and the love which ye have to all the saints, as often as we pray for you, we thank God, the Father of our Lord Jesus Christ, on account of the hope laid up for you in heaven'" (1856: xxxix). He continues: "That is to say, the report of their faith and love prompted him to give thanks, but as he gave thanks, the final issue and crown of those graces rose into prominence before him, and he adds, on account of the hope laid up for you in heaven. Their faith and love, viewed not merely in present exercise, but also in their ultimate consummation and bliss, were the grounds of his thanksgiving" (1856: 9).

rooted, reflexively alive, template. The word that has come to the Colossians is "bearing fruit and growing" (*karpophoroumenon kai auxanoumenon*) in just the same way "in all the world" (*en panti tō kosmō*). Neither rhetorical excess nor poor geography, the image stands alongside God's disclosure of the extent of his promises for the whole world as magisterially given to Abraham in Gen. 12. In turn, the language of bearing fruit and growing, while a common image, in biblical (Ps. 1) or more general terms, most likely in this instance is generated from the same Genesis backdrop.[9] Human beings (*'adam*) are commanded to "be fruitful and multiply." The sin in the garden distresses but does not erase the divine intention, as can be seen after the flood (Gen. 8:17; 9:1, 7) and reiterated to Abraham and the ancestors, and coming to startling culmination in Egypt under Joseph and beyond, with a generation that Pharaoh cursed and did not bless (Exod. 1:7). In the unit soon to follow, Paul will speak of Christ as "the image of the invisible God" (Col. 1:15), another evocation of Gen. 1. The word coming to Paul is that the command to humankind is undertaken by the one Lord Christ and in his hands made to prosper in the entire cosmos, befitting the scale of that opening chapter of sacred scripture. The gospel is creating descendants throughout all creation, new sons and daughters, saints, in fulfillment of that first command, now brought to fruition by Christ. The Colossians are part of that scenario. Paul is part of it, in a role of specially commissioned diaconate (1:23). That role he now shares with his associates in prison, who pray on behalf of the new saints in Christ in Colossae, Laodicea, and Hieropolis. Paul is a point on a map of enormous scale and of enormous temporal breadth, stretching back to the very creation of time itself. It is this particular note that Colossians sounds above others and that accounts for the scale and grandeur of Paul's imagery and the compounding we witness in this long sentence, which continues, **so also among yourselves, from the day you heard and understood the grace of God in truth learning it in this way from Epaphras our beloved fellow servant**.

Again, the reason for the piling up in the sentence structure is the movement back and forth on Paul's map as he speaks of what has occurred to them, what it means as he plays it back to them, and how all this is now being accomplished on a grand scale in which he is himself as much actor as confirmer of prior action. The gospel has been "heard and understood" (*ēkousate kai epegnōte*)—common enough verbs not to require biblical correlation, though they are all over the gospel of Isaiah, as a generation that will not hear or understand (6:9–10) becomes one that has ears and understanding (43:8–10), and in that new graced life, gives hearing and understanding to the nations (52:11). The messenger of good tidings was Epaphras, most likely a convert of Paul during his ministry in Asia Minor,

---

9. In Gen. 1:28 the verbs combined are *auxanō* and *plēthynō*. This same pairing is what appears subsequently in 8:17; 9:1, 7; 17:20; 28:3; 35:11; 47:27; and Exod. 1:7 in the Septuagint. Of course the question may be fairly asked, if not easily answered: is Paul constrained by a translation we are familiar with, in which the verb here used in the pair (*karpophoreō*) is very rare (Hab. 3:17), or does he operate more freely working from memory or adapting to his present purpose?

though Paul does not dwell on that if it was so. He is a beloved fellow servant. The truth of that is borne out in how Paul now concludes his long opening sentence: **Who is faithful on our behalf, the servant of Christ, and he has made known to us your love in the Spirit.**

Paul speaks of the day (*ap' hēs hēmeras*) when the Colossians heard and understood the grace of God in truth. The first day of new creation was the "and God said" day when Epaphras communicated a new creator to them. And Epaphras in turn has made known, as an extension of their coming to know, "to us your love in the Spirit." The Spirit that hovered with word and God at creation is active to bring about comprehension across time and space. The day of understanding in Colossae has a corresponding day of hearing and confirmation in Paul's prison church, and it is on that note that he chooses to proceed.

OUR PRAYERS FOR YOU AND OUR COMMON DESTINY IN CHRIST

(1:9–14)

1:9–14 And so, from the day we heard of it, we have not ceased to pray for you and to ask that you be filled with the knowledge of God's will in all spiritual wisdom and understanding, so as to lead a life worthy of the Lord, fully pleasing to him, bearing fruit in every good work and increasing in the knowledge of God. May you be completely strengthened by virtue of his glorious might, for all endurance and patience with joy, giving thanks to the Father, who has qualified us to share in the inheritance of the saints in light. He has rescued us from the dominion of darkness and transported us to the kingdom of his beloved Son, in whom we have redemption, the forgiveness of sins.

Several things are significant by way of summary. First, the language in these six verses reverberates from what has already been said in the preceding text. Prayer was referred to in 1:3; knowledge in 1:6; God's will in 1:1; spirit in 1:8; bearing fruit and increasing in 1:6; giving thanks in 1:3; Father in 1:3; saints in 1:2, 4. Second, Paul here focuses on what can be said of his concerns on their behalf (1:9–11), but again with a clear sense of a common destiny shared by them and by Paul and his associates (1:12–14); indeed, the cosmic scope of what is at stake is never relinquished even through 1:23. And finally, the verses move forward as well as backward to extend what was expressed in 1:3–8, for by speaking of the common destiny carved out for them by the Father's action in the Son (1:12–14) the space is opened up for a focus on their relationship one to another, as set forth in shimmering detail in the passage to follow (1:15–20).

As noted above, Paul picks up on his language of "the day they heard and understood" in Colossae and refers it now to the day in his own context, that is, **the day we heard of it**. The concerns mentioned in these first verses flow naturally from the context of enthusiasm and joy that Paul and his friends have noted. It is important that a purported false teaching not be given center stage when it has yet to make any appearance. The gospel is bearing fruit and growing in all the world, and so Paul wants to underscore that the prayers that are unceasing on their behalf have as their outcome the same fruitfulness, outwardly (**in every good work**) and inwardly, in the increase in the knowledge of God. The recycling of language from 1:3–8 is a clear signal that Paul is continuing in the same basic vein. What has come to them by way of Epaphras is to be augmented, now by virtue of Paul and Epaphras's (and others') common and unceasing prayer on their behalf. Unceasing (*pantote*) thanksgiving (1:3) has its precise counterpart in the prison praying of Paul and his associates. The general and unspecified realm of this augmentation and growth is made evident by the repetition of **all**: so "in all [*pasē*] spiritual wisdom" (1:9); "fully [*pasan*] pleasing" (1:10); "in every [*panti*] good work" (1:10); "in all [*pasē*] power" (1:11); "for all [*pasan*] endurance" (1:11). Paul does not give indication that his prayerful petitioning for them is occasioned by a specific problem hounding them in their religious environment. Rather, his prayers are for their growth in the knowledge of God and their response to that—in every and all exhibition, including endurance and patience. This is all to happen in the context of joy, which spills into *eucharistountes*, the shared thanksgiving life (1:12).

I discussed above the preference for staying with the first-person-plural reading (so NA[27]) consistently throughout 1:12–14. The one Father of Paul and the Colossians has given common reason for thanksgiving, as in his action in Christ he has made them all saints in light. God's holy people have become Jew and Gentile both, in consequence of the Father's action of rescue and transporting. The term **inheritance**, as noted by commentators, is redolent of Old Testament implication. It can draw on the promise of inheritance in the ancestor narratives and can also refer to the promised land. The promised inheritance of the Suffering Servant is also a theme of Isa. 53 and the final chapters of Isaiah (54–66), where the servants of the servant proliferate and also find the dividing wall of Israel and the nations collapse, as now fully in Christ. The wilderness darkness of rebellion and sin and death, figurally repeated in exile, birthed a new generation in the former day and in the latter day a forgiven Zion, servants, and children she knew not, by the accomplishment of the servant. The promises to David extended to the servants (Isa. 55:3) is a prefigurement of **the kingdom of his beloved Son** (Col. 1:13), by means of the redemption and forgiveness Isaiah referred to and Christ prosecuted by the cross. Thus far, however, the emphasis in Colossians is on the Father's initiative in all this. He qualified, rescued, and transported us. With this emphasis in place, Paul will now shift his focus to the identity and achievement of the Son (1:15–20).

Paul has brought the story of creation, redemption, inheritance, and kingship/dominion into a shared narrative of the saints, now enclosing the Colossians and aiming at the entire world as its creation-intended target. Nothing in these verses is focused on anything more specific in the realm of false teaching or the anticipation of that. Paul is seeing the Colossians and the spread of the gospel through a wider lens than had previously been his instinct, precisely due to his imprisonment and the emergence of a new form of apostolic life, in prayer and letter address, an extension of these vocations against a now wider canvas. His prayerful exertions and the form he gives expression to them in the letter thus far serve to emphasize growth in knowledge and increase in good works generated by thanksgiving for what God the Father has done for them all. The narrative of redemption and the manifold patterns of that, in Genesis–Joshua or in Isaiah, leech inevitably into Paul's fresh articulation of the gospel as he conveys this in thanksgiving to "those brought near" in Colossae.

Excursus: The Knowledge of God

When Paul prays that the Colossians will increase in the knowledge of God, what does he have in mind? Does one move through various grades in the knowledge of God, in terms of quantification? Is this what he means? In some measure, the answer is yes. One comes to know God more and more. To come into relationship with God is in the nature of the case to be brought more deeply, by that relationship, in obedience, to the knowledge of him. One goes from sight to sight, even against the backdrop of seeing darkly compared to what we will know when he is seen face to face. So at the burning bush God reveals himself as "I am who I am" and yet the knowledge of him unfolds in relationship to obedience or to disobedience and judgment: "The Lord is compassionate and merciful, slow to anger and of vast kindness, but by no means will clear the guilty, visiting on generations." In the *visitations* of kindness, forbearance, and judgment, the revealed Lord makes himself known. He begins with particular relationships and by means of these he witnesses and is witnessed to. So, Ruth comes to know and to name the Lord and to live in his light. The sailors bound for Tarshish come to know the Lord by virtue of his judgment over a disobedient prophet—the ironic prophetic announcement of Jonah after all. Nebuchadnezzar praises the God of Daniel when he is sundered in his pride and brought low. The non-Israelite (or pre-Israelite) Job confesses that he was aware by hearsay but knows by perseverance that he beholds God as God is, an adumbration of the "I am" whose disclosure to Moses extends and augments what was known by the ancestors and by Job in promise and in pledge. The great *'elohim* who is Yhwh "will make himself known" to Israel, the nations, and all creation, as the narratives of Exod. 3–15 display that.[1]

1. See "The Call of Moses and the 'Revelation' of the Divine Name" (Seitz, *Word Without End*, 229–50).

When Paul speaks of the action of the Father in Col. 1:3–14, does he refer to Yₕwₕ the Triune God or to the Father of Jesus Christ, or can that be untangled? Luther famously experimented with a translation of the opening line of Ps. 110, "Der Herr sprach zu meinem HErr" and by orthographic means sought to distinguish in the one YHWH an ontological distinction being made known—as a gift of the Holy Spirit—to David. The one LORD (HEER) speaks within his divine identity to the Son, "my Lord" (HErr). David was the prophet who spoke by the Holy Spirit, and for Luther that meant, who could see the inner life of Yₕwₕ in certain special places, like Ps. 2 or Ps. 110.[2]

The issue is important precisely because Paul is bringing the one horizon of the oracles of God entrusted to the Jews into coordination—because God has so made it known to him—with the new life of the Colossians in Christ, making him and them "saints" both in a new creation. The Yₕwₕ who is the willing and active *kyrios* of scriptural declaration, the protagonist in a drama from creation to new creation, has qualified his saints to an inheritance he promised as that protagonist to an elect people. A kingdom eternally guarded and kept by solemn promise and covenant is by Yₕwₕ being enlarged by virtue of his Son's obedient work, now enclosing all who in various ways lived in darkness and sin. The Father is he who raised Jesus from the dead, but at the same time Yₕwₕ is God and by his word and Spirit he is eternally who he is. The ambiguation cannot be underdetermined (Yₕwₕ and the Son are unrelated) nor overdetermined (Yₕwₕ is the Father alone).

The challenge for Christian theology is proper handling, appropriate to its character as a two-testament witness, the biblical witness to God in Christ. The easiest paths are (a) emphasizing diversity by simple fact of the sheer majesty and range of the two Testaments, together and apart, by historical-critical or by literary-critical declension; (b) turning the Old Testament into a falsely "Lutheran" melodrama, in the manner of Jung or Walter Brueggemann, whereby God's "dark side" is evolving haphazardly into self-knowledge and individuation; (c) Kantian selection, where who God is comes to us by naturally imparted Geiger counter in the form of "God can't be like that" and so "must be like that instead"; and (d) economic educationalism, where God hides behind language accommodating itself to the seasons of his otherwise genuine, but unstated, life with creation. Over against these options, Paul the Biblical Theologian shows us a better way.

His scriptures are not christotelic in some "tradition-historical" or "salvation-historical" sense primarily, whereby they live their own life en route to an economic denouement, whose culminating chapter Paul happens to share in time. Rather, they contain within their own providential unfolding an organic connective tissue that partakes of Christ and his work. The point will be made insistently in the unit to follow (1:15–20). But it also inheres with what he has been saying of God's work in Christ thus far (1:3–14), whereby the pattern of redemption stretching from creation to inheritance is shown to be figurally operative with Israel as a type that informs and clarifies the present life

2. Christine Helmer, "Luther's Trinitarian Hermeneutic and the Old Testament," *Modern Theology* 18 (2002): 49–73.

of the saints. Y$_{HWH}$'s promise and fulfillment in relation to Israel, his "I will be with you as I will be with you," is what it is for the saints of former days, but also at "the same time" the Father's action of redemption, inclosing Gentiles and Jews by one cross in one dominion marked by Christ's forgiving blood. The economic unfolding of Y$_{HWH}$'s triune life with creation, Israel, the saints, is inextricably a disclosure of his character and his ontology, the love of the Father for the Son, as the Spirit makes it known.

The scriptures that Paul calls the "oracles of God" are not a receptacle of diversities to be correlated after the fact by theological labor. Theology properly speaking follows Paul in apprehending who God is as disclosed in scripture, and how the work of God in Christ accords with that, economically and ontologically. Paul rehearses the significance of the pattern of redemption, as this has been his own theological DNA, and at the same time the extensional potential of that pattern sheds light on Christ's work of redemption in time, backward and forward. The figural dimension of scripture is paramount, not its salvation-historical "BC over here and then AD." And this serves as well to explain the next chapter of his address to the Colossians and why it follows in this place. Having spoken of the Father's action in qualification, rescue, and transfer, Paul now explains how this is at the same time the work of the Son, who is his very image. To know God and to increase in the knowledge of him is to see as deeply as possible how the scriptures speak of Y$_{HWH}$ and in doing so speak of the Father and the Son as the Spirit has disclosed and is disclosing that.

HYMN TO CHRIST
FROM HIS SCRIPTURES

(1:15–20)

▬ *Excursus: Transition to Colossians 1:15–20*

We now enter that stretch of terrain where, for differing reasons of evaluation, three of the best-known texts of Paul's letter to the Colossians are said to reside (1:15–2:23).[1] To speak in this way is to move past some obvious questions, for example: (a) Why would such texts wait to make an appearance fifteen verses into the address of the letter if they are so crucial to our interpretation of Colossians? (b) If they are prominent for *different* reasons, what is their relationship to one another in the argument of this central section of text? (c) How do they pick up from the opening fourteen verses and also relate to the material in Col. 3–4? This question is particularly pertinent to the final text in question, as it is held to reflect a context of false teaching. Yet the tone of exhortation follows without much slowing down through the entirety of Col. 3. How do we then understand the sharpness of the alleged context of "false teaching" against a more extended concern for general exhortation? The three texts to which I refer are:

the Christ hymn (1:15–20)
Christ afflictions *in extenso* (1:24–29)
the threat of false teaching (2:8–23)

The prominence of the last of these was not lost on an earlier history of interpretation, but the manner in which it now asserts itself is in proportion to the promise held out by historical-critical methods to bring precision to the religious situation on the

---

1. Moo 2008: 107 writes, e.g., of 1:15–20: "This passage, the most famous in the letter."

ground in Colossae. Indeed, the hopefulness about this quest has been such that the true occasion for the letter's composition has also said to have been discovered. Paul wrote Colossians to address the false teaching in the Lycus Valley, though exactly how he knew about that and why he waited until Col. 2 to pick up the main theme of his address differs among interpreters.

The centrality of this problem-solving model for reading Colossians also spills into the interpretation of the Christ hymn. The text had been prominent previously because of the place it held in dogmatic articulations, including creedal language in the Nicene-Constantinopolitan creed, and was hammered out in debate over texts like Col. 1:15–20; John 1:1–14; Prov. 8:22–31; Gen. 1:1–27; and others. But in the modern period the centrality of its interpretation is tied to the religio-historical environment and how the hymn would anticipate teaching errors and foreclose certain false routes being held up as attractive in the world of Colossian Christianity, which Paul knows and which he begins to thwart by means of this hymn.[2] He either chose the hymn and adapted it to this purpose. Or fortuitously it was there to hand and said what needed to be said in the context of his rejecting false teaching. Or he composed the hymn himself always and only for this purpose. The diachronic investigation is attuned to determining the extent of the inherited hymn; Paul's redaction over against its original thrust; whether Paul wrote it (how it compares with other linguistic and syntactical distinctives in Colossians, like the sentence structure of 1:3–8); whether its Christology reflects a novum over against the genuine letters. The emphasis on the text as such within the limits of 1:15–20 comes to the fore, as against its relationship (if any inherent one there be) with the passage that precedes this one (which does refer to Christ and his kingdom).

The second text's prominence in some measure trades on the simple challenge in what is being said. How can the afflictions of Christ be extended, a deficit completed, something lacking be made up, and so forth? Elsewhere in Colossians Paul holds to the notion that the one cross was once-for-all, and nothing further of this sacrifice is needful for salvation (1:22; 2:13–15). So what is being said here, and how is it to be understood? The idea of a thesaurus of merit, such as emerged in certain exegesis in the history of interpretation, became an obvious flashpoint at the Reformation. But leaving that particular debate to the side, the text is challenging enough on its own to deserve a label of "best known" in Colossians, even if the question of its relationship to the Christ hymn and to the religious challenges enumerated in Col. 2:8–23 remains to be explored.

One final issue requires mention at this juncture, involving the first text and the context said to be crucial to its interpretation. Some hold that Jewish wisdom/Torah occupies the place where Christ—so it is here being argued—truly resides and that the text wants chiefly to register this point. Others see the true context of the hymn not so much revealed through alleged contemporaneous Jewish influences (Philo and

2. "Paul obviously uses the language and concepts of the hymn as christological ammunition in fighting the false teachers" (Moo 2008: 110).

Sirach), but in relation to arguments Paul is making on the basis of scriptural texts like Gen. 1; Prov. 8:22–31; and the like. To clarify the distinction, the first has Paul addressing a contemporary Jewish theological conviction, based upon a scriptural deposit and derived from it; the second has Paul working out the implications of the scriptural deposit himself without primary or secondary considerations of what alternatives there may be in postbiblical or parabiblical reflection. Moreover, he is doing so as he has done thus far with his Gentile audience. That is, he is not assuming their knowledge of these texts, but is rather commending a logic the judgment[3] of the scriptures actually makes, as he sees it, and that could be defended should he be pressed, in the name of his primary purpose: to speak of Christ and his relationship to the one God, "who made the world and everything in it, being Lord of heaven and earth" (as he put in another context of faithful translation to non-Jews; so Acts 17:24).

One problem with the first manner of proceeding has been touched upon already. Those who hold that Paul is here anticipating a distinct realm of false teaching must correlate that with what they believe is true of the audience being addressed, and this is especially true of the Christ hymn. Would a largely Gentile audience know Philo or Sirach well enough to have to be warned of elements in them (e.g., Torah is wisdom) that they ought not to confuse with Christ's preeminence?[4] Hooker wants to reject the false teaching context and instead view Paul as simply making general warning statements. Yet in the end she brings back the false-teaching idea by a different means, when she tries to understand the force—not of Col. 2's presentation, but of the hymn in 1:15–20:

> The logic of Paul's argument is clear, and the link between the christology of Col. 1 and the exhortation of Col. 2 is explained, if this section in 1:15–20 is, as has been suggested, an exposition of Christ as the replacement of the Jewish Torah, in terms which have been taken from the wisdom literature. . . . For the Jew, the Wisdom of God is identical with the Torah [a footnote cites Sirach 24:23 and Baruch 4:1]. In claiming for Christ what had been said of Wisdom, Paul is claiming that he has replaced the Jewish Torah; it is Christ, not the Torah, who is older than creation, the instrument of creation, the principle upon which creation itself depends and to which it coheres. . . . What the Law could not do, God has achieved in his Son (Rom. 8:3).[5]

Note what happens here. The real audience now being addressed is those who like Hooker have read contemporaneous Jewish texts and believe, by an act of inferential speculation—for Col. 1:15–20 does not actually take up the topic of wisdom or the

3. The term belongs to Yeago ("New Testament and Nicene Dogma").
4. Dunn 1996: 89; J.-N. Aletti, *Colossiens 1:15–20: Genre et exégèse du texte* (Rome: Biblical Institute Press, 1981); and Ben Witherington, *The Letters to Philemon, the Colossians, and the Ephesians: A Socio-Rhetorical Commentary on the Captivity Epistles* (Grand Rapids: Eerdmans, 2007), 128–36, make much of the wisdom influence of contemporary Jewish texts.
5. M. D. Hooker, "Were There False Teachers in Colossae?" in *Christ and Spirit in the New Testament: In Honour of Charles Francis Digby Moule*, ed. B. Lindars and S. S. Smalley (Cambridge: Cambridge University Press, 1973), 315–31 at 330–31.

Torah as preeminent—that "Christ has replaced the Jewish Torah."[6] But why would the *audience of Colossians* need to be disabused of an idea they are arguably unacquainted with and would unlikely have accepted anyway if they were, knowing neither the Jewish sources nor even their biblical basis and not being in any way familiar with their logic or the purported centrality of their hold on certain Jewish thinkers or certain Jews of the period? In actual fact, the hymn would have to be saying something like, "Should you run into this idea, here is the answer to give in response; or here is the proper way to think about this difficult theological concept," but then the actual point of Paul's composing the hymn—to combat a known teaching, or a bona fide contextual reality—is no longer in place, but only the anticipation of it: "Here is a very complex constellation of Jewish thinking, in which, by a combination of biblical texts and a reflection on their inner nerve, the God of creation is thought of in terms of both self and agency. If you run into it, here is the alternative." The danger here is having a reconstructed Paul talking chiefly to himself or to a circle whose knowledge of contemporaneous sources must match his own (so it is held) and is his chief area of concern, when none of this is actually clear in 1:15–20.

The properly historical question to ask for the interpretation of Colossians is "what was Paul most likely trying to say and how did he go about that?" and also to keep that firmly connected to his hopefulness in being heard by the audience being addressed. This puts interpretation solidly in the position argued for above, namely, of Paul seeking to use the scriptures of Israel in a way that is defensible, captures their literal and extensional senses both, and offers this word in a persuasive way to the Colossian church, which does not share his scriptural DNA. To move the historical question into comparative sources or wider etic knowledge is to raise questions about what Paul genuinely knows and is worried about, in the context of an act of communication to an audience without his precise background.[7] This kind of approach is not more historical but represents a specific kind of etic account, as against Paul's own emic frame of reference. The latter requires historical precision as well, if it is to describe the communicative intention of texts like 1:15–20 in a manner that joins Paul's frame of reference with that of an audience he is communicating with.

As we seek to understand the provenance of terms like "image," "icon," "firstborn," and "beginning" in 1:15–20, we must also ask if Paul's commendation of these in respect of Christ is intelligible, even if that means an assumption on Paul's part that he has said enough that is comprehensible and true that he can be trusted in respect of his

6. They must also see Romans—which has a different audience—as directly relevant to Colossians at this point, on a text that has no obvious analogy in Romans.

7. "Emic knowledge and interpretations are those existing within a culture, that are 'determined by local custom, meaning, and belief' . . . and best described by a 'native' of the culture. Etic knowledge refers to generalizations about human behavior that are considered universally true, and commonly links cultural practices to factors of interest to the researcher, such as economic or ecological conditions, that cultural insiders may not consider very relevant"; M. W. Morris et al., "Views from Inside and Outside: Integrating Emic and Etic Insights about Culture and Justice Judgment," *Academy of Management Review* 24 (1999): 781–96.

claims, should one argue against them or seek to know how they grasp the scriptural word and the Christ to whom they point, both. In my view the contemporaneous Jewish discourse is derivative in a different sense of this same scriptural word, and for different reasons and toward different ends. It offers an obliquely comparative lens against which to understand Paul's achievement more than a historical context truly of primary importance for Paul or his audience.

As fundamental to the contribution this commentary seeks to make, the historical and hermeneutical points are crucial, are related, and need underscoring. A properly historical reading is one in which first importance is given to the text's own determinations of priority. It is possible through an act of historical imagination to give priority to an account of Colossians' meaning in which Paul is closely informed by Epaphras as to the character of problems/challenges in the church at Colossae. These include certain Jewish or Jewish Christian influences in which the Torah is held to have preeminence, because it is so held with conviction, or because such views have a grounding in Philo or other contemporaneous sources, and on the basis of these as such or because their own exegesis of scripture is persuasive and held to be true, Paul writes a hymn to Christ or bends one he has received from the "First Roman Church of Christ" to his purpose. He means by this to defeat such teaching and give preeminence to Christ, Torah's replacement and wisdom's true referent.

But the letter to the Colossians does not give priority to such an account as critical to its own historical-hermeneutical character and literary unfolding. The meaning of Colossians is not an inferential description of circumstances said to be operative behind the scenes, as the literal sense gives evidence for. Moreover, this cannot claim to be a historical reading *simpliciter* but a particular species of it, in respect of interpreting Colossians. It is an inferential-historical reading, or a reading concerned with *inferentiality*. It will also remain the case that inferential reading of a historical-evidentialist sort will be unable to declare whose reconstruction is correct. This is so in the nature of the case, because it turns on which inferential descriptions are given priority as these are brought to bear in the act of interpretation.

It could be argued that the space occupied in the history of interpretation by a certain species of allegory, pejoratively rejected as allowing a "resultant system" to override the "way the words go" in the literal sense, in the modern period is covered by a genre of historically sophisticated reading. Both are highly sophisticated in rendering the literal sense into a different context of association: (1) in the case of allegory, by means of elaborate lateral verbal associations (*verbi*) across the Testaments, and (2) in the case of the modern historically contextual reading, by means of elaborate associations in the realm of contexts (*facti*) and comparative sources behind the text. Independently of the letter to the Colossians, we can learn much about the historical "lateral world" of Colossae and Asia Minor. But at issue is determining *Paul's own frame of reference* as Colossians gives that and how it means to communicate in the light of it, based upon what the text relates in its own plain sense.

In the case of 1:15–20 several things stand out. First, the collocation of terms we find in these six verses best suits the primary source of scripture and not the refraction of that in Philo or other contemporaneous Jewish sources. Genesis, Psalms, and Proverbs make their influence felt with a distribution and density that keeps them closer to their primary field of reference than any secondarily refracted one. Second, the message of 1:15–20 is best grasped by hearing it in relationship to 1:1–14 and consistent with emphases I noted there. Paul is not quoting scripture to an audience for whom that kind of appeal has a special force. Rather, he is allowing scripture to make its sense in the light of Christ's work in relationship to the one Lord God, in a way those who do not know scripture (1) can otherwise grasp and (2) could find scriptural confirmation of should that become important. Finally, the genre of "hymn" may come with the suggestion that something is being recycled here or adapted by Paul for a new end. The text does not tell us that but only offers suggestion. The syntax seems to shift in the final verses, and the beginning and ending of the unit are enticingly two things at once, involving "firstborn" in 1:15 and 1:18, or "heaven and earth" in 1:16 and "earth and heaven" in 1:20. This means the transitions from what precedes and what follows are not as sharp as a theory of a self-contained hymnic unit may imply.

If Paul is not writing chiefly from within a contemporaneous Jewish context where establishing the priority of Christ over Torah or wisdom or word is his chief concern, dislodging the latter in the name of the former; and if he is not at the same time, or more especially, seeking to dislodge such views or the anticipations of them within the context of his audience, for whom his communication in Colossians is intended, what then is his concern? My conclusion is that Paul is working in the realm of what, variously and without precise dogmatic formulation, the earliest church fathers and exegetes of the Old Testament called the "rule of faith." This conclusion may also permit us to see a complete consistency and continuation of concerns as they have been set forth in 1:1–14 with the so-called hymn to Christ in 1:15–20.

Paul is arguing, as he has been doing thus far, in a very sophisticated way, bridging a largely Gentile audience he is addressing, with the scriptures he regards as the oracles of God, whose extensional sense preaches the gospel now in surprising but also in providentially prepared ways. He is teaching the Colossians from the inherited scriptures who Christ is, what he has done for them and for the saints of the old covenant, in one cross, qualifying, rescuing, transporting them into the dominion of David, which is properly the Son's. Who is this Christ, if not Adam, or Abraham, or Moses, or David, or the Prophets when seen in toto? What do the scriptures, the Law and the Prophets, declare? If Paul can get this right, in a register that proves from a scripture he knows, and one that in time his audience will study as well, he will have begun to speak in language we will in time come to call "the New Testament," en route to which we have these essential "rule of faith" declarations. Colossians 1:15–20 is one such *regula fidei* within the New Testament canon itself. Origen, Clement, Tertullian, Irenaeus, and others will formulate similar ontological declarations of the one God's life with the Son and Logos, yet working from the single old scriptures. This is Paul's chief work in 1:15–20, and it is a continuation of work he began in 1:3–8 and 1:9–14. The hymn to Christ rhymes with what he has been saying thus far about the Father, our Father, the Father of our Lord Jesus Christ, and the saints:

> **He is the image of the unseeable God // the firstborn of all creation,**
> **that is: in him everything was created // in heaven and earth, everything was**
> **created through him and for him (including thrones, dominions, principali-**
> **ties, authorities).**
> **Moreover, he is before all things // and all things hold together in him.**
> **Further, he is the head of the body, the church // he is beginning, firstborn of**
> **the dead,**
> **so that in all things he should be preeminent // for in him all the fullness of**
> **God was pleased to dwell.**
> **And through him everything was reconciled in him // making peace through**
> **the blood of his cross,**
> **whether on earth or in the heavens.**

It has become commonplace in the scholarly literature, as noted, to refer to 1:15–20 as a "hymn." Several things may be implied by this genre label. First, it refers to the particular syntax and form of the verses as a whole, or at least in 1:15–18. Colossians 1:19–20 may then be treated as a further elaboration, with the difference between 1:15–18 and 1:19–20 the subject of evaluation. Second, it refers to the self-contained and indeed prior life of the unit. Paul has picked up a hymn in circulation and adapted it. Hence its (allegedly) abrupt beginning and an ending now tailored to the following context, or occasioning it (with a focus on reconciliation). Third, it declares the intention of the unit: it is a hymn of praise to Christ. Hymns work best without elaborate prose markers and with an instinct for repetition.

Of course Paul has in fact a "hymnbook" of his own, and he refers to it in 3:16 when he writes, "Sing psalms and hymns and spiritual songs with thankfulness in your hearts to God." The Psalter is the "hymnbook" *par excellence.* The thankfulness to God is expressed here, at this juncture in Paul's address, by penetrating the reality that God's unique self, worthy of praise and worship, encloses from eternity the unique Son. I have set the text in a deliberate way above because of the patterning that exists in Israel's hymns, namely of "A yea B." So, for example:

A The earth is the Lord's
B and the fullness thereof.

A Come let us sing unto the Lord
B and shout for joy the Rock of our salvation.

The Psalter is the preserve of sacred repetition. Sacred repetition is required properly to speak praises to God, because saying something once will not be up to the task.

This also has theological significance. It serves as a caution against isolating phrases or individual words when it comes to Col. 1:15–20. If "A yea B" is the hymnic way to speak of God, then one cannot look at A alone, or find phrases in A or B and focus on them alone. This is the error of Arius (and others) well known in the tradition.[8] One further comment at this point is in order. Hebrew poetry, it is said, is marked by terseness and avoidance of prose indicators (direct object marker, subordinating conjunctions, and so forth). This is easier to achieve in Hebrew because of the relative paucity of such linguistic elements generally speaking, over against Greek. The literalistic translation of Symmachus was notable for wanting to replicate the Hebrew direct object marker 'et in Greek *syn*, probably wanting to rectify the "impoverishment" of Hebrew at this point or for reasons of hyperaccuracy vis-à-vis the Christian scriptures in rival Greek translation. A and B lines interpenetrate one another, and the full significance of A is grasped only in relation to B and vice versa.

If this poetic structure has found its way into the hymn to Christ, as we believe it has, it means that theological significance is conveyed when one reflects on the lines in relationship to one another. It is a very close matter standing alongside to say that *only this kind of poetic phrasing is suitable for the subject matter itself*. How is God in Christ? How is it appropriate to worship Christ and also to preserve with conviction the fundamental theological monotheistic reality, "The LORD our God is LORD alone"? The answer in 1:15–20 is given in the form of Hebrew poetry, as the only form up to the task of making "the LORD, the LORD compassionate and merciful" rhyme with "Jesus Christ, to the glory of God the Father."[9]

My translation is not a way to force an artificial form into place so as to score a theological point. But in my view it does caution that Christian dogmatics will often fail in the hands of rigorists and literalists, as arguably the tribes of Arius were, when they fail fully to observe and be obedient before "the way the words go" in their entirety and according to their form. No one ever grasped this sacrament better than Donne in his reflections on the literal and metaphorical God, both required in their A-ness and B-ness together, to use the logic of Hebrew psalmody.[10] I have tried to render the effect of Hebrew poetry in the translation. Like Hebrew poetry, of course, there are also exceptions proving the rule. I take "including thrones, dominions, principalities, authorities" to be a clarifying gloss and so place it in parentheses, as stipulating what "the everything created through him" entails, appropriate to the specific case of the Colossian address. I find unpersuasive the argument that Paul's chief business, or even oblique concern, is showing that the place held by Torah or Wisdom is in fact held by

---

8. The discussion of Col. 1:15–20 is therefore understandably widespread in the writings of Athanasius, alongside the text that proves so critical in exegetical-dogmatic reflection on "of one being," that is, Prov. 8:22–31. Unsurprisingly, that Old Testament text is also likely making its own presence felt in Colossians as well. C. F. Burney's "Christ as the ΑΡΧΗ of Creation," *Journal of Theological Studies* 27 (1926): 160–77, remains astonishingly fresh and full of insight.

9. See the fine discussion of this and other texts in Bauckham (1999).

10. My *God*, my *God*, Thou art a *direct God*, may I not say a *literal* God, a God that wouldst be understood *literally*, and according to the *plain sense* of all thou sayest? But thou art also (*Lord* I intend it to thy *glory* . . .) a *figurative*, a *metaphorical God too*: A *God* in whose words there is such a height of *figures*, such *voyages*, such *peregrinations* to fetch remote and precious *metaphors*, such *extensions*...such *curtains* of *Allegories*. . . . O, what words but thine, can express the inexpressible *texture*, and composition of the *Word*. (*Devotions upon Emergent Occasions*, XIX, *Expostulation*)

Christ, who places them in inferior position or rejects them thereby. If there is a concern over priority in the created realm that Paul is rejecting, and forcefully for his Colossians audience, it could be the position said to be held by rival authorities, requiring placating or confused and fearful obeisance. Genesis 1 does not highlight these forces, even as it could be shown to intimate them, by way of underdetermination in the literal sense.

One of the strongest reasons for arguing that Paul's primary context of reflection is not contemporaneous Jewish literature or Philo is the density of reference to a single scriptural text: Gen. 1. "Image," "heaven and earth," and "beginning" are words with obvious Genesis association. At the next tier are "all creation" (*pasēs ktiseōs*), "created" (*ektisthē*), "before" (*pro*), and "principalities" (*archē*). *Prōtotokos* ("firstborn") belongs in this same orbit but requires special attention, as it is linked to both "all creation" (genitive) and "the dead" (preposition "from") and surely cannot mean "first of a series of like things," even in special rank, as Arius claimed. Proverbs 8:22–31 usually appears in dogmatic-exegetical discussions of a similar nature as Gen. 1 or Col. 1:15–20 because it speaks of agency in association with the divine reality, using the (troublesome) Greek verb pair "make" and "create" and so masking the more intriguing "beget" in Hebrew parlance.[11] In Proverbs this agency is called Wisdom, but it should be noted that, however close the text may be in kindred dogmatic reflection, the term *prōtotokos* does not appear in Proverbs. At most the association of Wisdom and Torah and Word with agency in God's creation, in Jewish literature of the time, is derivative of the primary Genesis context. It is the primary context for Paul's reflections as well.

1:15 he is the image of the unseeable God // the firstborn of all creation—He obviously picks up from the preceding unit and refers to "the beloved Son" into whose kingdom (*basileian*) the Father has transferred the saints. Paul will now tell us whose kingdom this is and how the Son and the Father are related in the one divine identity, action, and purpose. My view is that we have an A and B structure here, reminiscent of Hebrew poetry, where the two lines mutually inform one another. The apparent rogue term in the verse is *prōtotokos*. It does not appear in Genesis, and its use here must also take into consideration "firstborn from the dead" in 1:18.

As provocative and as challenging is the (rare) idea of being made in the image of God, in the Old Testament, one thing is not being said in Genesis in the context where the term *selem* appears. Genesis 1:26–27 does *not* read as follows:

> And God said, "Let us make man like us, and to resemble us, so that they may rule over the fish in the sea and the birds in the air and over the livestock and all the wild animals and over all the creatures that move along the ground." So God created man to be like him, like him he created them: male and female created he them.

Rather, the Hebrew text uses a nominal form. It speaks of the "image of God." God created humankind, male and female, "in the image of God." It uses the

11. Above all, see the extremely thorough discussion of the early church fathers' translations in Burney, "Christ as the ΑΡΧΗ of Creation."

A plus B syntax in its own poetic rendering. God has an image (*eikōn*). He is unseeable (John 1:18). This means that if he is seen, as we frequently hear in the Old Testament, it must be that the "old fathers" saw God's image (or the Logos), that which can be seen and which nevertheless perfectly and faithfully transmits God by his presence, his glory, his effulgence.[12] The acoustic icon (YHWH) has a counterpart, and it is in this image that humankind is created. The image belongs to God's interior life, and Paul declares that the Son is this interior divine person. God is invisible, but the Son, the only begotten, who is in the bosom of the Father—to use the language of John's prologue—has made him known. When the Word of God—to use John's language—is made flesh and dwells among us, humankind then beheld God's glory. Colossians 1 uses Gen. 1 in its own way, just as has John 1. They both make distinctive contributions in seeing in the Genesis text a literal sense with inherent extension. John's account involves the economy of God, the word-becoming-flesh dimension, as well as the essential, ontological dimension. In Colossians, Paul lets the focus stay with the ontological, as he bridges the movement from 1:14 and 1:21 so as to explain how the dominion of the Son and the action of the Father in qualification, rescue, and transfer are one and the same in character and intention.

What then does it mean to speak of "the firstborn of all creation"? The Hebrew equivalent can mean the distinctive eldest: the firstborn son who inherits. This is true whether other sons follow or not, but if they do follow, the term clarifies the distinctiveness of the eldest in respect of them. This appears to be what Arius heard when he isolated the term from its larger poetic context. Christ is the unique "firstborn" and so distinctive vis-à-vis other creatures, but nevertheless in kindred relationship to them, created in time like them. Would this make him worthy of worship alongside God, the Father, the uncreated? If so, then only somehow derivatively.

To understand Paul's use of the term it is important to grasp the sense of the genitive being deployed ("of all creation") and where he draws the term from for use in the context of creation, for which it is not an obvious one. Already in the Old Testament the term has been drawn into a wider circle of significance. Israel is God's firstborn son, ransomed in place of the firstborn of Egypt, by sacrificial act and the marking of blood. Israel, in this context, is not the first distinctive thing in a series of kindred things. Israel is made something by contrast with something else. Equally, Ps. 89 speaks in this way about David (who of course is not by act of procreation the "firstborn"—any more than Jacob/Israel is):

> Once you spoke in a vision,
> to your faithful people you said:

---

12. So Irenaeus holds that when the OT reports that the "old fathers" saw God, they saw the Logos. For the prominent place given to ontology in the exegesis of the early church, see Gerald Bray, "The Church Fathers and Biblical Theology," in C. Bartholomew and E. Botha, eds., *Out of Egypt: Biblical Theology and Biblical Interpretation* (Grand Rapids: Eerdmans, 2004), 23-40.

"I have bestowed strength on a warrior;
I have raised up a young man from among the people.
I have found David my servant;
with my sacred oil I have anointed him.
My hand will sustain him;
surely my arm will strengthen him.
The enemy will not get the better of him;
the wicked will not oppress him.
I will crush his foes before him
and strike down his adversaries.
My faithful love will be with him,
and through my name his horn will be exalted.
I will set his hand over the sea,
his right hand over the rivers.
He will call out to me, 'You are my Father,
my God, the Rock my Savior.'
And I will appoint him to be my firstborn,
the most exalted of the kings of the earth.
I will maintain my love to him forever,
and my covenant with him will never fail.
I will establish his line forever,
his throne as long as the heavens endure."

David is appointed to be firstborn. His kingship is preeminent not in the sense of being better than others in a series, but due to its fully *sui generis* character in relationship to the only God: "He will call out to me, 'You are my Father, my God, the Rock my Savior.'" His dominion will be forever. The covenant with him will never fail.

The colloquy with God is David's alone to enjoy as firstborn, itself opens onto the truly divine colloquy, as David, inspired by the Holy Spirit, sees the love of the Father for the Son and the obedience of the Son in relation to the Father: "You are my Son, today I have begotten you" (Ps. 2). This "today" is the "today" of eternity, in the rendering of a large block of the history of interpretation or, in Calvin's reading, following the lead of Acts, the "today" of resurrection (Acts 13:33–34). In the resurrection of the Son by the Father, the uniquely begotten character of the Son, eternally so, is made known. He is "firstborn from the dead" as Col. 1:18 will state it in resumption of the basic idea, now in respect not of creation but new creation.

In the fuller context of 1:15 in its entirety, Paul speaks of "firstborn of creation" in a similar way. The image of God, referred to in the creation account of Gen. 1, is the Son, eternally and as he becomes flesh and the glory of God is beheld. The language Paul uses here, rich in Old Testament background, "firstborn of creation," does not refer to the first distinctive thing in a series of like things. It refers to the status the Son has vis-à-vis God himself. The firstborn is heir of all things of the Father. He is image, he is firstborn of creation, that is, creation is the work of the image alongside God himself. Like David, Christ's dominion is a unique dominion (Col. 1:13). His kingship is unique: it is the new-covenant confirmation of the old-covenant promise held in pledge by David. That kingdom is grounded in eternity in essential relationship with God, whose likeness/icon is the Son. The next verse offers the clarification should there be any doubt of how Paul means "firstborn of creation" to function in the hymn. "Firstborn from the dead" completes the picture in respect of new creation (1:18).[13] In order properly to interpret individual phrases in this hymn, it is necessary always to keep the entire hymn in view. This is true as well of Prov. 8:22–31 and how it is properly used in dogmatic exegesis of the period.

1:16 that is: in him everything was created // in heaven and earth, every-thing was created through him and for him (including thrones, dominions, principalities, authorities)—I have intentionally set the text out in such a way that the parallelism can be observed. This involves taking **including thrones, dominions, principalities, authorities** as an explanatory gloss on **everything** of the B component and so shifting it to make the A and B components clearer. The verse obviously rules out the idea of Christ as first in a series of creational acts. In, through, and for him is the created realm. The **heaven and earth** of B picks up the merism of Gen. 1:1, meaning, that is, the totality of all things (e.g., including even the sea creatures, hidden from the eye, as referred to in 1:21): "In the beginning God created the heavens and the earth." In Col. 1:18 we have the terse declaration "he is beginning" (*hos estin archē*). Genesis 1 is opening up its logic in such a way that Colossians and John both see there, in the unusual substan-tive with which the whole of scripture opens its pages (*reshith*), a sign of agency. In him, in *archē*, God created the heavens and the earth. He is at the beginning of scripture; he is the beginning of scripture; he is the agent of creation, literally alongside the *'elohim* who is the subject of the verb *bara'* in Gen. 1:1. *Archē* and *'elohim* are Yhwh, with the Spirit in mysterious (sacramental) association ("and the Spirit brooded over the waters"; 1:2).

Genesis speaks immediately of the earth being "chaos and void" (*tohu wavohu*) in some underdetermined but concrete sense (the B line is "and darkness was over the surface of the deep"), prior to the fashioning that is God's *bara'*, the "let there be light" of 1:3. "The light shone in the darkness and the darkness comprehended it not"—as John speaks of the Logos in his particular reading of Genesis. Here Colossians provides its distinctive New Testament catalog, as an explanatory gloss on these opening verses of Genesis. The everything created in, by, and for the *archē* does not exclude the invisible realms intimated by Gen. 1's opening verses, where we hear of chaos, void, darkness, and deep. Paul will use his own vocabulary to speak of the everything that exists in creation and that is not outside of the Son's

---

13. Basil in reply to Eunomius: "If he be called the firstborn of the dead, because he is the cause of their resurrection, then, by parity of argument, he is the firstborn of the whole creation, because he is the cause of its existence" (quoted in Eadie 1856: 48). Here Basil shows how critical it is to read the text in its entirety and thus grasp its whole logic, as against individual words in isolation.

sovereignty, shared with God himself. "Visible and invisible" he writes, explaining, "whether thrones or dominions or principalities or powers" (Col. 1:16). The list intends to communicate: "From a to z, whatever the proper titles may be."

I have intimated that the fourfold list serves as a kind of explanatory gloss on **invisible** without committing to any elaborate diachronic view about that (see, e.g., the discussion in Moo 2008: 121–22). I also hold that the background for the idea of (refractory) invisible forces exists in an underdetermined way in Gen. 1:2—a text that in its own right raises questions. Are chaos and void and darkness and deep preexistent? Do they represent a surd inside the created realm, an outlier? Genesis may not be poised to answer such questions on its own and that, given its priorities, arguably lie elsewhere: in the acts of creation themselves. I should also note that this listing gives the clearest evidence of relationship to other texts in Colossians (and Ephesians, for that matter), thus pushing back against the idea that the hymn to Christ is an independent composition only awkwardly accommodated to its present context. Colossians 2:10 speaks of Christ as "the head over every rule [*archēs*] and authority [*exousias*]"; and 2:15 likewise shows a victorious Christ who has "disarmed the principalities [*archas*] and powers [*exousias*]." Whatever their more precise background and provenance (can they refer to earthly as well as spiritual powers? are they angelic powers and so capable of being good as well as evil?), in Colossians Paul wants his audience to know that they are under Christ's authority and that whatever ill they might do or be claimed to do, they are robbed of root and branch. Moreover, if one might be tempted to think of them as a surd, Colossians insists they are not so in respect of Christ's authority, and that from all eternity. The proximity of Ephesians to this same basic venue of teaching has been noted. Colossians ties the defeat to the work of the cross (2:14–15); Ephesians to the raising of Jesus from the dead (1:20). He sits at the right hand of God, the iconic equivalent of closest imaginable proximity and shared rule in "the heavenly places" (1:20), that is, "far above all rule and authority and power and dominion"—a slightly altered catalog whose purpose is however identical to the fourfold list of Colossians, bespeaking totality. The four corners of the world; the four essential elements of earth, wind, fire, rain; the fourfold gospel collection—fourness being a number and a comprehension both. Ephesians also offers a further clarification: "above every name that is named" (2:21), which elsewhere has implications for the divine name and its unique place (Phil. 2:9) and also, as somehow tied to these antithetical spiritual realities, "the prince of the power of the air" (*archonta tēs exousias tou aeros*) (Eph. 2:2).[14]

Less clear is whether and how these enumerated spiritual forces might be related to the *stoicheia* referred to in the same context as "spiritual forces" in Col. 2:8 and 2:20. The basic lexical meaning of the term is "component parts" of a system (an alphabet, table of contents, elementals, scales), and we do not know

---

14. Reference to spiritual powers are found, apart from Colossians and Eph. 1, elsewhere in 1 Cor. 15:24; Eph. 3:10; 6:12. *Archē* in Luke 12:11; Rom. 8:38; and Titus 3:1 refers to earthly rulers.

if Paul is using the term as it exists in a system already (the material universe components, divinized and manipulated; a philosophical grid), or whether he is using it in his own properly polemical conceptuality. He says the Colossians have died to this context and been given a new context in Christ (2:20). It is therefore difficult not to see some relationship between the disarming of the fourfold/twofold authorities in 2:15 accomplished by the cross of Christ and the displacement of "elemental spirits" (*stoicheion*) by Christ. We will need however to examine the issue below. At this juncture, the hymn to Christ clarifies without exception that the Father and the Son share an ultimate authority over all creation, as creator and agent in creation. A threat that emerges in the invisible realm of spiritual power is no rival, or independent authority, but is always subject to God's higher authority, rule, power, and dominion. As we have seen, whatever claim God has given to his firstborn David in respect of earthly kings and their thrones, it is but a type of Christ's firstborn authority over the spiritual realm said by others to control and effect all human traffic, in pagan religion, magic, art, sexuality, and procreation.[15]

1:17 Having clarified and anticipated in part the argument of Col. 2, the hymn resumes with its main theme: **moreover, he is before all things // and all things hold together in him**. Often it is held that Prov. 8:22 lies behind this statement, with its emphasis on the anteriority and agency of Wisdom vis-à-vis creation. It is hard to know how Paul might have heard the Hebrew original, if he had this in view. "The LORD begat me as the beginning of his ways with his works of old" is one way of hearing the verse. This would link up with the claim in Col. 1:18 to follow that Christ is *archē* ("beginning"). To "beget" is to possess *from within oneself*, though the term is not easily rendered in English or Greek. Colossians is content to say "he is before all things" and to let the emphasis lie with that, not with the manner of its being so. "Begotten of his Father before all worlds" is the way the language will eventually come to form in the controversies of Nicea and its aftermath, based not on a single text like Prov. 8:22–31, as crucial as this would be in the discussion, but upon this and a range of kindred texts in the Old Testament and New Testaments.

1:18 The idea of things holding together in him (*synestēken*) can be found in a variant form in Eph. 1:22. Christ is head. The body has its life in him. Sirach and Philo can use the verb to convey the idea: "by his word all things hold together" (Sirach 43:26); and Paul may be thinking along these lines here, with Christ as this power holding together all things, by means of his headship.[16] So we read:

---

15. Compare the statement of N. T. Wright, quoted in Moo 2008: 123.

16. "For after making mention of the creation, he [Arius] naturally speaks of the Framer's power as seen in it, which power, I say, is the word of God, by whom all things have been made. If indeed the creation is sufficient of itself alone, without the Son, to make God known, see that you fall not, from thinking that without the Son it has come to be. But if through the Son it has come to be, and 'in him all things consist,' it must follow that he who contemplates the creation rightly, is contemplating also the word who framed it, and through him begins to apprehend the Father" (Athanasius, *Against the Arians* 1.14.12).

further, he is the head of the body, the church // he is beginning, firstborn of the dead.

1:19 By being firstborn from the dead, Christ has inaugurated a new creation. It is crucial that this eschatological act was grounded in a protological "beginning and firstborn of creation," the language with which the hymn began. God is doing in and by and through his Son what was his first intention in him. The first word of scripture, "in beginning," is scripture's middle and last word because of God's raising of Christ from the dead, thereby creating the church and revealing its eternal head. **So that in all things he should be preeminent // for in him all the fullness of God was pleased to dwell.** Here one has a sense of resumption and conclusion, reiterating and summarizing the main point the hymn has emphasized.

1:20 Whether the final verse is Paul's own contribution to a hymn he has commandeered for this special purpose in the larger flow of Colossians, we cannot say. The text does not choose to tell us this in any straightforward, exegetically significant way. What can be said is that 1:20 achieves a fine transition to the following unit in 1:21–23. The reconciliation it speaks of continues the majestic theme of totality, typical of the hymn. But it also refers to the economic manifestation of that in time and space: the unique blood shed by the unique Son at the cross, "who suffered under Pontius Pilate, was crucified." This anticipates the reconciliation of 1:20, "in his body of flesh by his death." As if to round out the hymn before transitioning, Paul ends as the hymn began, with the reference to "heaven and earth" now in reverse order to emphasize Christ's earthly work: **and through him everything was reconciled in him // making peace through the blood of his cross, whether on earth or in the heavens.**

Excursus: Brief Theological Postscript

With a greater appreciation of the foundational role the scriptures of Israel play in dogmatic reflection, including the "earliest high Christology" formulations now being emphasized by Larry Hurtado, Richard Bauckham, N. T. Wright, and others, it is important to be clear about how these scriptures are said to speak of Christ. Moo is not atypical when he writes approvingly, "Through Jesus's mighty acts, and especially in the light of his resurrection and exaltation, Christians began quite early to 'redefine' Jewish monotheism by including Jesus Christ in their understanding of God" (2008: 114). In my view a better way to describe what Paul is doing is not to speak of redefinition in the light of economic acts; even these acts make little sense independent of the essential claim that they are "in accordance with the scriptures." That phase does not mean "by means of redefinition" but rather, it is a confession that our understanding of what God is doing in Jesus Christ penetrates to the heart of the message of the one scripture. Paul did not redefine Jewish monotheism. He saw into its heart and grasped its inner logic.

The same thing can be said about the otherwise very alert evaluation of Richard Bauckham in God Crucified (1999). Several sentences from this very important treatment of the "earliest high Christology" by Bauckham will help illustrate the point.

Bauckham here discusses Paul's use of Deuteronomy for christological purposes. I offer a slightly different phraseology to clarify the concern, and place my own comments in the brackets within the quotation from his work.

The text in question is 1 Cor. 8:6, whose final clause will remind us of our present text in Colossians: "Yet for us there is one God, the Father, from whom are all things and for whom we exist, and one Lord, Jesus Christ, through whom are all things and through him we exist."

> Paul has in fact reproduced all the words about Yʜᴡʜ in the *Shema* ʿ (Deut. 6:4: "The Lord our God, the Loʀᴅ, is one"), but Paul has rearranged the words in such a way as to produce an affirmation of both one God, the Father, and one Lord, Jesus Christ. It should be quite clear that Paul is including the Lord Jesus Christ in the unique divine identity. He is redefining monotheism as christological monotheism [or: he is penetrating to the heart of biblical "monotheism" by acknowledging its christological basis and essence]. If he were understood as *adding* the one Lord to the one God of whom the *Shema* ʿ speaks, then, from the perspective of Jewish monotheism, he would certainly be producing not christological monotheism but outright ditheism. The *addition* of a unique Lord to the unique God of the *Shema* ʿ would flatly *contradict* the uniqueness of the latter. The only possible way to understand Paul as maintaining monotheism is to understand him to be including [or: recognizing or acknowledging] Jesus in the one God affirmed in the *Shema* ʿ. But this is in any case clear from the term "Lord," applied here to Jesus as the "one Lord," being taken from the *Shema* ʿ itself. Paul is not adding to the one God of the *Shema* ʿ a "Lord" the *Shema* ʿ does not mention. He is identifying Jesus as the Lord whom the *Shema* ʿ affirms to be one.[17]

The last sentence puts the matter as correctly as can be done. This is also, in our view, the way Paul is working in the hymn to Christ in Col. 1:15–20.

---

17. Bauckham 1999: 38. Compare my "The Trinity in the Old Testament," in *The Oxford Handbook on the Trinity*, ed. G. Emory and M. Levering (Oxford: Oxford University Press, 2011).

CHRIST'S
RECONCILIATION
AND PAUL'S VOCATION

(1:21–29)

The next three verses (1:21–23) present a bridge between the hymn to Christ and the following passage devoted to Paul's discussion of the character of his afflictions (1:24–29), one of the more ambitious statements of this theme and also one that calls for careful treatment. In the present three verses we pick up aspects of the theme set forth in 1:14 "in whom we have redemption [*apolytrōsin*]" and then culminating in the hymn's final declaration: "To reconcile [*apokatallaxai*] to himself all things" (1:20), "making peace by the blood of the cross." The redemption language appears in 1:22 (*apokatēllaxen*). Lightfoot 1997: 78 goes so far as to begin a new unit in 1:20, stretching to 2:3, which he labels "The Work of the Son—A Work of Reconciliation." This serves to underscore that strictly defining the subunits of the text is made difficult precisely by the integrative character of Paul's unfolding address. I make the decisions I do on this front partly for reasons of practicality, as well as for signs of Paul's own transitions in his argument.

It is important to underscore the manner in which the ambitious statement regarding Paul's afflictions in 1:24 exists within the wider context of his address and cannot properly be evaluated apart from that. Recall that what Paul says is confined to just a single verse (1:24) and does not represent in his articulation a sustained bit of theological reflection on the complex idea of "filling up what is lacking in Christ's afflictions." He says what he says literally *in passing*. That the comment has given rise to much ink and not a little disagreement and confusion still needs to be considered in terms of the proportion it actually manifests in the letter.

Formally, the interlocking character of the wider context is revealed by word pairs and repetition within 1:21–2:7. Only at that point (2:8) do we move to the topic of false trails Paul is warning the Colossians (and Laodiceans) off, extending for sixteen verses to the end of Col. 2 (2:8–23). In 1:21–2:7 Paul speaks of his ministry of commendation of the one cross of Christ's reconciling work and of his specific efforts in this regard. Paul has become a minister of this gospel (1:23 and 1:25).[1] His ministry entails a presentation (*parastēsai*) of those he stewards in Christ (1:22 and 1:28: one is Christ's, one is his). This ministry costs Paul, and the cost borne is suffering (1:24), affliction (1:24), toiling (1:29), and striving (2:1). There is a great mystery (1:26 and 2:2) to be disclosed, and its specific extension to the Gentiles is what Paul is at pains, literally, to make clear (the language used here has a clear counterpart in Eph. 3:1–13). This is in turn the ground of their hope (Col. 1:23 and 1:27). The idea of maturity and stability is mentioned twice as well (1:23 and 1:28). Also note the fourfold reference to "flesh" (1:22, 24; 2:1, 5). In my view this emphasis stands out and provides an important clue as to how to understand Paul's representation of his own work. Christ did his reconciling work "in his fleshly body" (1:22). Paul has his own fleshly embodiment of that, appropriate to his role on this side of the cross ("in my flesh I complete"). He does this fleshly work for those who have not seen his face (*to prosōpon mou en sarki*). Though absent in body (*tē sarki*), he is present in spirit (2:5). Christ is absent in the heavens, and his cross cannot be viewed with the eye, but his work reaches through all time. Paul is absent and hidden by distance from the Colossians, but his work is effective all the same, by the Spirit's ministrations. There is an Old Testament context for this idea we will need to explore below.

Before we look at the central text in more detail, it is important to set out the key components of Paul's thinking so as to anticipate misunderstanding. The idea of "affliction," as is frequently pointed out, is not typically associated with the actual work of Christ on the cross, which in no way does Paul delimit or suggest requires supplementation (especially the unequivocal statements at 1:20, 22; 2:14). Paul is considering his own ministry and the cost of that, as an extension, a shared living-out, of Christ's work. He is considering this not in simple introspective terms but as part of a larger mystery, whose beneficiaries are the Colossians and others for whom Paul strives. Nowhere does Paul speak of this cost in terms of anxiety about false teaching and how to best head that off. That overstipulates in a way the text itself does not choose to, and it further displaces the centrality Paul gives to the basic fact of the cost of his ministry as such, borne now in prison, after a long career, much labor among the Gentiles, and awaiting the adjudication of sentence, itself caught up in the vortex of commitments he has made and kept

---

1. See commentary on 1:23 for discussion of the past-tense phraseology "became" (*egenomēn*). Compare Eph. 3:7.

as a minister of the gospel of one cross for Jews and Gentiles. To speak as though Paul is studying a list of false-teaching concerns and is preoccupied with that is, in a way, to intellectualize Paul's ministry of affliction on behalf of the Gentiles, with the extreme cost that must be borne in that ministry.[2]

In this section Paul presents seven elementals of his ministry of affliction:

1. I am a minister/**I have become a minister** of the gospel: the one cross of saving reconciliation.

2. The gospel discloses a **mystery**. The mystery has been hidden in previous generations. It goes back to the first word of Genesis, and it is now disclosed to the saints (cf. Ephesians).

3. I make this mystery of the gospel known in my vocation to preach to the Gentiles and to every creature under heaven, and **it costs me**.

4. The cost is not the cost of one cross; that has been paid in full; **it takes the form of affliction and toiling**, and this consists in practical terms: cell, prayer desk, tattered map of the Roman Empire, my letter writing, my Bible study for the gospel.

5. This cost is borne in the name of Christ, and so **the afflictions are his**: they represent the shared outworking of the one cross in the world for salvation for Jew and Gentile. They are Christ afflictions as the gospel takes hold in a groaning creation.[3]

6. They are **"on behalf" of those Paul ministers to**, and so they are beneficiaries of his exertions, as we are all beneficiaries of the work of the one cross.

7. These exertions are "on behalf of every creature under heaven," and until they communicate what Christ has accomplished "for us all" there is work still to be done; something is lacking, and **my work is to fill up that lack**, as I am able.

These components are overlapping and interlocking. They represent "the table of elements" and the "component parts" directing his address to the Colossian

2. Lightfoot writes: "Here, however, the inner struggle, the wrestling in prayer, is the predominant idea" (1997: 86), and he compares 4:12. This is closer to the literal sense presentation though it may not say enough. Moo, by contrast, makes far too much of a scenario whereby the afflictions and toiling are focused on false teaching and anxiety about that.

3. As Paul wrote in Rom. 8:18–25: "I consider that the sufferings of this present time are not worth comparing with the glory that is to be revealed to us. For the creation waits with eager longing for the revealing of the sons of God; for the creation was subjected to futility, not of its own will but by the will of him who subjected it in hope; because the creation itself will be set free from its bondage to decay and obtain the glorious liberty of the children of God. We know that the whole creation has been groaning in travail together until now; and not only the creation, but we ourselves, who have the firstfruits of the Spirit, groan inwardly as we wait for adoption as sons, the redemption of our bodies. For in this hope we were saved. Now hope that is seen is not hope. For who hopes for what he sees? But if we hope for what we do not see, we wait for it with patience."

church, not in component-part form but in narrative address. They and not the *stoicheia* (2:8 and 2:20) of the world are the true measure of reality and the true meaning of God's creation and his intention for it in Christ. They constitute a "rule of faith" whose proper grasp leads to the ordered life of faith (2:5). This is why Paul gives them pride of place before he addresses alternatives to this life. He also is able to underscore the relationship between Christ's work and his own, in such a way as to make clear how precious is the faith Paul is commending and at great cost "for your sake."

1:21–22 and you, who were once estranged and hostile in mind, doing evil deeds, he has now reconciled in his body of flesh in order to present you holy and blameless and irreproachable before him—The opening phraseology is similar to Eph. 2:1 and 2:11, and in both places Paul is speaking specifically about Gentiles. This is explicit in Ephesians. The former life is described in detail in Ephesians and in summary fashion in Colossians. Gentiles were "alienated from the commonwealth of Israel" (Eph. 2:12), and in Colossians the word is used to describe their *dianoia* or "bearing, mind, orientation." The alienated or estranged orientation is effectively hostile to God and inclined, as with gravitational force, to "evil deeds."

This is the first time the "you" of differentiation comes through so clearly in the letter thus far. It is not surprising in a section where Paul is about to emphasize his own role. His role is both "because of you/on account of you" and their condition—that is, the distinctive destiny of Gentiles vis-à-vis the household of Israel—and "for your sake"—that is, his ministry of affliction redounds to their salvation and benefit. The failure to quote scripture extensively in this letter is not to keep them from wrongly prioritizing a scripture with which they are not familiar (they are estranged from Israel), nor is it to intimate that Christ stands where Torah once stood. The oracles of God entrusted to the Jews do not make this latter claim as a first-order affair anyway: it is a derivative notion, which can be observed in Philo and Sirach. Paul understands that one critical aspect of scripture is the existence of the book of Genesis, which he mines precisely because it stands prior to the law in the strict sense and yet is part of the Torah; here is an important scriptural testimony with significance for Paul's understanding of the law and of Christ.

Paul does not quote scripture in Colossians, arguably *because his audience does not know it*. His work of bringing them to maturity entails accustoming them to scripture's main patterns and themes, in a language they can comprehend. Once that is in place, scripture can be opened and read "in Christ"—that is, in something of the manner Paul is reading it "for your sake." This is his main theological work—showing the scriptures to be in accordance with Christ—and it also can be called part of Paul's toiling in the broader sense.

One major achievement of Paul's scriptural toiling is his describing the distinctive dilemma marking off the Gentile condition—estrangement, alienation, "without God in the worldness"—as against that of Israel, and yet maintaining one cross for God's single work of reconciliation in his only Son. He began with the common reality and used the language of first-person plurality (1:1–14). He shifts here to "I, Paul" and "you" (1:21–2:7) in order to speak of his ministry and their specific condition in relation to that. The first-person plural does not disappear entirely, but reasserts itself when Paul speaks of the reconciling work of the cross, a work he may share but only as its first forgiven recipient (2:14–15).

Christ's fleshly reconciling work was for the purpose of his presentation of recipients **holy and blameless and irreproachable** to himself (1:22). The "once-for-all" fleshly work was to the end of ultimate blameless presentation back to himself. We might have expected Paul to speak of presentation by Christ to the Father, but by leaving the emphasis on Christ's singular, ongoing role, he paves the way for his own personal development of the theme. Paul has a work of presentation in view as well, as he will strive mightily "with the energy he inspires in me" to bring the Colossians to Christ as mature men and women (1:29). His presentation is grounded in the intention of Christ himself both to reconcile and to present those reconciled in a state acceptable and commensurate with his grand fleshly accomplishment. Little wonder Paul, following this counterpart thinking, moves with ambition to consider his own afflictions as in some sense carrying on where Christ left off (1:24).

1:23 **provided that you continue in the faith, mature and steadfast, not shifting from the hope of the gospel that you heard, that has been preached to every creature under heaven, and of which I, Paul, became a minister—**The blameless and irreproachable presentation by Christ to himself must contend with the temporal, fleshly reality of this life. The hope of the gospel is the marker buoy in the restless sea of challenges, within and without in the life of faith. This is so for the Colossians, but it is always and everywhere so, because the ambition of the gospel is to reach every creature under heaven. Christ means for his body to reach that far, and until that is so, there remains a lacking in respect of that body's fullest extension. The one gospel word that came to them by the agency of Epaphras is the same word to every creature under heaven, as far as Abraham was given to see and even for him, beyond his ability to see altogether. Paul stands somewhere inside all that ambitious reach, critical to its unfolding but an agent of a much larger destiny all the same.

Does Paul's introduction of this grand perspectival canvas occasion as well a retrospective note in his self-declaration, **of which I, Paul, became a minister?** Paul has had a long ministry. It is now long enough to consider on its own scale of unfolding, hard laboring, and completion. The fleshly work of Christ had a beginning, a middle, and an end, and Paul is of course focusing on that end work and its grand, crowning achievement. Paul's fleshly work has moved through stages and has reached a probable culmination in his imprisonment, the final vocation of absent letter writer, man of prayer, striving scriptural proclaimer. The scale of the work of Christ is enormous, and Paul has had his role to play. He is now giving thought to the character of that role and the work it has been his privilege to discharge, under the shadow of the one cross.

1:24 now I rejoice in my sufferings for you—The theme of suffering in Christ is not introduced here for the first time. It serves as the prominent opening theme in 2 Cor. 1:3–7. Philippians 3:10 speaks of Paul's ardent hope that "I may know him and the power of his resurrection, and may share his sufferings, becoming like him in his death." Here Paul explicitly links his own personal suffering with the Colossians as true beneficiaries. What he undergoes is not isolated but has a genuine larger purpose and in some measure imitates or participates in the vicariousness whose once-for-all prototype was and is the cross of Christ—mention of which frames carefully what is said here (Col. 1:21–23 and 2:1–15). The fleshy achievement of Christ has a fleshy counterpart in Paul, and the reality of the character of his ministry as entailing suffering is seen by Paul to be related intimately to Christ himself. The term "suffering" (*pathēmasin*) does not derive from Christ's work on the cross. It describes rather Paul's own understanding of his condition as minister of the gospel, which then, in turn, he sees as having its source and rationale as a form of fellowship with Christ. What holds them together is not a one-on-one relationship of equivalent and shared suffering, once for all on the cross and in the ongoing work of Paul, as this theme is not prominent in the accounts of the work of the cross as such. What holds them together is the conviction that they are kindred affairs and that they both share the critical element of vicariousness "for you." Christ died *for us*. Paul suffers *for you*. Neither event is tragic. Both are acts of loving intention, the former providing the deep rationale for the latter. **I rejoice in my sufferings for your sake**. And because Paul speaks of this "for you" in the context of the worldwide spread of the gospel, it can also point to his understanding of his specific role as minister to the Gentiles. That is, it is because of Christ's fulfillment of the vocation to reconcile all nations that Paul finds the mandate and warrant for his present condition. It is for their sake and it is because of them, too. The same can be said of the cross of Christ. Christ died for the ungodly: at their hands and for their sake.

Moses and a whole series of major scriptural figures loom over this "for you" talk. It is indeed Israel's unbreakable reality as one people that undergirds any notion of communal solidarity and of doing for the whole. God proposes to break up the solidarity in the name of working with Moses and a subsection (Num. 14:12; Deut. 9:14), and perhaps as well sending a subaltern to do what must be done (so the drama of Exodus 33–34). Moses's greatest act is his intercession on behalf of this promised solidarity (Deut. 9:18–29), by insisting it is God's solemn intention and strikes therefore to the heart of who he is and what his "I am whom I am" is fundamentally and inextricably about. The name will go with Israel. The name will go with all of Israel (those under twenty, so Num. 14:31) and not a new portion emerging in some sense from the isolated and righteous Moses himself. And how is this made possible? Moses lays his life on the line in the solemn intercession (Exod. 32:32). He suffers because of and on behalf of (Deut. 1:37). And he will find his counterpart in Elijah, Samuel, Jeremiah,

Ezekiel, and especially in the Suffering Servant of Isaiah. The "for us" language of the final tribute is the leitmotif of the servant's accomplishment: "We esteemed him smitten, stricken by God and afflicted, but he was bruised for our iniquities and the chastisement that was ours was laid on him." In that hymn the "we" speak up and confess what Paul here states is so from his own side. Above all, it is Israel's unbreakable solidarity in God's self that sets the ground rules for how it is that Christ will go the way of the cross for sinful people. Paul lives in the same universe of significance and so speaks of it as he seeks to understand what he is accomplishing, rejoicing that it is so.

And I complete in my flesh what is still to be carried out: in respect of Christ's afflictions for the sake of his body, the church—There is Christ's fleshly work, and there is Paul's fleshly work. There is the "for you" work of suffering by Paul for the Colossians, and there is the "for you" work extending to the whole of Christ's church, everywhere, which is his body. In temporal terms, this work will require a vast unfolding, as it entails a preaching to every creature under heaven. At present that work has only begun. It will extend far beyond Paul's own day. But he has his own particular role to play in completing what is lacking. The work of proclamation will be costly for reasons that derive from the cross's reconciling work itself. It faces opposition, it stirs up the "hostility of mind" Paul referred to in 1:21, which is the baseline Gentile condition.

1:25 The afflictions of Christ can therefore find intimations in the rabbinical reflections associated with *hable messiah*. The scriptures show that the coming of the Messiah is accompanied by severe tribulations (Zech. 13), even the groaning of creation itself. By inaugurating that era, in cross and empty tomb, and then by prolonging the (now) "second coming," these tribulations and afflictions stretch through time and are not focused on one-time events (if indeed they ever really were in that strict sense). The gospel portrayal of end-time afflictions, in their present location *before* the cross and passion (Mark 13 et passim), permits a reading that discloses the cross itself as an end-time event (with betrayal, cosmic disturbance, politic upheaval) in proleptic, eschatological form. The reason for the extension of end-time times is of course that the "full number of the Gentiles might come in" as Paul will put it in Rom. 11:25. And because his ministry is poured out for that very purpose, it has the potential to be labeled a **completing what is yet to be accomplished of the afflictions of Christ for the sake of his body**. That the language is open to misinterpretation is all the more reason to press for its proper framing. Here Paul identifies in his suffering the completing of the larger purpose of the once-for-all cross, the "for you" ministry of Paul for the sake of the Gentiles, including here particularly the Colossian church. As he continues: **of which I became a minister according to the divine office given to me for you, to make the word of God fully known**. That is, Paul's ministry is against the backdrop of the "every creature under heaven" referred to in Col. 1:23. But it is also specifically **given to me for you**. Paul's ministry is to make what they have heard more **fully known** and lived out.

1:26–27 And this brings us to the specific "fully making known" Paul has been leading up to: **the mystery hidden for ages and generations but now made manifest [*apokekrymmenon*] to the saints**. Romans 11, mentioned above, speaks of this mystery, as does Eph. 3. Indeed, if I were to indulge a speculation, it would be that when Paul speaks of "briefly writing" about the mystery disclosed (*apokalypsin*) to him (Eph. 3:3), he is not referring to something previously said in that same letter, but to what is being said here in Colossians. "When you read this" in Eph. 3:4 does not sound, as has been long noted, like a cross-reference to something already said, but to a kindred treatment somewhere else, and in the language that follows "not made known to the sons of men in other generations" (3:5), we hear the same expression employed in Colossians. Paul is about to speak of the church in Laodicea (Col. 2:1), and he will close his letter to the Colossians with the charge to have it read in the church of the Laodiceans, and their letter in Colossae (4:16). In my view "the letter to the saints who are faithful in Christ Jesus" (Eph. 1:1), now commonly referred to as Ephesians, is this letter. Paul is a steward of the mystery (Eph. 3:2) as it finds expression in both Colossians and Ephesians, as well as in Rom. 11–13 in fullest form. An exchange of letters will allow the churches elsewhere in the region to read what Paul has written briefly about the mystery in his letter to the Colossians. In Col. 1:24–29 they would hear of the character of Paul's ministry on behalf of the Colossians, Gentiles who have been made to know, because of Paul's exactions, of **the riches of the glory of this mystery, which is Christ in you, the hope of glory** (1:27). Confirmation of this for the Colossians will come from the reading aloud of the letter to the Laodiceans, as Paul will charge should take place among them. He strives mightily for the congregations in both regions that have never seen his face (2:1). At issue is the disclosure of the gospel mystery to the saints, for **to them God determined to make known how great are the riches of the glory of this mystery among the Gentiles, which is Christ in you, the hope of glory**.

In Rom. 9:23 the phrase "riches of his glory" appears, and it is in the identical context of God's mercy extended beyond Israel to the Gentiles. Paul also dwells on the idea of the "beforehand" character of God's action in this regard, in the same way he speaks of the mystery being hidden away for generations until the time appointed for its full disclosure. When in the final chapter of Romans Paul ends the letter with a solemn doxology, he chooses again to focus on this theme: "Now to him who is able to strengthen you according to my gospel and the preaching of Jesus Christ, according to the revelation *of the mystery that was kept secret for long ages but is now disclosed and through the prophetic writings is made known to all nations . . .* to the only wise God be glory for evermore through Jesus Christ" (Rom. 16:25–27, emphasis added).

The mystery has been hidden but equally it has always been there, for it is by means of the prophetic writings that it is now being clearly perceived. They announce the hidden mystery and make known the "riches of his glory" (9:23). Paul speaks of "vessels of mercy prepared beforehand" as well as the means of their declaration now in Christ via the prophetic writings, and he refers specifically to the Gentiles (9:24). He uses Hosea and Isaiah as classical witnesses from the "prophetic writings" (16:25), quoting the prophet Hosea—"those who were not my people I will call my people" (Hos. 2:23)—at the start of a catena of references. So it is not only that the sacred writings have the innate capacity as scripture to disclose a hidden mystery, "the riches of his glory," but also that they speak within their own scope of a referent and a glorious hope in respect of them, that until now has not found the fullest revelation because the work of Christ was required to bring them near, within hearing and seeing range. The message was always there, but the declared recipients of it were not. The "dial tone" that was Israel's could become a "party line," but only at the moment of proper disclosure, which in turn could be accomplished only by the cross.

Paul's unique ministry is now becoming clearer. It is a work on the other side of the one cross, though the earthly ministry of Christ could be said to prepare one for it, as it is available to testify—not in the letters of Paul, but—in the fourfold gospel record coming to form where the gospel among the nations is surely a persistent if "still-to-be-fleshed-out" theme. That is, it belongs to Paul's special ministry among the Gentiles to tell them of a great mystery that includes them as vessels of mercy alongside Israel, *and the means of its declaration as already speaking of them and to them in the oracles of God entrusted to the Jews.* Their being read into a last will and testament is not a happenstance or a lovely surprise, but was always God's plan, and Paul has the means at his disposal to show that it is so. The hope of glory was always theirs, but to make that known is to deliver a gift beyond all gifts. That is the force of Paul's understanding in this section of Colossians, confirmed by Romans and Ephesians. It also explains why the ministry he has been entrusted with must reach to every creature under heaven: that is what the scriptures themselves say (1 Cor. 2:6–10). The "riches of his glory" is the availability of a beforehand testimony, which discloses the Colossians to be recipients of "the hope of glory" that is "Christ in you." Paul is the steward of a mystery with implications for every creature under heaven.

1:28–29 him we proclaim, warning every man and instructing every man in all wisdom, that we may present every man mature in Christ—The threefold repetition of **every man** is striking. The "Christ in you" promise of glory has as its target everyone, and so Paul has a solemn ministry to make sure all whom he meets share in this hope or have the opportunity to do so via his warning and exhortation. They must further be taught the character of this hope of glory and the nature of its declaration: from the scriptures, long promised, achieved by the blood of the cross. Paul's reference to this form of being taught as "wisdom" (*sophia*) brings to mind his associating the specific form of Christian wisdom with "a secret and hidden wisdom of God, which God declared before the ages for our glorification" in 1 Corinthians. There he clarifies the distinction between "worldly wisdom" and the wisdom the scriptures disclose by the Spirit's working (1 Cor. 2:6–10). The rulers of this age failed to grasp this kind of wisdom, and so "they crucified the Lord of glory" (2:8). But the scriptures foresaw all that as well, given the unique character of wisdom they manifest and impart (Paul quotes Isaiah). The work that Christ has accomplished on the cross intends as its final goal a presentation of those so saved, the "vessels of mercy" targeted from before all time, as "holy, blameless and irreproachable" (Col. 1:22) to himself. That is Christ's fullest cruciform intention. Paul's ministry is to underscore the mystery that makes this intention clear, its source, its present revelation, its merciful targeting of everyone so that he may fulfill his special vocation "for your sake" (1:24). Christ's presentation entails Paul's own, **that we may present every man mature in Christ. For this I strive, contending with all the energy he inspires in me in power**. Paul here and in the following verse describes his exertions for the Colossians and the Laodiceans and indeed "for all who have not seen my face." It is however Christ who supplies the energy for this striving. The participle translated here "contending" (*agōnizomenos*) can have a primary athletic meaning: "to compete, to engage in a contest." Paul here and elsewhere likens his work to that of a highly trained athlete. One can almost hear the runner Eric Liddell when he explains to his sister, who objects to the time he gives to his training, "When I run, I can feel his pleasure." The power is granted in relation to the task at hand. Paul is not here adverting to his concerns for the false teachers at Colossae, a popular way to consider the context of striving. Closer to hand is the statement at 4:12: "Epaphras, who is one of yourselves, a servant of Jesus Christ, greets you, always remembering you earnestly [*pantote agōnizomenos hyper hymōn*] in his prayers, that you may stand mature and fully assured in all the will of God." As with Paul's language here, the concern is with the Colossians abiding "in love and in all the riches of assured understanding in the knowledge of God's mystery" (2:2). The context is a positive one. Paul speaks of "all the riches of assured understanding." This is the ground of their hope, a bulwark against any challenges, and Paul strives in prayer to petition God on behalf of the maintenance of this "assured understanding."

Erasmus provides a paraphrase on Paul's suffering:

> It is not enough in these circumstances for us to be brave and fearless. No, it is fitting, rather, that we should even welcome sufferings eagerly, joyfully giving thanks to God the Father because he deemed you worthy of this honour: that, although previously you had been worshipers of images and demons, he saw fit to enrol you in the company of the Jews, who were holy (in contrast to you) on account of their worship of the true God, and to admit you to the same inheritance of immortality.[4]

Though the passage Erasmus is dealing with is earlier in the letter (1:12), it is striking how well integrated it is with the material we have been looking at in 1:24–29. Erasmus is speaking about suffering, the theme of 1:24–29, but does so at 1:12 because he is otherwise alert to another prominent topic, often not

4. "The Paraphrase on the Epistle of Paul the Apostle to the Colossians by Erasmus of Rotterdam," in *Collected Works of Erasmus*, ed. R. D. Sider (Toronto: University of Toronto Press, 2009), 400.

sufficiently underscored in a Gentile Christian context where the particularity of election is either unnoticed or judged Christianly inappropriate, a holdover from "Jewish religion" Christ finally got rid of. God the Father has enrolled us "in the company of the Jews," to use Erasmus's language, by the work of the one atoning cross for Jew and Gentile both. This enrolling enables us to worship the true God, to admit us to the same inheritance of immortality and the privilege of suffering, having been deemed worthy of this honor. Here in 1:24–29 suffering and the great mystery are brought into conjunction. In 1:12 our "sharing in the inheritance" was referenced, and in 1:24–29 it is unrolled more fully (2:3–4).

On the far side of Immanuel Kant and the notion of universal religion and conscience, it is refreshing to see Erasmus not only retain the election-adoption particularity of God's act in Israel and in Christ, but further to highlight its provision of true religion, immortality, and the sufferings now being born in Christ's body.

For Paul, Christ has graciously transferred non-Jews into the eternal covenant and life everlasting. This is a matter for which he gives thanks. He calls this a "mystery," a sacrament, hidden in the older times (the eternal invisible grace) but now made manifest (outward and visible sign).[5] Suffering is the way Paul thinks about his labor on behalf of the gospel for the Gentiles. This is an extension of Christ's own suffering, now happening in the apostolic ministry on behalf of the head, who is seated at the right hand of God, his earthly sufferings and afflictions at an end, but still being poured out in his body and experienced as such. "Saul, Saul, why do you persecute me?"

By contrast, for modern men and women, we are thought to be somehow naturally religious (or not; there was no practical atheism in antiquity). Christ crowns that natural achievement, when we choose him. We ought to do this, and the church ought to commend that we do this. Christ is an entity unrelated to the Jews except as a kind of accident, or incidental, having to do with his cultural heritage. The Jews have their own religion, and a difficult idea about God.

For Paul, again, this is an impossible description. The only natural religiousness is idolatry and death. Christ transfers us from this realm—in Col. 1 Erasmus calls this realm the realm of Satan—into the worship of the true God, the God worshiped by the Jews, that which makes them holy (set apart as different from the natural religiousness), "the saints in light" (1:12). The movement from Old Testament to New Testament is not from law to gospel, but from estrangement to adoption, by the covenant of blood, the fulfillment/end point of the holy law.[6]

---

5. Thomas Aquinas writes at this point: "To make known the riches of the glory of this mystery, because by the fact that such things had been hidden, God now appears superabundantly glorious. For God was formerly known in Judea, but through this mysterious conversion of the Gentiles the glory of God is made known to the entire world" (2006: 39).

6. Christopher Seitz, *Word without End: The Old Testament as Abiding Theological Witness* (Grand Rapids: Eerdmans, 1998), 41–50.

STRIVING MIGHTILY
FOR YOU

(2:1–7)

2:1–3 For I want you to know how greatly I strive for you, and for those at Laodicea, and for all who have not seen my face in the flesh, that their hearts may be encouraged by virtue of being knit together in love and in all the riches of assured understanding in the knowledge of God's mystery: in Christ is hidden all the treasures of wisdom and knowledge—It is important to reiterate a comment made above about structure and rhetorical units in the letter to the Colossians. We have seen how Paul builds his argument by returning to and repeating key phrases as he moves along, stitching together his remarks in this way. Colossians 2:1–7 introduces the topic of "beguiling speech" (2:4) and Paul's concern about delusion entering in, countering the "good order and firmness of faith" of the Colossian church (2:5). The unit can serve to introduce the section on false teaching that follows, yet it depends for its logic on the bulk of the presentation already provided in Col. 1, where Epaphras's teaching and Paul's thanksgiving for their solid faith are front and center. In 2:6–7, there are provisions of a reprise and a culmination of that theme from Col. 1.

The concern with false trails and delusional belief/philosophy begins properly speaking in 2:8 and extends for sixteen verses until the end of Col. 2. But 2:9–15 is also a summation of the *positive* work of Christ and its *positive* effect in the Colossian church. Moreover, the "if then" language of 2:20 is picked up again clearly in 3:1–4, so the dividing line between the heresy section and what follows is not overly sharply drawn. Dying (2:20) and new life (3:1) are an obvious pairing. The same rough idea is pursued, moreover, in 3:5–17, with the contrast between "put to death" (3:5) and "put on" (3:12). The point is that in truth there is no specific concern with false trails and deluding belief that is not woven into the argument of the letter as a whole and balanced by its positive commendation of the Colossians' faith. Paul focuses on what Christ has done and what the Colossian church has received in abundance, and only from that perspective does he turn to the concern with the threat posed in every church with beguiling speech and delusional enticements of various description.

When, then, Paul speaks of **striving** (*agōna*) on behalf of the Colossians and the Laodiceans (2:1) we ought not import to that what has not been clearly said. The language of striving extends what Paul has already said of his suffering and affliction: it is for their sake (*hyper hymōn*). It is not borne of anxiety or worry as primary indexes, or the specifics of false teachers and their infiltration into the Colossian church. The text does not choose to indicate this with anything like the expected detail. Paul's flesh (**all those who have not seen my fleshy face**) is engaged in a combat for their sake. It takes up all the life he has to give, much as we heard in 1:24–29, "For this I strive, contending with all the energy he inspires in me in power." Moreover, it is the detail of his being absent from them that gives rise to the expression of urgency and intensity. He is not there and so must emphasize that what they cannot see or know is nevertheless the case. It is not exhibited by his movements among them, by his personal address, his lived life in their midst, as teacher and pastor. But it is happening all the same. It is hard not to find the relationship between striving and prayer as Paul attributes this to Epaphras (4:12) as equally the situation here. His absence from the Colossians and the Laodiceans "and all who have not seen me face to face" is not in any way a hindrance to Paul and the work he now undertakes on their behalf. The shift from second-person plural to third-person plural is simply the way Paul seeks to make clear that the Colossians ("you") and any and all are all recipients of Paul's striving, as his ministry now unfolds in respect of "every creature under heaven" (1:23).

The goal of this striving is not the identification of false teachers and their correction, as 2:2 states it. Rather, it is so that hearts may be encouraged—a thoroughly positive emphasis and outcome. And by means of this, all those who have not seen Paul will find a common currency **in love and in all the riches of assured understanding in the knowledge of God's mystery**. This is what Paul is striving mightily for. The return to the theme of mystery will wrap up that particular emphasis at this point in the letter (1:26–27). **In Christ himself is hidden all the treasures of wisdom and knowledge**. Hiddenness referred to the way the mystery was imbedded in the scriptures of Israel and was found there in latent form. In Augustine's dictum: the New Testament latent in the Old Testament and the Old Testament patent in the New Testament. As Paul says in Romans, it is the prophetic writings themselves—the old scriptures—that are now disclosing and making known the mystery they had stored away in their literal sense, "according to the command of the eternal God" (16:26). The mystery had been kept secret, but it was truly there and now makes itself known from these selfsame scriptural deliverances. It is Christ himself who is this mystery, for in him and through him

God's word went forth of old, "according to the command of the eternal God." Whatever may be known of God can be known only through Christ. He is God's mystery and in him alone reside all the treasure houses of wisdom and knowledge.[1] We likely have here an anticipation of rival claims to knowledge and wisdom, as these will be referenced by Paul in the coming verses.

2:4 this I say, so that no one might delude you with beguiling speech—This refers to God's own mystery, Jesus Christ, in whom true wisdom and knowledge reside.[2] Paul is aware that rival accounts of wisdom and knowledge are there to make themselves known and their claims taken seriously. The true mystery of God is a single truth, and not one that merges and overlaps with systems that ask that they be taken seriously for their own accounts of God, human life, creation, and the rules for living. Paul does not provide any detail here in this single brief verse. His emphasis is on Christ and the sufficiency and overabundance of what he comes to give. **Delusion** and **beguiling speech** are intentionally comprehensive terms, not intending to address particularities at this juncture of Paul's argument.

A further caution is in order at this point. As commentators note, attention needs to be given to the genre to which this kind of language conforms.[3] Paul is not giving us empirical facts about the content of a false teaching or the message of false teachers. He is alerting the Christians he addresses to the character of what they may confront. This is Paul's rhetorical concern. Christians are to stand on firm ground based upon what they have been taught and what Paul reinforces in respect of that through the medium of this letter. They are not to be enticed or beguiled by alternatives. This is roughly the equivalent of warning about "silly myths" arising to lead Christians astray (2 Tim. 4:4). "Silly myth," like "beguiling speech," is a category of comprehensiveness aimed not at accuracy in describing a phenomenon in the history-of-religion, but instead registering a broad appeal to stand firm on what has been passed on. The term translated "beguiling speech" or "plausible argument" comes from the single Greek word *pithanologia*. Plato contrasts the term with "cogent proof" (*apodeixes*), hence translations like "fine sounding argument" and "arguments that sound reasonable." The cogent proof is Christ, as against deceptive alternatives. He is the treasure house in which all truth resides and against which counterfeits can be exposed for what they are.

1. Prov. 2:1–8 speaks of "wisdom" (*sophia*) and "knowledge" (*epignōsis*), and there as well we find the rare Pauline word "treasure" (*thēsauros*). One is to search for wisdom and knowledge as if it were hidden treasure. This will give understanding into the fear of the Lord.

2. So most commentators. Lightfoot thinks "this" refers forward to the end of the verse, as in "what I mean is this: let no one lead you astray." In part this is because he sees the start of a new unit here (1997: 89–90). I take it as a continuation of the thought of 2:1–3. Paul is wrapping up his appeal as he moves to the discussion of possible threats to the faith the Colossians are rooted in.

3. See the useful compact discussion of Barclay on the matter of genre recognition: "Even when we have identified where the attack is directed, we still have to judge how much it reveals. If a politician attacks his or her opponents as 'a bunch of crooks' we are not likely to consult police records to identify them: we know this is a general piece of abuse that tells us nothing about the character of the opponents" (2004: 50).

2:5–7 For though I am absent from you in the flesh I am present with you in the spirit and rejoice to see how well ordered [*taxin*] you are and how firm your faith in Christ is. So then, just as you received Jesus Christ as Lord, continue to live in him, rooted [*errizōmenoi*] and built up in him, established in the faith as you were taught, and overflowing with thankfulness.—Thomas Aquinas reads these three sentences closely together. Moo properly calls 2:6–7 "the heart of Colossians" (2008: 177). The synonymous expressions **ordered**, **firm**, **rooted**, **built up**, and **established** are obvious in 2:5 and 2:7. Clearly all that Paul has been emphasizing up to this point is here summarized. Paul's absence is an irrelevance; indeed, it gives him even greater joy to see the independent work of the gospel. It grants him a spiritual presence greater than any fleshly counterpart. The faith they have received is solid and has everything they need to sustain them. "First, he calls to mind the goods that they have; and second he shows how these should grow within them" (Aquinas 2006: 49). Finally, the thankfulness that it is his to know because of them and their faith (1:3–7) is to be shared with them, in the character of its own overflowing abundance. One senses that the opening address is here being reprised. What is true for Paul and Epaphras—rejoicing in the faith manifested in the Colossian assembly—is to be their truth as well.

To **receive Jesus Christ the Lord** retains the critical personal dimension. But it must be emphasized that in this letter Paul underscores the apostolic teaching about Christ as fundamental to what it means to have "received him as Lord." The verb *paralambanō* is the term of choice when Paul refers to teaching being passed on. This teaching is to serve as a bulwark against anything that emerges to rival it, and by its own character it exposes what is counterfeit. I have already stressed the crucial conjunction of **Christ** and **Lord**. It is the simplest form of what the earliest church fathers will call the "rule of faith" now governing Christian confession and Christian handling of the scriptures of Israel, as disclosing the "mystery of God, that is Christ." To call Christ "the Lord" is to confess his ontological identity with the God of Israel, YHWH. It is to uphold the core conviction of Israel's creedal life: "The Lord our God is Lord, him alone" as Jesus himself attested (Mark 12:29) before the questioning scribes, while at the same time to confess this Lord Christ as enclosed within the eternal life of YHWH, "who with the Father and the Holy Spirit lives and reigns forever and ever." Paul is introducing the Colossians to the basic grammar of Christian faith. Yet he is doing it in such a way that the scripture's literal sense is both upheld and extended in the single purposes of God, the scriptures bearing witness to him and allowing an extensional idiom to emerge as Paul speaks to those outside the covenants. This is the highest accomplishment of the mature Paul as he exercises an apostolic vocation he probably did not anticipate, itself now disclosed from the mystery of Christ and the scriptures that effect that disclosure.

What they have received, they are to continue to live within. That is Paul's chief concern: that the positive and full-orbed life of the gospel, as they have received it, will continue the sole path of their lives. **To live in him** is literally "to walk in him" (*en autō peripateite*). One thinks of the common Old Testament phrasing,

"Blessed is he who has not walked in the counsel of the wicked" but instead "their delight is in the law of the LORD." There is a way of the righteous, and it is the only path God knows and blesses. The way of the wicked is doomed. The Psalter opens quite properly with this threshold in the life of faith it sets before Israel in 150 episodes. Psalm 2 describes the installment of God's Son. God rebuffs the counsels of the wicked on behalf of his Anointed One, and in so doing he marks out the path that the blessing of God will chart for the faithful. That Anointed One has come. In him, as foreshadowed with the faithful Israel of old, one finds the path of life, and in him one walks for life. This is the sense the translation "live in him" seeks to communicate.

Psalm 1 may well continue its—unconscious or conscious—pressure in Col. 2:7. **Rooted** (*errizōmenoi*) is language from the field. It corresponds nicely with the image of Ps. 1:3: "They are like trees planted by streams of water, bearing fruit in due season." Paul describes the "walking in him" as enabled in three aspects: **rooted and built up [*epoikodomoumenoi*] in him, and established in the faith**. The second image is a constructional one, as in building a house. It corresponds in many ways with the thought of Eph. 2:20, just as rootedness is the language of 3:17. The household of God contains now sojourners and saints both, Jews and Gentiles brought near, for it is a house built on the foundation of "prophets and apostles, Jesus Christ himself being the chief cornerstone" (2:20). Paul's prayer in 3:16 reminds one of his striving on behalf of the Colossians, which is the topic of the present context. He prays there that "Christ may dwell in your hearts through faith; that you, being rooted and grounded in love may comprehend what is the breadth and length and height and depth, and to know the love of Christ that surpasses knowledge, that you may be filled with all the fullness of God." The two passages second one another and will explicitly do so should the letter in the Laodicean church (Col. 4:16) be in fact the letter we know as Ephesians.

The rooted and well-constructed walking in Christ Paul rounds out by speaking not of Christ as such, but of being **established in the faith** (*bebaioumenoi tē pistei*). There is some question as to how this is to be taken as the third image in the sentence. It could mean that rootedness and construction in Christ is "established by means of faith." This has a nice personal appropriation overtone, of the sort beloved of certain Christians. I am inclined to take the definite article seriously. The sense would then be "by means of this rootedness and inbuilt walking with Christ, thus established in the faith (which is the church's life)." If this is so, Paul is concerned as much with the public witness to Christ that is enabled by life in him, as he is with saying yet again that this life is to be found only in proportion to our rootedness in him. This would help explain the change in syntax and his decision not to just have passive participles conjoined by "and." We shift from "in him" to "the faith," and that change is a part of the way Paul formulates the sentence.[4]

4. "He now repeats without a figure what he had said in metaphors, that the following of the way, the support of the root and the foundation, is the firmness and steadfastness of faith. And observe that

The final phrase, "established in the faith," is glossed by **in the manner/just as you were taught**. This serves nicely to return us to the very opening notes of Col. 1. What has transpired already in the Colossian community has every good potential to sustain and be sustained. The faith they received then is able to weather the journey. Their walk in Christ has the compass of what they have been taught to direct it, and the letter they will receive from Paul will remind them of this and second it by means of Paul's own passionate address. As he was thankful for what he had heard from Epaphras, they also are to be thankful, indeed **overflowing with gratitude**. This final phrase is not an afterthought. One can properly think of the positive role that thanksgiving plays in sustaining the life of faith and of defeating the challenges to it. Calvin remarks on overflowing/abounding: "He did not want them merely to stand immovable, but to grow every day more and more.... And certainly, ingratitude is most often the reason why we are deprived of the light of the gospel, as well as other gifts of God" (1996: 328–29).

---

this argument is set before them because they have been well taught in the past, in order that they may securely and confidently plant their steps in the faith which had been known to them" (Calvin 1996: 328). Calvin refuses to see a distinction between subjective and objective faith. "Faith" is "the faith" that must be taught, received, and passed on.

THE SO-CALLED CONFLICT AT COLOSSAE

(2:8–23)

We have arrived at a crucial juncture in Paul's letter to the Colossians. The last three verses (2:5–7) are the culminating high notes of Paul's encouragement to the churches in the Lycus Valley. He brings the themes of his opening address to a passionate conclusion.

He has just previously spoken of the threat of "fine-sounding arguments" in 2:4, which we hold to be an intentionally comprehensive and open-ended way of referring to them. Paul does not move to the false trails he is about to explore, however, directly from 2:4. He pauses to speak in detail of why they need not be distracted or deterred. They have Christ, in whom are all the riches of assured understanding. They have him, and they are to walk in him. "Good order" and "firmness of faith," "rooted and built up" in Christ, "established in the faith"— these are the character traits and sure possessions of the Colossians. They are the factuals against which Paul will warn of alternatives. The alternatives in my view do not belong to a single religious system on the ground that Paul knows well and that could be combined to give a factual description of life in Colossae. To approach it from the other side, by an etic description of religion in Colossae, might well misconnect with what Paul knows, with what concerns him, and with how he proceeds to address this church in 2:8–23. Moreover, this way of dealing with the exegesis of 2:8–23 and indeed of the central purpose of the letter, has only given rise to a myriad of reconstructions—all of them plausible but none of them capable of dislodging the others. The alternatives Paul sets forth in 2:8–23 are better characterized as counterfactuals. The point of the strong commendation in 2:5–7, then, is to establish what is true, so that upon receiving this exhortation and encouragement from Paul, they will in general terms be able to stand aside from challenges that arise, for which Paul is about to give three examples. It is Factual 1 to be contrasted with the following counterfactual.

2:8 Counterfactual 1: **see to it you not end up a captive by means of vain and deceptive philosophy, according to human tradition, according to the elemental spirits of the world and not according to Christ**—"Rather than on Christ" might be a good way to bring focus to what concerns Paul in this particular case. He has been forthright in emphasizing (a) the centrality of Christ as the source of all wisdom and knowledge and (b) the thankful nature that characterizes walking in him and being firmly established in the faith. The **elementals** (*stoicheia*) of Christ and of his role as afflicted apostle on their behalf and how this fits with the mystery of the scriptures now disclosed—Paul has been at pains to set this forth with passion and clarity. The Colossians have "received Jesus Christ the Lord," and this is their rule of faith and the means by which the common scriptural witness now discloses its eternal purpose. Paul has not emphasized in practical terms (via formula citation) the role of the scriptures of Israel as they might be of use to the Colossians, but has instead used them in a translated medium to declare the work of God in Christ. It is this work—this faith that has been taught them and that they have received—that remains the decisive and instrumental bulwark on their behalf. That said, certainly within his own operative frame of reference, within his own reflexive world of scriptural knowledge and appeal, the idea of a privileged account of God and all that goes with that—as opposed to the general wisdom of the world or the specific systems purporting to convey that wisdom—is fundamental. The scriptures are the "oracles of God entrusted to the Jews," and they bear witness to the reality that "in Judah God is known." The Lord Christ himself bears witness to this fundamental conviction about the sole source of all truth and all knowledge of God.

These scriptures are well aware of rival accounts of truth and of the knowledge of God. The term they employ for God (*'elohim*) is one shared by neighbors both friend (Ruth) and foe (the Assyrian Rabshakeh). It will take the subtle argumentation of an Ezekiel (who refers to *'elohim* with a scatological gloss) to acknowledge that and reduce it to an epiphenomenon, a kind of accident of language whose only point is ironic. But even with that shared language and the positive potential it has for extension of the knowledge of the one true God, the scriptures know that God's name (YHWH) is not written into the general scheme of things. It is vouchsafed to a people God has chosen to provide with a "dial tone" (Deut. 6), and it is not an "abracadabra" but a name with a history of judgment and forbearance known within a specific relationship of trust and obedience and failure and forgiveness.[1] All this the nations must observe, and on occasion—as with the Philistine kings and Abraham and Isaac; the Pharaoh who knew Joseph or the Pharaoh who did not; Ruth, the sailors bound to Tarshish, or Nebuchadnezzar

---

1. C. Seitz, "The Divine Name in Christian Scripture," in *Word Without End*, 251–62.

the Great—they bear witness to the outskirts of his ways, in mercy or in dreadful judgment. Job remains the profound testimony to how the named God can break through without thereby unnaming himself.[2]

This is Paul's frame of reference. This frame of reference is far more decisive, in my view, than seeking to learn what the specifics of religious practice were in the Lycus Valley and then finding a way to determine with certainty what Paul might know of that and how he might know it. The letter of course does not raise the issue with any reference to this kind of information. Striking is the way Paul simply moves through the challenges and false trails and interweaves this with positive statements of what he knows from his own frame of reference and from one he is laboring to remind the Colossians is one they share fully, having been carefully taught.

Minimally, whatever Paul is communicating we must assume he believes will be intelligible to those addressed. The various terms (philosophy, elemental spirits, principalities, rules) need to make sense in general terms to those Paul is communicating with. Less obvious is whether they all refer to a single system threatening the Colossian church. One term in particular, because it stands at the beginning as well as at the end, may be critical, and that is the Greek word translated "elementals, rudiments," "elemental spirits," "elemental spiritual forces," and so forth (*stoicheia* at 2:8 and 2:20). What the larger thrust of the passage conveys is that Christ has defeated through the cross the power of any and all threats and rival systems (2:15) and that the Colossians are now dead to them and their potency (2:20). That it is very difficult to relate the "elemental spirits" to "principalities" and to "rules" belongs to the actual manner in which Paul speaks about them. He does not explain their relationship. He either assumes the Colossians know what this relationship is, or he speaks as he does in order to be comprehensive and to allow his audience to make connections on their own side.

I mention this because a certain imprecision almost seems imbedded in the discourse at points. This is especially true, in my view, of 2:8. We have four nominal expressions: (1) "philosophy," (2) "empty deceit" (*kenēs apatēs*), (3) "human tradition" (*paradosin tōn anthrōpōn*), and (4) "elemental spirits." The first two are joined by "and," and the others are linked by "according to" (*kata*). Does this encourage us to find a single tidy way to conjoin the four syntactically? The first two could then be combined into "vain and deceptive philosophy" as is frequently done, clarifying that a word like "philosophy" is not inherently negative (Josephus describes the parties in Judaism as "philosophies"; *Against Apion* 1.54; *Antiquities* 18.11); here Paul would then be referring to a species of false thinking. Is this then clarified further by "according to human tradition, according to the elemental spirits of the universe," and if so just what does this mean? The only clear thing here is that the repetition of "according to" sets up the contrast with "according to Christ" with which the sentence concludes.

2. C. Seitz, "Job: Full Structure, Movement, and Interpretation," *Interpretation* 43 (1989) 5–15.

The view taken here is that Paul is himself unable to refer to the challenge spoken of in the first case by a single term, and that is significant in itself. The extended predication is an indication that the challenge itself is not simple or univocal but needs elaboration—for Paul himself to be sure, but perhaps also for the Colossians. Paul struggles to give a single name to the threat and must qualify and stipulate. It is a vain and deceptive philosophy; it is according to human and not Christ-generated *paradosis*—that which they received (*parelabete*; 2:6) and which established the faith (2:7). It is a vain and deceptive philosophy; it is based on elemental spiritual forces within the universe.

We get some further help with "elemental spirits" because the term appears on its own in 2:20. There the Colossians are told they are now dead to the "elementals." To live in/by them is to "belong to the world." It further entails submission to various regulations (2:20–22). Paul explains what the "regulations of this world" sought to do: through rigor and self-abasement they sought to check indulgence in the flesh (2:23). Paul declares that this kind of "wisdom" is counterfeit. It belongs to the human realm, not to the new realm of Christ, where the Colossians now live. If the vain philosophy finds its grounding in elemental material realities, as the word *stoicheia* means in some places (earth, air, wind, fire); and if living and not dying to these—because Christ has defeated them—means submitting to human regulations demanding self-abasement with the hope of checking indulgence in the flesh, then we are apparently in the realm of an ideology with a heavily practical dimension. Paul is casting the net in broad terms so as to describe the significance of very specific alternatives: the wisdom of Christ and the life lived in him and not in intellectual or spiritual systems of behavioral control. The philosophical system is counterfactual to the new life in Christ, in terms of wisdom and knowledge and the means of living one's new life in him. Paul has said enough about this positively that the counterfactual needs only to fit in general terms the situation on the ground in Colossae, whatever that might in fact look like in detail.[3]

At one point Moo speaks of a hermeneutical knock-on effect of the difficulty of specifying in detail the challenges Paul is addressing in Col. 2: "For it means that we can apply Paul's teaching in the letter to a wide variety of historical and contemporary movements that share the general contours of the false teaching" (2008: 49). This appears to suggest that a modern historical-critical difficulty in

---

3. Calvin writes: "Observe, however, that he opposes Christ both to the elements of the world and to the tradition of men; by which he means that whatever is hatched in man's brain is not in agreement with Christ, who has been appointed by the Father as our sole Teacher, that he might retain in us the simplicity of the gospel. But that is corrupted by even a small leavening of human traditions. He means also, that all doctrines are foreign to Christ which place the worship of God (which we know to be spiritual, according to Christ's rule) in the elements of the world, and also which hinder man's mind by these trifles and frivolities, whereas Christ calls us directly to himself" (1996: 330). Calvin does not overstipulate but by the same token we get sufficient sense of Paul's meaning and also the possibility of its being grasped in Colossae. He also keeps the balance between what Paul is saying positively and its factual prominence and traction vis-à-vis a counterfactual possibility.

recovering the religious world of Colossae reveals a kind of accidental benefit of wider appropriation. But the actual issue may not be all that different for Paul than for us. Paul is trying to speak about a set of circumstances he may himself struggle to give univocal precision to, and he does not judge that disqualifying of his task. So long as he gets the description of the new life in Christ, and the "elementals" of that, in clear and compelling and accurate terms, he can be free to speak in intelligible if not also elastic terms regarding false trails not to be followed.

One final comment on 2:8 and on the wider subject of false teaching in Col. 2. Those who argue that Paul is speaking in a sustained way about Judaism throughout 2:7–23 must confront the obvious fact that this is simply not stated by Paul.[4] It would, moreover, require a very clever audience of Gentiles excited about Judaism and accommodating Christ within it—the putative target—to pick up on Paul's irony and sarcasm, required for this interpretation. So, Paul is speaking about a false philosophy, and the Gentiles at Colossae are to know that with this word Paul is classifying Judaism as another religion of the world. Then, he tells them not to be a "prey" (*sylagōgōn*), and they are to hear in this word a "contemptuous pun" on the word "synagogue"—"see to it that no-one snatches you as a prey (see RSV) from the flock and locks you up within Judaism" (Wright 1986: 105). On his reading, Paul is describing Judaism as another "human tradition" and its regulations as worldly and of no value. To worship angels is to worship the Torah so given by angels, and so forth. It is one thing to argue for an arch and ironic Paul making contemptuous puns and describing Judaism as a "human tradition," and another thing entirely to believe this would be an act of communication with obviously clear reception in a Gentile church. Wright produces an arch Paul speaking ironically to himself and fellow Jewish Christians, and overheard on those terms by outsiders. If the Gentile church is attracted to a Judaism on offer, how can they have lived in it and died to it already, as Paul says is true of them in 2:20? This reading cannot be held up as a more historically cautious and precise reading of the literal sense, as Wright hopes, but is instead an imaginary scenario best suited to an internal Jewish discussion, if even there. This is manifestly absent in the Colossian correspondence. History needs attention to plausible reception as well as (in this case) sarcastic Jewish insider-speak in hypothetical form.

The ground meaning of the word *stoicheia* is "member of a class of things" (letters in an alphabet, days in a calendar) or "fundamental principles." The primary elements from which all things are composed are *stoicheia* (in antiquity: air, fire, water, earth). "How does the universe hold together?" engendered speculations from Judaism as well. Sometimes this focused on systems of stars (*stoicheia* as

---

4. I agree with Barclay concerning the distinctive language of Colossians: "This is indeed a major flaw in N. T. Wright's argument that Paul here addresses something much like the situation in Galatia" (2004: 29). He continues: "But if the topic of conversation differs, we cannot insist that Paul always use the same language!" The situation of Colossians is indeed different, and Wright overreaches in trying to make a letter whose language and arguments and audience are distinctive conform to a single pattern, which in addition sounds its note in such an oblique way.

"constellation") or angels in charges of various dominions and the invisible realms of principalities, powers, authorities, and thrones.

The tradition often saw the interpretation of "elements" as influenced by the literary context in great measure. So what might be a neutral term linguistically, or what might refer simply to component parts, tends in the direction of "things in their complexity, speculative differentiations" on the one hand and "minutiae, things of lesser significance, rudimentary" on the other. One standard interpretation of *stoicheia* comes from Gal. 4:9–10, which speaks of "beggarly elements," that is, focusing on minutiae rather than the larger picture. In that instance, as well, the "elemental spirits" were false gods of a former life, to whom they were in bondage, and that included "observance of days." Because the text speaks of "observance of days" it is clear that in this instance the "elements" are the component parts of a calendar system. They can be referred to as "elements" and then described negatively as "weak."

"Elements of the universe" can also be seen by the tradition as somehow connected to calendar observance, but by extrapolation. Chrysostom concludes regarding 2:8, "Now he sets about to reprove their observance of particular days, meaning by the elements of the world the sun and moon" (2004: 285). But "elements of the universe" can mean for Thomas Aquinas simply preferring to focus on secondary causes rather than primary ones and so misdirecting one's proper apprehension of God. But he is also not doctrinaire and is willing to offer different interpretations, "measuring the truth of faith according to creatures" being one of the more general. He speculates about idolatry: "Worshiping idols and saying Jupiter was the heavens" (2006: 53). He knows that Galatians leans in the direction of "according to bodily observances" but is not convinced that meaning is proper in Col. 2:8. Yet in 2:20 the context does appear for him to move *stoicheia* in this direction (2006: 70–71).

My view is that in 2:8 the term is associated with a philosophical system that is vain and deceptive and that depends on complexity and minutiae rather than on the one cross and one Lord. In sum, it is intellectual idolatry. In 2:20 intellectual idolatry is attached to disciplines enjoining self-abasement, which are complex and rigorous and promise much, but are vain. These could be observances from the law, but what is clearer is that false trust has been placed in their power when compared to the work of Christ. In both cases it is the power wielded over those who attend to the "elementals" that concerns Paul, as well as their counterfeit wisdom. The "elements" are "spiritual forces" that seek to occupy the place of power and new life Christ has died to bring (Lincoln 2000: 565–67).

2:9–15 Factual 2: **(For in Christ) the fullness of deity dwells in all substantiality. You have been brought to fullness in him. He is the head over every power and authority. In him you were also circumcised with a circumcision not performed by human hands. Your whole self ruled by the flesh was put off when you were circumcised by Christ, having been buried with him in baptism, in which you were also raised with him through your faith in the**

working of God, who raised him from the dead. **When you were dead in your sins and in the uncircumcision of your flesh, God made you alive with Christ. He forgave us all our sins, having canceled the charge of our legal indebtedness, which stood against us and condemned us; he has taken it away, nailing it to the cross. And having disarmed the powers and authorities, he made a public spectacle of them, triumphing over them by the cross**—Paul does not decide to engage a single religious system whose details are well known to him and in a sustained way familiar with what we see in Galatians and other letters to refute its premises and its purveyors (the "false teachers" so conjectured). Rather, having warned about becoming prey to vain and deceptive philosophy in a single verse, he immediately returns to his positive commendation of the work of Christ and stays with that theme. Christ, not intellectual or spiritual systems, is deity in himself. He requires no further religious amplification or systemization, and indeed that is what makes faith in him and in the God with whom he is in fullest union different from philosophies. Christ is not a lower deity, nor is he capable of being ranged alongside high religious ideas or disciplines for checking indulgence of the flesh. He is not in this category of reality. "Bodily" (*sōmatikōs*) does not refer to the specifics of the incarnation, but here, as in 2:17, means "really" and "without remainder." That being said, the point may well be to emphasize the total identification of God with Christ, in earthly manifestations as well as ontological identity. The lack of gap between God the Father and God the Son disallows any intruding religious system from generating a population of angels, principalities, conceptual or disciplinary realities demanding our attention and preoccupation. All divine substantiality is focused in one place: Jesus Christ.[5]

2:9–10 As there is no gap on God's side, so too there is none of the side of those incorporated—*sōmatikos*—into Christ. **You have been brought to fullness in him**. The fullness and substantiality is God's gift and not a human achievement, the movement through levels or grades in a system. The image is developed of a body with a head as the means for describing this incorporation. Paul wants us to know that the head is not rivaled by any system or any power "visible or invisible" purporting to animate and regulate divinity or human conduct. **He is the head over every power and authority**. The same point and similar language emerged in 1:16. Whatever exists in the created realm was created through Christ; the only system for their synthetic relationship is him (1:17), and we know he is

5. The church fathers preoccupy themselves with the term "bodily." Is it used because the church is Christ's body? Is it used because Paul will shift to a discussion of Christ as head, thus meaning, "God dwells in Christ bodily inasmuch as Christ is the head"? That is, "bodily" means with respect to Christ being the head. But surveying the material it is not clear that any one reading ruled the day and that all may contain a measure of truth. God dwelt in Christ bodily in the incarnation—Paul is about to speak of Christ's bodily work on the cross. God has made Christ the head over all things, and so he embodies God in respect of dominion over all creation. Less obvious is the reference to the church as body. As Chrysostom notes: why did Paul not just say this (2004: 285)? Calvin concludes, after noting disagreements: "I do not doubt that it is employed imprecisely for substantially." That is: "The sum is that God has manifested himself to us fully and perfectly in Christ" (1996: 331).

preeminent over them all (1:18). There too we learn that "in him all the fullness of God was pleased to dwell" (1:19).

We do not attain incorporation by means of craft or bodily disciplining or movements through grades of self-knowledge and divine knowledge. God has crafted us. He has circumcised us **with a circumcision not performed by human hands**. This incorporation happened by God's will for us in his Son—not by human hands in obedience to the command of God, but by God's own hands in his Son. On the cross God carved out for us in his Son a new circumcised life for which the former circumcision by hands was a pledge and earnest. The only way adequately to describe this surgery is to say that we died. The problem in us was not piecemeal, and it did not reside in one faculty or another. It was not amenable to religious applications, intellectual exertions, or bodily disciplines. These not only failed to produce the wanted results, they were threatened by their exposure as inadequate and rose up against God in the form of crucifixion, seeking to kill he who was God's true Son and source of life and health in all fullness and comprehension.

2:11–12 your whole self ruled by the flesh was put off when you were circumcised by Christ—This translation is found in some versions as a way to avoid the dualism of flesh/body and spirit as it sometimes comes across when the word "flesh" is used. "The whole self ruled by the flesh" is in Greek simply "the body of flesh." But it was not the body only that was put off in this circumcision and the dying it accomplished, but the whole self ruled by the flesh and so bent toward rebellion and inevitable corruption. All of this, with nothing remaining, was circumcised by Christ: the foreskin of the body and the foreskin of the heart and will and mind. Here Paul speaks about the sacramental "new rite" corresponding to the former sacrament of circumcision. How is this action of God in his Son that gives us new life now manifested? How do the hands of God accomplish this circumcision? We die by going down into the waters of baptism, so Paul continues, **having been buried with him in baptism**. Baptism is the means by which we are buried **with him**. Paul will speak shortly of our being dead in our trespasses, of this being the condition of our natural man, but here he speaks about dying and being buried **with him**. A natural deathliness meets the transforming death of God's Son, and something new happens in consequence. This deathliness becomes transformed in these waters, because they are "waters" of Christ's own baptized life and death and peculiar to them is God's eschatological raising: **in which you were also raised with him through your faith in the working of God, who raised him from the dead**.

We may struggle with the articulation of baptismal theology only to find Paul's careful declarations, here and elsewhere, in their totality, marvelously fit to purpose. The sacrament's "outward and visible sign" (water consecrated to the purpose of joining us with Christ) and the inward and invisible grace (the Holy Spirit's transforming work of us by this rite) are two sides of a single coin, in Christ. The new and raised life is a reality as sure as Christ is himself raised from the dead by the power of God the Holy Spirit, by the will of God the Father. This is what God has in Christ accomplished for us and has given us fully in the sacrament of baptism. But there is also the Holy Spirit's gifting of a faith that brings this home to us and allows us to grasp what God has done and is doing. It is this faith that allows us both to see and to grasp what is the working of God. Our faith is raised to life as surely as God raised Jesus himself from death, and it is that new life in faith that engenders and releases in us who we now are in him. Our lives are now "hid with God in Christ" as Paul will put it in Col. 3, where he dwells on this sacramental mystery in greater detail. Neither baptism nor any other sacrament is ever merely a transactional *opera ex operata*. Something sure and final has transpired, and of that there is no doubt; God is faithful in what he promises. But the finality and the sureness are conveyed to us by the working of God, alive in us by faith. Without this, we hold deeds to a great mansion but do not live in it.

2:13 **when you were dead in your sins and in the uncircumcision of your flesh, God made you alive with Christ**—Here there can be little doubt that Paul narrows his vision to speak specifically of Gentile Christians in Colossae. But he never does this as if to lose sight of the work of one cross for Jew and Gentile. There is a dilemma peculiar to the uncircumcision, but seeing it from the standpoint of Christ's saving work for all, it becomes a species of something larger. Gentiles, as Paul tells us in Ephesians, and earlier in Colossians, are "without God in the world." The deathliness of their condition means being lost in a world of sin without being apprised of its full or partial reality and the consequent verdict of death over it. So Paul announces from inside the world of covenanted revelation what is the truth of the Gentile condition outside it. But all that matters little in the light of the victory secured by Christ for Jew and Gentile both. Knowing the rules of the game and failing to live up to them or living as though there were no rules both amount to the same consequence of death from which Christ has made us all alive. Hence the possibly unanticipated move from second-person plural to first-person plural. **He forgave us all our sins**. The possible distance separating Paul from his Gentile addressees is overshadowed by one cross, not two doing duty for conditions distinctive or unrelated.

2:14 Paul continues with the first-person plural and now uses language with its own particular relevance in the light of the one cross: **having canceled the charge of our legal indebtedness, which stood against us and condemned us; he has taken it away, nailing it to the cross**. The move from "you" to "us" is not accidental but in every way attaches itself to Paul's great insight into the human condition without losing sight of the special way God has decided to dispense his grace. Israel lived in a covenant relationship. Israel was entrusted with the oracles of God, which spoke clearly to God's people and also contained extensional mysteries only now perceived and only now delivering their address as clearly as the prophets had spoken of old. Insofar as that single oracular word spoke in two ways, so too the cross of Christ spoke in two ways at the same time. So Paul lets the difference collapse at the foot of that cross and now he speaks of "our" and "us" as he had just spoken of "you" and "you were dead in your trespasses."

Having erased the writ against us, with its decrees, which was opposed to us. This he evacuated, nailing it to the cross—The key to the interpretation of this very important verse lies with taking it as a totality, considering all its various expressions together.[6] Critical in this regard is the phrase "in respect of its decrees" (*tois dogmasin*), which sits rather inelegantly as a dative in relationship to the main image of a "writ" (*cheirographon*) or "document, bond, IOU, note of debt." This *cheirographon* has been the subject of much discussion as it is a rare word in New Testament Greek, though it is used sufficiently in Greek in other places and goes back to concepts of debt and debt notes familiar from the wider biblical presentation. "Forgive us our debts" (in the Lord's Prayer) and several New Testament parables make the general concept clear, as do the book of Tobit, the Testament of Job, and images of a heavenly court with record books. One is in a situation of debt, where a note is drawn up to acknowledge this and signed by the debtor in a public manner. The question is how Paul is thinking. Does his mind move toward Gen. 2–3 and the debt of Adam? Does it move toward a record book of good and bad deeds opened in a heavenly court and judged according to a divine standard (God's law)? Is he thinking of Torah itself? Versions of these positions can be seen in the Christian tradition's history of interpretation. In my view much of how one inclines is based upon the phrase "in respect of decrees" even if this is not acknowledged as crucial in the first instance as governing what we understand by the main image of a writ.

Those who hold that Paul is speaking of the Law (Torah) encounter several problems, and these are noted in the tradition (Theodoret) and most recently in modern scholarship. The IOU is signed by the debtor, not by the one to whom repayment is due, so if that is what is referred to, God's law cannot be a writ in this strict sense. Second, it would require Paul to use a phrase as an extrapolation in application to the law, and that is not obviously the case in this verse. Third, and importantly, Paul is speaking in the first-person plural here. Those referred to in 2:13 are Gentiles. By a careful transfer to the first-person plural in that verse, Paul anticipates reference to the cross in 2:14 and its overshadowing all humanity. He includes himself in its work and its address of the human condition alongside the "uncircumcision and dead in trespass" Gentiles of 2:13. If a note of debt at all, the agreement is to comply with God's law (Theodoret cites Exod. 24:3): "Is the Jews' bond not all people's?" (2001: 94). But in this light we also need to ask what the word *dogmata* means and in what way it might refer to commandments of the law.

In discussing the matter Sumney makes the obvious but significant point that an interpretation of *cheirographon* as law "does not fit the context because Colossians has no discussion of the Mosaic law in the life of the believer" (2008: 144).

6. This is true regardless of whether one could be successful in declaring, e.g., *tois dogmasin* a gloss and assessing the significance of an addition to inherited traditional material.

I registered the same point above against the idea of a contemptuous and ironic reference to the law as "human tradition" that would further require a subtle apprehension by Gentiles nowhere consistent with the tone and substance of Colossians. Sumney notes the early interpretation (see Chrysostom 2004: 286) of the term *dogmata* as the positive application of gospel teaching, leading to "having canceled the debt by means of Christian teaching"—a reading also roundly rejected in the tradition for voiding the centrality of the cross in the verse (see Eadie's thorough survey: 1856: 163–65). Another proposal was that the *dogmata* refer to the false teachings: regulations being imposed on the Colossians. But this is a most oblique reading, and it raises the question whether we are making Paul too literally engaged with the details on the ground. As he remarked earlier in respect of "elements of the world," Sumney correctly cautions against the idea that *stoicheia* or in this case *dogmata* correspond to the *specifics* of false teaching as the teachers themselves believed them: "Rather, the author gives a polemical evaluation, denigrating their teaching by associating it with the *stoicheia*" (Sumney 2008: 131). In this instance, the *dogmata* are aspects of the character of the "note of debt" and must be interpreted in reference to it, inside Paul's own thinking on this matter.

So what does *dogmata* mean in the context of 2:14? Barth and Blanke note: "The term occurs only five times in the New Testament, and even then never in this sense" (1994: 370). Ephesians 2:15 is the only reference that comes close to this idea, and like Colossians it is dealing with the fate of Jew and Gentile together. Ephesians is not speaking of a "note of debt" and its *dogmata*, however. In our context, *dogmata* likely moves not in the direction of legal commands (a familiar translation, so NRSV) but in the direction of "decrees." This is the way the term is used in Luke 2:1 and the Codex A reading of Heb. 11:23 (the decrees of Herod and Pharaoh, respectively). If in rabbinic Judaism the term refers to law as the means by which the decrees of God are known, then the heavenly judgment would be rendered by this standard, and it cannot then be that the law is a "note of debt" that condemned us. It is God's righteous disclosure of his will, and by its standard righteous judgments are rendered positively as well as negatively.

For this reason the association with Adam and all humanity seems more persuasive. This foundational episode is revealed by the law but is not the law as such. As a consequence of the debt of Adam, God rendered a decree of death that encompassed all humanity. In the Syriac literature of the early church, surveyed carefully by Gary Anderson, we see the dramatic narrative enactment of the key episodes.[7] Adam signs a public note of debt. Satan receives the note by virtue of the decision to become enslaved to him. All humanity suffers in consequence, everyone, through all time. Christ tricks Satan into believing he is another mortal, because he comes in the flesh. He waits for an opportune time to strike, having sought to test the enslaved DNA (so he thought) of the mortal Christ in the wilderness. The

7. Gary A. Anderson, *The Genesis of Perfection: Adam and Eve in Jewish and Christian Imagination* (Louisville: Westminster John Knox, 2001).

cross is this final moment. All the forces of debt slavery and satanic disobedience and death, accumulated through all time and exhibited by all in Satan's power, with his note of debt testifying to it (implicating every descendant of Adam, Jew and Gentile), are unleashed at the cross. But Christ is no mere mortal but a second Adam and God's own Son. By a second tree the effects of the first tree are canceled (Irenaeus). The *cheirographon* is nailed to the tree. "God made him to be sin in whom there was no sin" (2 Cor. 5:21), so that in killing this Son of God, the note of death is killed, canceled, and rendered null and void.

Those who think the regulations of the law are under discussion here must wrestle with the assumption that the law is nailed to the tree, and frequently this takes the turn of dividing the law into ceremonial and moral dimensions. Often the discussion, especially at the Reformation, becomes very convoluted. But even in the modern period, someone like Dunn, having argued for a reference to the law, realizes that the implications for ongoing reception of the law by Christians must be carefully thought through. In my view this is why recourse to the categories of moral and ceremonial and such like entered into the picture, rather than because they were functional in Col. 2:14 or even in Paul's argument here in address to Gentiles. Paul is again engaged in an active theological translation. He does not displace the deep patterns of God's word as disclosed to Israel, but speaks of them in terms that are accessible to Gentiles who do not know the law (much less details about its ceremonial and moral distinctions) but whom Paul believes are addressed by the law all the same. Working from the one cross of Christ, he describes a debt cancellation that reaches back to Adam and encloses both the circumcised who have reflected long on the character of debt and guilt, as well as the uncircumcised, who Paul nevertheless believes, on the basis of Gen. 2–3, will grasp what he is intending to say: that one cross avails for both Jew and Gentile. The tradition will speak of the memory of Adam's disobedience in the conscience of the Gentile, itself betokening and illuminating what Paul says when he speaks of a *cheirographon*.

Thomas Aquinas is his usual comprehensive self in his listing of interpretative options. He notes Eph. 2:15 and assumes that Paul is speaking of the regulations of the law at this place in Colossians as well. Yet he also notes that the term "bond" has a wider range and could include the harassing of the devil in human consciousness via the memory of transgression. So he wants *cheirographon* to retain two meanings: "The law, because it gave humankind a knowledge of sin, but did not help [in overcoming sin], and the memory of our transgressions, for which we deserved to be punished." Yet at the same time, he concludes by adding what he calls "another interpretation." He notes that Paul is speaking generally here and "not just about the Jews." So he suggests Paul has in view the first command (Gen. 2:16): "But man violated this law, and the memory of this violation became a bond that stood against us. And Christ canceled this" (2006: 61). This final interpretation tracks well with the movement we have described taking place in Col. 2:13. Paul is seeing the dilemma of Gentiles ("you were dead" and "your flesh") from the standpoint of one cross and so includes himself via the first-person plural "all our trespasses." The one bond that stood against "us" (Jew and Gentile) was revealed in the Genesis account of the disobedience of Adam. The new Adam canceled that bond when he nailed it to the cross in his own dying and rising. He evacuated it and its force. So Paul then continues.

2:15 he disarmed the principalities and powers and made an open spectacle of them, triumphing over them in him—The final *en autō* could conceivably refer to the last word of the previous verse ("the cross") but I opt for the referent being Christ. The main verb in the sentence (*apekdysamenos*) leads to two different interpretations in the tradition. As a middle voice it usually has a reflexive force, and indeed in 3:9 that is the case: "you have put off, stripped off (of yourselves)." So an older interpretation leaned toward "he stripped off from himself the powers and principalities" or even with an applied object "flesh" ("he stripped off his flesh/mortality").[8] Thomas Aquinas, for example, knows the second of these meanings as well as the one reproduced in the translation above. Christ put off his flesh and made an example thereby of the powers. By death and the grave, Christ raised up a new life and routed the forces of darkness. Citing Rom. 6:9; 1 Cor. 15:50; and 2 Cor. 5:15, the idea is that Christ traded mortality for immortality and is no longer to be regarded as mortal. In consequence the forces arrayed against him were defeated, the cross and empty tomb given public display of that. "Open spectacle" has been linked to a "victory parade" where the defeated are led in chains. It may be that by speaking of the cross so specifically in Col. 2:13, here Paul widens the referent of "public display" to the resurrection and ascension. Thomas Aquinas is very concerned, for example, to include in his discussion the "saints who died before Christ's passion" (2006: 62). He cites "captives of the waterless pit" (Zech. 9:11) and "captives of the mighty" (Isa. 49:25) and means by that those freed from devils in the lower world. Christ "descended into the lower world of the saints and ascended into heaven" (2006: 63) captures the sequence in its entirety.

My translation follows the more usual modern one. There has been no indication of a change in the subject of the verb from "God" in Col. 2:13. God "made alive" and he "canceled" and he "disarmed" and all this took place "in him," that is, in Christ. God despoiled the anarchic powers in Christ, and the means by which this happened was the cross and empty tomb. "In him" God released all captives against whom the bond declared their service to death, enslaved to invisible powers.

---

8. Lightfoot is usually cited for the modern version of this rendering: "Christ took upon himself our human nature with all its temptations (Heb. 4:15). The powers of evil gathered about him. Again and again they assailed him. . . . The final act in the conflict began with the agony of Gethsemane; it ended with the cross of Calvary. The victory was complete. . . . The powers of evil, which had clung like a Nessus robe about his humanity, were torn off and thrown aside forever" (1997: 96–97). The Greek patristic writers usually had this conception. For example, Theodoret: "Since the demons had influence over us through the body's passions, he by being clad in a body proved superior to sin. He abolished the influence of the adversaries, and made their weakness obvious to all people, granting all of us victory over them through his own body" (2001: 94).

This is the *Christus Victor* model of the atonement, which Aulen otherwise labels the "classical model."[9] It can move through time and so has contact with the Holy Saturday themes as these appear in the church's liturgical life. Though one associates this often with the Eastern churches, the reference to this understanding is obvious in the Thomas Aquinas quotations above as well, who speaks of "those saints who had died before Christ's passion" (2006: 62). The trampling of death is however part of an entire sequence, with cross, empty tomb, and resurrection and ascension all interlocking aspects of the "open spectacle" referred to in 2:14–15.

Anticipating the verse to follow, and the counterfactual it introduces, Paul wants to insist that in Christ everything God needed to do he has done. The forces hostile to God are not brought to heel by calendar or dietary observances about which one faces another worldly judgment as to proper execution. The judgment of God has come and its public demonstration is attested. In Christ, the Son of God, God accomplished the canceling of Adam's debt and its transmission throughout all humanity throughout all time. No rite or observance exists now except those that keep this fact preeminent. The conscience is not to hold itself under a new judgment, this side of the cross. The only "elementals" worthy of our attention are those that articulate the great mystery of redemption as Paul labors to describe that in 2:9–15. The only rite that Christ endorses is the one baptism, whose sole purpose is to describe our death in Christ and our rising to new life in his new life (2:12). Christ needs no regulatory assistance to achieve a victory over hostile and enslaving powers. God has in him accomplished everything necessary, canceling a debt hanging over humankind through all time and nailing it to his one cross of new life.

We need to be clear about Paul's achievement here and the way it matches what we have seen of this elsewhere in Colossians. On the one hand, Paul's understanding of the cross and empty tomb is informed by the specifics of the character of the human condition as these exert their pressure from the scriptures, "the oracles of God entrusted to the Jews." In his mind are Adam and the decrees of God, and possibly their reflex within the commandments themselves. But at the same time and more crucially, Paul must translate the eternal truth of these specified scriptural realities into the Colossian frame of reference, where for example the commandments (*entolē*) of the law are not a factor as such and are never referred to with this word. The image of a "writ opposed to us" does not have to match on-the-ground details of the Colossian church perfectly (if we could know that), but it will have to be persuasive and understandable as a truth about the human condition. (Here I suspect is the one detail noted by those who see in *cheirographon* an appeal to conscience and memory, general enough in its location in the human condition to find reception and redolence.) Paul can be creative in his choice of language, and a "note of debt" is certainly something that is concrete

9. G. Aulen, *Christus Victor: An Historical Study of the Three Main Types of the Idea of the Atonement*, trans. A. G. Herbert (London: SPCK, 1945).

and understandable. His further gloss, "in respect of decrees," may come more from his side of the register than their own, if he has in view the specific decree over the couple in the garden (Gen. 3:16–19) and the debt note held by demonic powers. But is he also anticipating the use he will make of *dogmata* later on, where the term covers the decrees or regulations seeking to impose themselves on the Colossians? Certainly that is possible. Paul is negotiating several realms at once: (1) his scriptural frame of reference, (2) his creative application and translation of this for his audience, and (3) his general sense of what may be a threat to the Colossians over against the faith that has taken hold among them and that Paul seeks to bolster and inform. How he is able to do this is by reference not to three things but one: the cross of Christ. From that reference point the character of the human dilemma, its resolution by God in Christ, and the implications of that for false understandings of God and the human condition all flow.

This depiction of Paul's achievement helps us also avoid false trails. Paul cannot be majoring in his own frame of reference in respect of the law and its command-ments (*entolē*; see Rom. 7) because he has in mind the character of the Colossians as outside the law strictly speaking. But not outside all expressions of God's will for humanity in general. The law is a particular and commandment-thick expression of God's will, but it has its specific character in relation to God's will for human-ity in general, such as we find it in the law's own opening book of Genesis, and elsewhere in the scriptures' spilling out into the nations (Amos 1–2; Isa. 13–23; Nahum). Romans works hard to describe the relationship between the revealed law and its ramifications otherwise for the whole human family.

It must not be the case, then, that the details of Paul's exhortation require perfect matching up with religious realities on the ground he knows in detail or that we readers could uncover through rigorous investigation of the religious and philosophical texts of the Lycus Valley. Paul is negotiating the scriptural reality and the audience's ability to comprehend it in an idiom Paul is creatively deploying, which he hopes and prays will bridge the two realms. It is the work of the one cross that enables him to do that, because of the comprehensive way it addresses the human dilemma in its fullest sense, breaking down the dividing wall of religious comprehension.

In Ephesians Paul uses the word "body" to explain this. There was Jew and Gentile but now there is one body, one Christ, and in the light of that, one new man in his body the church (Eph. 2:13–22).[10] Striking is how prevalent the term is in Col. 2:9–23.[11] In the light of the one body sacrifice of Christ, we are in a new realm that puts the former realms of Jew and Gentile in the shade. There has been a death to an old life and a former body and regulations for its conduct. This is all

10. "That he might create in himself one new man in place of two" (Eph. 2:15) and "might reconcile us both to God in one body through the cross" (2:16).

11. Consider the following: "dwells bodily" (2:9); "putting off the body of flesh" (2:11); "but the body is Christ" (2:17); "not holding fast to the head, from whom the whole body . . . grows" (2:19); "severity to the body/indulgence of the flesh" (2:23).

because of the body of Christ in one sacrifice and his new risen body the church, where we have a new life in a new body. This theme overlaps the present and the next two paragraphs (2:16–19 and 2:20–23).

In sum, Paul seeks to be an excellent preacher. To do that he must be truthful (in respect of the scriptures), compelling (persuasive and creative), and comprehensible. He must be sufficiently clued into who he is speaking to, without knowing every jot and tittle of what is going on with them. He is like a "guest preacher" who has been given some general sense of "St. Albans Church" from "the rector" so he can avoid false trails and have some general sense of his audience. But he is also seeking to draw the congregation into a new frame of reference, one that will reorient their living and dying and will help to recast what may be challenges facing them, which come of course in many forms. The "rector" of "St. Albans Church" did not provide Paul with a laundry list, but Paul has his own idea about what kind of challenges most get in the way of Christ and God's accomplishment in him. He was once nearby and spent a three-year stint preaching and persuading people like the Colossians. He knows enough to do the work of translation, from the scriptural world to the world of Colossae and its challenges. The one cross provides him all the access he needs. The one cross has given rise to a new one-body existence. That has distinct implications for any system of calendar or dietary regulations designed to order the life of a former body. It also rules out adventures in spiritual realms that divorce one from the true head and his new body.

2:16 Counterfactual 2: **therefore, let no one pass judgment on you in matters of eating and drinking or with regard to a festival or a new moon or a Sabbath**—However we understand the particularities implied by "eating and drinking" and "festival or a new moon or a Sabbath"—if by that we mean the particularities in Paul's articulation and in his own thinking—it is crucial to keep in mind how the concern is introduced. Paul does not say, "avoid X and Y, they are wrong." He does not refer to the promulgation of Jewish regulations or teachers who promote rites in which one participates so as to gain religious experience and insight (2:18). That must be inferred. Instead he is clear that what is at issue is passing judgment on the basis of these matters: "Let no one judge you" (Eadie 1856: 175 has "test your piety by such a criterion"). This matches almost perfectly the context of Rom. 14. There the matter of the calendar and dietary observance has been put in the shade. Paul can speak of proper use of these matters, as well as a certain indifference about them. At issue is not allowing them to divide the community because they are used to pass judgment on one another. The Jewish and Gentile background of such a concrete concern is not explicit here (the "strong" and the "weak" brother). There is no reference to the "law of Moses," and the term "commandment" (*entolē*) is absent. Indeed the reference to "eating and drinking" is vague to the point of generic (the Old Testament does not spend much time on the subject of drink regulation). Paul appears to be seeking to be comprehensive. Let judgment not be passed on anyone due to food or drink. Of course the Old Testament had rules governing not just food but the proper manner of its preparation, a matter of some concern given non-Jewish culture and the implications associated with food and drink in them, which are invariably religious in nature (see 1 Cor. 8). "Food offered to idols" bespeaks that eating is participating in some system of "elementals"—pagan or, in the case of Israel, as regulated by Torah.

In my view Paul is not offering any analysis of religious systems here, such as would commend his exhortations due to the accuracy of his descriptions. His comments about the religious systems—Jewish or pagan—are too lapidary and seem to be generic in nature. Any calendar system or dietary system cannot be the means for pronouncing judgments in the new body of Christ. There has been one judgment and one body and one cross. Any festival, new moon, or Sabbath is now a shadow (Col. 2:16). Is Paul using categories known to him from the law, or is he imagining himself into a different frame of reference, where pagan calendars and dietary rules assist in gaining religious insight and experience? As it stands, his language could make its way into either context, either because that is his intention or because he uses the language of his own context to apply to possible non-Jewish counterparts. The triad is a common enough one in the Old Testament (Hos. 2:11; Ezek. 45:17; 1 Chr. 23:31; 2 Chr. 2:4; 31:3), though one needs to look at these contexts more closely (and none of the references are in the law of Moses strictly speaking).

Lohse is somewhat typical in appreciating the challenge of these verses when he writes that "Jewish tradition" is the source of the terms, but he believes they have been "transformed in the crucible of syncretism to be subject to the service of 'the elements of the universe'" (1971: 116). Another way to put this would be that Paul uses terms known to him in such a way that they can comprehend challenges facing the faithful in Colossae, which Lohse is otherwise at pains to give history-of-religion precision to in the name of a syncretism on the ground. It is worth underscoring in this regard that the triad is not a familiar one in the law as such. In Hosea it emerges in the context of prophetic indictment: they are "her yearly festivals, her new moons, and her Sabbaths"—that is, unfaithful Israel's "appointed feasts" (2:11). The reference in Ezekiel encloses the triad in a wider set of rites properly to be conducted when the new temple is constructed as Ezekiel himself sets forth. True to its narrative conception, and in that sense closer to the perspective of Ezekiel, Chronicles is looking backward and writing a history so as to reconceive something for the future in the postexilic Israel (or eschatological Israel). What is Paul thinking of when he uses the triad? Is he referring to contemporary Jewish practice that is somehow a real or possible threat to the church? In my view it is simply not possible to give this kind of precision to his language. I prefer the view that Paul is being precise in what he does not stipulate and in how he is content to frame the matter generically as he does. Perhaps Hosea's negative ambiance is in view, and if so, that would say nothing about the appropriateness of the rites as such, but rather their deformation or potential distraction. So Paul clarifies.

2:17 these are a shadow of something to follow later, not Christ's body— Some translations interpret the first part of 2:17 epexegetically, "these are a shadow of the things that were to come" (NIV), and so adopt something of the temporal perspective implied in Heb. 10:1. "These were a shadow" would accomplish the same thing, even as the verb in Greek is *estin*. The older KJV, translating literally, had "which are a shadow of things to come, but the body is of Christ." At issue is not just how the second part of the verse is rendered ("the reality, however, is found in Christ"; NIV), but what the pair *skia* ("shadow") and *sōma* ("body") mean and how the temporality is to be rendered. The pairing is not unattested in sources like Plato, but more familiar is "shadow" and "form" (*eikōn*). Philo speaks of the Old Testament letter as shadow vis-à-vis the substance of his allegorical interpretations (in a notable reversal of our modern historical conceptuality).[12]

At issue is whether the contrast is between something past that is now substantially and differently viewed, literally "put in the shade," or, more strongly, oppositional; or whether the thought is of the general provisionality of any rite vis-à-vis the true age to come. If the latter, Paul is not making a statement of the pastness of the rites and their coming to an end, but of their inherent provisionality *at present*. They are matters about which the passing of judgment is disallowed because that would deform the work of Christ. The rites and Christ belong in different realms of existence altogether and are not linked temporally on a shadow-form basis. They are shadow. Christ is body. In the body the eschatological finale is now a reality. The rites have sense only as shadows of the greater reality that is now the church as such. Hosea equally saw the provisionality of a rite in the sense that it could be improperly observed and so belonged to a season of judgment. Such rites would simply be taken away, until the true bride was restored "in that day" (2:16). The shadow is in contrast with, not in opposition to, the bride.[13]

Paul has referred to the cruciality of baptism as bringing about the new life in the one body of Christ. Calendar observance and food and drink regulations cannot be the arena for judgments that would destroy the confidence of Christian faith in the work of Christ and in the new rite of baptism for creating that. But Paul now goes further and speaks of something of the attitude that lies behind the passing of judgments, in the form of religious practices to which he refers. I am tempted to introduce the translation and the discussion both with a long quotation from

12. Brevard S. Childs, "The Sensus Literalis of Scripture: An Ancient and Modern Problem," in *Beiträge zur Alttestamentlichen Theologie: Festschrift für Walther Zimmerli zum 70. Geburtstag*, ed. H. Donner (Göttingen: Vandenhoeck & Ruprecht, 1976), 81–93.

13. It seems to me that Sumney is on the right track by noting the difficulty of the translation and the contrast between *skia* and *sōma*, with the link to Christ's body: "This reading allows that those regulations may have had some value before the arrival of the fullness of blessing available in Christ; they are not illusory or completely without value, only less valuable than what is available in the church." Colossians does not assert "that observance of regulations from the Mosaic covenant was illusory" (2008: 153). I hold that the references Paul uses also are flexible enough to apply to any rite or calendar requirement and not just rites within his own specific Jewish frame of reference.

Augustine, where he confesses his befuddlement at what Paul means here. That sets the proper context for my exegesis. That is, there is a degree of obscurity in what is being communicated that probably in the nature of the case cannot be removed. It may be that Paul himself recited a litany of false religious activities that corresponded to no single religious system on the ground. Our task is to try to understand how his mind was working and what he was seeking to communicate and also have received as intelligible by his audience, at the same time.

2:18 **let no one disqualify you, seeking to do it by self-abasement and worship of angels, taking his stand on visions, puffed up irrationally by his fleshy mind**—Though the phrases themselves are a bit obscure, the only real translational difficulty is in rendering *thelōn*. The first imperative could be rendered "let no one rob you of your prize" or "disqualify you." *Thelōn* has the character of "will," and the question is whether it is attached to the imperative ("let no one disqualify you willingly") or to what follows (KJV has "voluntary humility"). As we have a series of four participles in a row, it seems best to let it have its own construction with what follows, as with the others as well. Some see *thelōn* as the Septuagint equivalent of Hebrew "delight in," though the phrase does not otherwise appear in this way in the New Testament itself. I opt for "willing/seeking/wishing to do it" by means of humility and the worship of angels. There is an affectation of humility and phony abasement whose ironic truth, as Paul states it, is a puffed up and fleshy mind—the very opposite of the *soi-disant* "abasement" practices themselves. Much ink has been spilled on whether the genitive in respect of angels is objective or subjective: "worship of angels" or "worship alongside the angels' own worship," as in an initiatory religion or the ascending claims of mysticism, namely, a worship like that of the angels from which humankind must learn. The view is not just a modern history-of-religion one but can also be found in the tradition as well (Tertullian, Luther). My view is that genitive of object is more obvious and that Paul has in mind here the eccentricities of religious practices that would purport to need objects of worship alongside Christ. It was for this reason among others that he devoted the central section of Col. 1 (1:15–20) to a description of the relation of Christ to God. It is a relationship of its own kind and belongs to the eternal character of God. However the scriptures (Old Testament) or other religions spoke of angels and ranks of plenipotentiaries, for the Christian church in Colossae all this would be distraction or worse. As with 2:16, the negative imperative sets the tone. Any such practices are bogus but the real problem is the way they could be used to disqualify the Christian or otherwise obscure the solid ground of their faith. Christ is the final and glorious abasement and the means of our salvation through his sacrifice once for all. No other abasement and no other worship have any warrant in our new life in him.[14]

14. For a compact, recent discussion of the possible history-of-religions context of the phrases here, see Barth and Blanke 1994: 346–48; C. E. Arnold, *The Colossians Syncretism: The Interface between Christianity and Folk Belief at Colossae* (Grand Rapids: Baker, 1996), 243–44; Sumney 2008: 153–59; and Lincoln 2000: 560–68.

It is striking that over against this depiction of religious life Paul has made no small effort in describing his own vocation, which includes abasement of a different kind. It is abasement whose character and purpose is only in the person of Christ himself. No one ranges alongside Christ and props up alongside him what one has done or imitates it in some religious rite. But equally, no one should pretend a false humility that, seeking to give high place to divinity, designs elaborate means to worship ranks of intermediaries instead. Whether the archangel Michael was worshiped at Colossae at this period in the manner Theodoret later references (in the fifth century) we cannot know. But the instinct to refract the ontological relationship between Father and Son into something other than "image" or "first-born" or "likeness" can inevitably lead to higher and lower estimates of God and Christ, vis-à-vis one another and in relation then to other realities. Paul warns the Colossians not to be beguiled by any such refraction. This is "mind of the flesh" thinking, and it is often marked by high self-regard and self-importance. Paul presents the solid ground from which our real growth is accomplished, contrasting this with rival schemes for ascending to God or generating self-regard and high-mindedness.

2:19 **not holding fast to the head, from whom the whole body, nourished and knit together in its joints and ligaments, grows with a growth that is from God**—Now the language of the second half of 2:17, compressed as it was, comes into clearer focus. Not a shadow in the form of rites or regulations but a real body, whose head is Christ. Not a mind of flesh that is of our own exalted making, through visions, but a head that gives us proper thinking and apprehension, when we remain in his body and seek not to leave our body by means of religious ascent or conform it by means of dietary regulation. Paul has spoken of Christ as head in 1:18, and the same term is found in Eph. 1:22. We are to grasp the head, and the participle is quite concrete: "lay hold of." We are not to conjure up, or seek after, or religiously confect, but grasp what is there for the grasping, Christ himself as head. The language of the second half of Col. 2:19, in describing the whole body as composed of joints and ligaments, working in coordination so as to produce growth, is very similar to the image of the church in Eph. 4:16. This organic life-giving existence in the body contrasts with a condition in which we are exposed, "tossed to and fro by every wind of doctrine, by the cunning of men and their craftiness in deceitful wiles" (4:14). It is hard to conceive of anything but the same thinking here at work in Col. 2:8–23. Paul is aware of what Christ has accomplished on our behalf, and equally he knows that without bodily rootedness in this reality we are exposed and under threat from rival systems of thinking, of living, and of worshiping. This is the factual contrasted with the counterfactual.

2:20–21 Factual 3: **since with Christ you died to the elemental spirits of the universe**; and counterfactual 3: **why, as though living in the world, would you be decreed to, "do not handle, do not taste, do not touch"**—And so we come to the third and final counterfactual Paul warns against in the light of Christ's one body new life. The **if then** opening of 2:20 finds its counterpart in

3:1, reminding us of the difficulty of isolating a single section of the letter dealing with false teachers. Dying (2:20) and being raised (3:1) are extensions of the fundamental insight given by Paul in positive terms in 2:11–13 with reference to dying and being buried and raised in Christ, in baptism. This in turn gives way to "put to death" (3:5–11) and "put on" (3:12–17). Melanchthon was keen to emphasize the rhetorical achievement of Paul in Colossians and to resist taking individual verses or units of texts abstracted from this larger achievement. The text itself gives reason for his concern.

If then could equally be rendered **"since then"** and some translations follow this. What hangs on this decision is probably not grammatical in either/or terms, but has to do with the character of Paul's rhetoric. "If" could raise the rhetorically charged "why then" in the direction of threat. The Colossians are then to be seen as potentially threatening a condition that should be theirs by possession. "Since" lowers the threat but raises in its place the nonsense of not living in the state of affairs that is a reality. In 3:1 "since" makes better sense in terms of the objective reality Paul is and has been proclaiming. I prefer it as well in 2:20 as pointing to a deliberate pairing.

The verb that I render **be decreed to** (*dogmatizethse*) is middle in Greek and so means "allow yourself to be, submit yourself to" the subject of however we are to render *stoicheia* in 2:8.[15] I do not believe Paul is referring specifically or exclusively to the commandments (*entolē*) of the law, for which a perfectly good term is available (see Rom. 7, where "commandment" is repeated six times). Rather, he is speaking to a threat—the attraction of rules for conduct—for which he uses the general term *dogmata* as decrees to be honored and respected.[16] Galatians also speaks of a *former* life of enslavement to elemental spirits and of the danger of reverting to it, and the basic idea is introduced by reference to their erstwhile bondage "to beings who by nature are no gods" (4:8) as constitutive of a life without the knowledge of the true God. Paul is concerned that their calendar observances are the manifestation of this life returning.

On my view the concern in Galatians with a former life is here Paul's more general concern with a present threat, which he describes as being in thrall to decrees of various kinds. They are dead to elemental spirits and are alive in Christ.

---

15. Middle can also be passive. The verb in this form appears only here in the New Testament. I adopt a subjunctive reading because I believe this is how Paul is thinking in this case. M. D. Hooker, "Were There False Teachers in Colossae?" in *Christ and Spirit in the New Testament: In Honour of Charles Francis Digby Moule*, ed. B. Lindars and S. S. Smalley (Cambridge: Cambridge University Press, 1973), 315–31 at 317–18, on slightly similar lines, renders: "why submit?" Sumney renders: "Why do you accept any commandments from the elements of the world, as though you were living in the world?" (2008: 159). This captures something of the hypothetical character of Paul's phrasing, as I see it. Sumney writes (160): "So it is better to connect the prepositional phrase 'from the elements of the world' with the following verb *dogmatizethse* ('dogmatize,' 'accept commandments')." "Elements" (*stoicheia*) appears in 2:8 and 2:20.

16. As noted above, the derivatives of *dogmata* appear infrequently in the New Testament. The verb in the Septuagint means "to establish or publish a decree" (Dan. 2:13, 15; Esth. 3:9; 2 Maccabees 10:8; 15:36; 3 Maccabees 4:11).

It would be a return to life in the world to attend to such things or to take them seriously as worthy of following. The description of these negative imperatives that follows in Col. 2:22–23 is sufficiently pejorative that it is hard to understand them as Paul's reference to commandments of the law especially (a) when he has never mentioned the law and does not in this letter and (b) as it would be hard, if he were speaking to Gentiles, properly to avoid their misunderstanding of God's commandments as "human precepts" and as having "the appearance of wisdom." For this reading to work, we must posit a threat from Judaizers that is otherwise never mentioned by Paul and that is not consistent with his concern, as we see it, to address the Gentiles positively with the scriptural witness of Israel, in an idiom they can grasp and in truthful delivery of its main themes, such that the one cross might be set forth in all its eternal significance. Did the one true God who sent his Son, who is his image, likeness, firstborn, give *dogmata* that were human precepts with the appearance of wisdom? More likely Paul is speaking of the threat of any and all systems for regulating human conduct that promise religious attainment and advancement or the propitiation of hostile elemental spirits. In Galatians these were associated with "beings who are no gods" and held in sharp contrast with the only God and the true knowledge of him. I will address the language "according to human precepts and teaching" in a moment. For now it is important to emphasize that the imperatives Paul is warning the Colossians not to heed are to be classified as human precepts. The term also appears in Mark 7:7; Matt. 15:9; and Isa. 29:13, and those passages need consulting if we are properly to understand what is being said here.

The three strong prohibitions—do not handle, do not taste, do not touch—are not obviously intended by Paul to send us on a search for more precise contexts and meanings. As commentators note, the first and third are barely distinguishable (Barth and Blanke 1994: 355; Moo 2008: 235–36; Sumney 2008: 162). (It is doubtful that the third has a more explicit reference to sexual touching, as in 1 Cor. 7:1.) Lohse puts it succinctly and perceptively, in my view: "In the form in which they are cited here, the imperatives have no object which might more exactly indicate what each prohibits; thus they appear to be an intense caricature of the legalistic commands" (1971: 123). Paul is again being comprehensive here. He is not trying to understand or speculate about the specifics on the ground and is relaying an exhortation that coordinates perfectly with that and is heard because of that. Rather, he is speaking of a climate of regulatory impulses that interfere with the work of Christ he is at pains positively to relate. To live in that realm is to live in the world and to place oneself in the service of elemental spirits and their alternative account of reality. Moreover, as we are about to learn, submission to this rival worldview and regulations cannot produce what it claims to be able to produce anyway.

2:22–23 Colossians 2:22 is so sufficiently compressed that it is difficult to perceive the meaning. Two possibilities have emerged and are reflected in the translations offered. Sumney (with helpful clarifying parentheticals) offers this reading: "these [prohibited things] are all destined for destruction by consumption [and such prohibitions] derive from human commands and teachings" (2008: 160). Alternatively, the NIV (and other contemporary translations) has: "these are all destined to perish with use, because they are based on human commands and teachings." Compare TNIV's "these rules, which have to do with things that are all destined to perish with use, are based on merely human commands and teachings." It is most doubtful that it is the rules that are destined to perish. Lohse offers a correct appraisal based upon his translation: "The things however—this is the message of the short critical note that follows—whose touching or tasting is forbidden by the taboos are things destined to be used by man." That is what God has ordained them for. He concludes that the regulations are "man-made commandments and teachings" (1971: 124). By filling in the blanks, NRSV elicits the likely sense: "All these regulations refer to things that perish with use; they are simply human commands and teachings."

It is most improbable that Paul is referring to Mosaic laws. As Lincoln rightly notes, Paul "would scarcely have dismissed what, in fact, had been commanded by God in the Torah as merely human commandments."[17] We really have nothing like this in Romans, for example. Moreover, we have here a likely echo of Isa. 29:13, which is also cited verbatim in Mark 7:1–8 and Matt. 15:1–12, in the dispute with the Pharisees over the clarity of God's law in the commandments. The language of the second half of Col. 2:22 uses terms that are very rare in the Septuagint (four appearances only), and they appear together as a pair only in Isa. 29:13 ("commandments" [*entalmata*] and "teachings" [*didaskalia*]). The prophet Isaiah contrasts proper worship and honoring of God with "commandments taught by men." The spirit of incomprehension has led to darkened minds and manmade religion (Isa. 29:1–12). Matthew and Mark show Jesus citing the passage as a way of making very clear the traditions of the elders that have obscured the divine commandments, as distinct from those commandments as such. They nullify the law for the sake of their tradition (Matt. 15:6; Mark 7:9). It is not necessary to be able to determine the status of the Jesus tradition as available to Paul in this case to corroborate a very similar use of the Isaiah passage. The text may well come reflexively to mind as Paul caricatures commands that are human constructions. The darkened minds of those in thrall to elementary spirits and their systems approximate the dulled incomprehension of Israel under judgment in the days of Isaiah. The book of Isaiah has hardly a more prominent theme in its

---

17. Lincoln believes Paul is not the author and so speaks of a "Pauline disciple" in this case (2000: 634). His interpretation is a rejection of the view held by Dunn 1996: 191–92 and others. Tertullian writes: "When Paul blames those who claim to have visions of angels, on the basis of which they teach that people are to abstain from meat . . . he does not mean to criticize the mandates of the Jewish law, as if he had been speaking at the instigation of superstitious angels. His intention, rather, is only to condemn those who do not accept Christ as the one who has authority over all such things" (*Against Marcion* 5.19 in Ante-Nicene Fathers 3.472). The tradition is by no means uniform on the question of rules/visions and their religious location. Ambrosiaster speaks of "pseudoreligion and sacrilege" (quoted in Bray 2009: 191).

first thirty-nine chapters, and it belongs to the center of the prophet's commission to make hearts fat and to dull hearing and seeing (6:10).

As we have seen in previous uses of the scriptures of Israel, to ask whether Paul is making an allusion and, if so, whether the audience would register this is to pose an unnecessary question—interesting though it may be for other reasons. In my view Paul accesses the letter and patterns and extensional senses of the scriptures not so as to seek, or find, confirmation that he has done so within his audience. He does so intentionally or reflexively, seeking to translate the literal world he knows innately into a context quite different from his own. Yet his goal is to assure that the translation activity is accurate, even as it must span two different contexts and move from one idiom into another. Paul sees the threat of false regulations and systems and knows they are "commandments of men." When he seeks to communicate this the language of Isaiah may well rise up in his head given the similarity, now as the new Israel confronts the challenge of darkened thinking in the world they have latterly, in Christ, had reconfigured through his death and resurrection. The negative counterpart to the new Israel is the old nature (as Paul puts it in Col. 3:9), because "you have died, and your life is hid with Christ in God" (3:3). To give attention to any other frame of reference would be to enter the land of judgment and incomprehension, such as Isaiah witnessed it in his own day. Commandments of men are also unable to produce anything but further incomprehension anyway. So the unit concludes: **These things, though they have the aura of wisdom, in self-imposed worship and humility and severe treatment of the body, are of no value in checking indulgence in the flesh**.

Theodore of Mopsuestia famously declared 2:23 incomprehensible. Actually, it is the final clause of the sentence that presents the only translational challenge, and it is not minor. The other possibility is along the lines of "they lead to gratification of the flesh."[18] The difficulty Theodore was likely referring to is the strange terms themselves, the triad of *ethelothrēskia* ("willing service" or "would-be worship"), *tapeinophrosynē* ("humility"), and *apheidia sōmatos* ("severe treatment of the body"). "These things" (*hatina*) most likely goes back to the prohibitions of 2:21, while my translation allows the entirety of what precedes not to be ruled out. In that sense, Paul is drawing his remarks to a close. "In sum" we might well think. I take the view of Lightfoot and others that the final clause refers to the failure of all this religiosity to do what it claims, rather than that all of this is in fact its own kind of fleshy indulgence. In Eadie's tidy phrase: "The paragraph therefore reprobates superstitious asceticism" (1856: 203). Is our grasp of this improved if we can give more precision to the actual religious practices on the ground, or in fact is Paul merely taking sufficient stab at something to serve to indict any proximate inclinations? My view is the latter. The phrases are clear enough. I note that absent the effort to match what is being condemned with

18. Along this line are translations in Barth and Blanke 1994: 337; Lohse 1971: 114; Sumney 2008: 160. Aquinas 2006: 72 appears to adopt a similar reading ("they serve only to indulge the flesh").

specific practices in the religious situation on the ground has not prevented an older commentator from drawing out significance for his own audience, but has in fact enabled it. I quote it at length as a masterful bit of Victorian prose. On *apheidia sōmatos*, Eadie writes:

> The physical condition is enervated and sickened. Yet its sinful tendencies are only beaten down, not eradicated. Job made a covenant with his eyes, but those fanatics would dim theirs by fasting. The whole process was a cardinal mistake, for it was a system of externals, both in ceremonial and ethics. The body might be reduced, but the evil bias might remain unchecked. A man might whip and fast himself into a walking skeleton, and yet the spirit within him might have all its lusts unconquered, for all it had lost was only the ability to gratify them. To place a fetter on a robber's hand will not cure him of covetousness, though it may disqualify him from actual theft. To seal up a swearer's mouth will not pluck profanity out of his heart, though it may for a time prevent him from taking God's name in vain. To lacerate the flesh almost to suicide, merely incapacitates it for indulgence, but does not extirpate sinful desire. Its air of superior sanctity is only pride in disguise—it has but a "show of wisdom," and is not. (1856: 206)

I might also add that the finale in 2:23 prepares us very nicely for how Paul now proceeds. We have died in Christ. Our lives are hid in him. Our bodies are not our own but belong to him. Colossians 2:23 speaks of both body and flesh, and a wrongful way to consider what is wrong with them and how they have been renewed and given new life. That is in the one body of Jesus Christ. He has made the full sacrifice for us and for all creation. We are new men and women, and our identity is not in an old Adam seeking to find his true self by means of systems, sacrifices, regulations, or victimization of ourselves. Our identity is hidden in Christ himself, who is raising us and asking that we put on his own new clothing.

PUTTING ON
THE NEW LIFE IN CHRIST

(3:1–17)

Excursus: Garmenting the New Adam in Christ

The English-Greek version of NA[27] includes all of 2:20 through 3:17 under the title "The New Life in Christ." That is, the discussion of false trails in 2:8–23 overlaps "The New Life in Christ" and cannot be isolated as its own brambly thicket of "false teachers and false teaching." Even portions of the thicket are broken up by positive accounts of the Christian life (e.g., 2:9–15), and the rubric provided by NA[27] for 2:6–19 is "Fullness of Life in Christ." I believe NA[27] sees the issue from the proper perspective. Paul continues his positive endorsement of this church he has not seen firsthand, only in this middle section warning about possible threats to their "good order and firmness of faith" (2:5) in various species of bramble. The "since/since" pairing of 2:20 and 3:1 has been mentioned already, as well as the theme of putting off (3:5) and putting on (3:10, 12, 14). I would be hard pressed to improve on "The New Life in Christ" and would only add an emphasis in 3:1–17 on "Clothing Oneself in Christ."

Some argue that the language of exchanging clothes points to ritual dress ceremonies in the mystery religions being condemned in Col. 2 (see discussion in Lohse 1971: 141–42). It takes little imagination to consider the way special vestments and ceremonial robes are central in the rites of sectarian, quasireligious groups of all manner: academic initiation; fraternity and sorority gatherings; the Masons, Elks, or Woodsmen of the World; the bizarre and clandestine gatherings of the recent Sherlock Holmes movie, plotting to bomb the English Parliament in their garments of dark intimidation. Also, Israel had special vestments for the priests and Levites. Is

Paul drawing on that general backdrop and adapting it for the new Israel and its new priesthood of all believers?

The answer is a qualified yes, but the logic of those vestments needs equally to be explored before one selects out this particular investiture as relevant here.[1] Modern and classical commentary properly note that—especially given the reference to "a circumcision made without hands" and "burial in him in baptism" in Paul's remarks in 2:11–13—the stripping off of worldly clothes and the putting on of new baptismal gowns is integrally tied up with what Paul is saying here.[2] The language of dying and rising in Christ, such as was introduced in 2:12, is unmistakable here as well (3:1–3). We have died (3:3), and because of this we are to put to death (3:3) a former way of life and attitudes and DNA that were part of that life (3:9). And the counterpart of death is the putting on of "a new nature, which is being renewed in knowledge after the image of its creator" (3:10). The new gowns given to the baptized concretely symbolize that new nature. In his baptismal charge, Chrysostom uses a verse from this section of Colossians when he addresses those to be baptized:

> It was not idly or without purpose that I anticipated the event and instructed your loving assembly in all these matters, but I did so that you might be carried on the wings of hope and enjoy the pleasure before you enjoyed the actual benefit. I did it, too, that you might adopt a purpose worthy of the rite, and as blessed Paul has exhorted, you might "mind the things that are above" and change your thoughts from earth to heaven, from visible things to those that are unseen." (quoted in Gorday 2000: 46)

The changing of thoughts, former ones enumerated in 3:5–10 and new ones to be put on in 3:12–15, has a visible correlate in the new vesture of baptismal incorporation.

In an illuminating essay on the garments of skin the first couple received when they exited the garden, Gary Anderson draws our attention to both iconic and painted representations of the weighty narrative of Gen. 2–3.[3] Oddly enough, given how the phrase "garments of skin" is usually taken, we see in much graphic and literary representation almost the opposite of what we might think. The couple in the garden is clothed. The clothes are resplendent. They are like the elaborate and costly robes of Israel's holy priesthood. Or, stated differently, the robes of the priests are like those of Adam and Eve, when they stood in glorious union with the God in whose image they were made, as yet undefiled, in fellowship with *yhwh 'elohim* in the garden he made for them. The perfect fellowship between God and humanity bespeaks not nudity—the idea of primitive, naked innocence is one latterly devised. It is as gloriously

---

1. J. H. Kim suggests Zech. 3:3–5 (Joshua exchanging filthy vestments for new attire suitable for a renewed sanctuary) and other texts dealing with vestments and robing as relevant to Paul's thought; *The Significance of Clothing Imagery in the Pauline Corpus*, Journal for the Study of the New Testament Supplement 268 (New York: T&T Clark, 2004), 25–69.

2. See the remarks of Moo 2008: 266–67; Sumney 2008: 201; Dunn 1996: 220–21; and others. Galatians 3:27 and 1 Cor. 15:53–54 are relevant.

3. Gary A. Anderson, *The Genesis of Perfection: Adam and Eve in Jewish and Christian Imagination* (Louisville: Westminster John Knox, 2001).

clothed that we find our relationship to God in its undefiled and sanctified character. The robes of the priesthood approximate this under the conditions of controlled and Torah-regulated access, now highly prescribed, cautious, and limited to those so set apart, "the holy" (the consecrated) in the presence of the Holy One.

It is only at the moment of disobedience that the couple first recognizes a condition they label, in search of a word, "naked." They have transitioned into a new state and find the glorious garments they had unconsciously worn replaced with self-regard, shame, and alienation from God. "The eyes of both were opened and they knew they were naked" (Gen. 3:7). They "knew" (not "realized," so NIV—that is too psychological) because they ate from the tree of knowledge. This disobedient act created the condition they now "know" to be their state of affairs before God. Now they seek to remedy this new, unknown-until-now condition, by sewing coverings (3:7). But this only makes manifest what has fatefully transpired. Adam says poignantly: "I heard you in the garden. I was afraid because I was naked; so I hid" (3:10). God replies by posing the obvious question: "Who told you that you were naked?"—for which there is no obvious answer—so God continues without pausing: "Have you eaten from the tree?" (3:11).

The decrees of God now follow, addressing in turn the serpent and then the woman and then Adam (3:14–19). The couple does not simply leave the garden in the coverings of fig leaves mentioned in the scene of exposure at 3:7. Rather, a scene intrudes before they are driven out and the garden sealed off (3:24) and after the decrees proper (3:19). Adam names the woman Eve (3:20). Then we have the report that "God made garments of skin for Adam and his wife and clothed them" (3:21). They are already clothed, as it were, in fig-leaf coverings, presumably available in and appropriate to a garden (though this is unremarked). Where did the garments of skin come from if the reference is to animal skins? The sources examined by Anderson suggest that the garments of skin are of skin itself, our skin, that is, our present corporeal and corruptible body. Michelangelo shows the couple leaving the garden naked (with fig leaves reattached!). The couple made in the image of God (1:27) is in the garden, before the disobedient eating of the fruit of the tree of knowledge, in resplendent garments as befitting full fellowship with God. We know them only by inference: by their forfeit into that condition the first man calls the consequent "nakedness." At baptism, however, we take off the old garments of Adam and Eve's disobedience and put on the new garments of Christ's rising. Our true new life identity is hidden in him (Col. 3:3) and will not be fully known to us until he appears. The glory that is his risen body is to be our own in him (3:4). On the Mount of Transfiguration selected disciples glimpsed Christ's body of glory, which he has had from eternity, in something of the way the Prophet Ezekiel saw "the appearance of the likeness of the glory of YHWH" (1:28). Jesus talks with the saints of old in the form they "saw" him in the former dispensation, and now he brings his chosen disciples into that privileged circle of apprehension—which of course they struggle to understand or fail to understand at all, depending on the evangelist's account. His skin cannot be more dazzling, because his body is in a condition approximating what will be its risen glory and so no human analogy for whiteness can be found.

Here we likely also find the logic behind the language chosen by Paul in Col. 3:10: "the new nature, which is being renewed *in knowledge according to the image of its creator* [*eis epignōsin kat' eikona tou ktisantos auton*]." The phrase is slightly enigmatic and is strictly speaking unnecessary, unless the connection to Genesis is in the air. In Christ we are being renewed in the image of God, and so are to put on those "clothes" that correspond to that divine intention before the fall. Instead of a tree of knowledge wrongly chosen and so the means of humanity's disobedience, we have reference in 3:10 to renewal in knowledge of a different, life-giving kind. This knowledge is the gospel itself and Paul's conveyance of it to the Colossians.

Though it is not specifically in reference to knowledge (*epignōsin*) in 3:10, Ambrose nonetheless raises the theme in general terms in connection with his reflections on Paradise (quoted in Gorday 2000: 46). A life was hidden in the garden and could have been chosen. This causes him to see a direct connection with Col. 3 and the trees in the garden:

> We should be aware of the fact, therefore, that where God has planted the tree of life he has also planted a tree of the knowledge of good and evil in the midst of paradise. It is understood that he planted it in the middle. Therefore, in the middle of paradise there was both a tree of life and a cause for death. By carrying out and observing the precepts of God it was possible for man to find life. This was the life mentioned by the apostle: "Your life is hidden with Christ in God." Man, therefore, was, figuratively speaking, either in the shadow of life—because our life on earth is but a shadow—or man had life, as it were, in pledge, for he had been breathed on by God. (*Paradise* 29, quoted in Gorday 2000: 46)

This returns us to the question of the decrees of God and the writ against us (2:14). I argued above that the best candidate for the writ was Paul's adaptation of the logic of Gen. 2–3 for the purpose of addressing the Colossian church, showing that the one cross of Christ had erased the writ against all humanity. Paul knows of this universal indictment from Gen. 2–3, and he seeks to make the logic of this account known to those outside Israel, but embraced, with Israel, by the work of one cross. The decrees (*dogmata*) are not the commands of the law but the announcements of judgment by God in the garden. Ambrose works the matter from a different direction but using the same core text. The precepts of God could have been obeyed, and life with God known, experienced, and preserved. This was forfeited, but the life remained in the form of what he called a "pledge." In Christ it has been hidden all along and preserved. He brought the pledge into present existence with all its promise of new life by his sacrifice on the cross and God's raising of him to new and glorious existence. We are in him able to put on a new life, a life that was had in Eden before the disobedient act and that existed in the glorious clothing of our fellowship with God. Baptism into Christ's death reenters us into that hidden place, and rising with him we begin to claim a new life that is his life shared with us. We put on this life by putting off a formerly clothed existence in our garments of skin and putting on the glorious garments recreated and provisioned by Christ.[4]

4. Paul "tells them that they must 'put off the old man' and put on the new man 'that is renewed after the image of him that created him.' Now may we all return to that divine grace in which God at the

It is anticipating a bit but we may also have here the explanation for the (rather abrupt) transition represented by the movement from the section I call "Putting on the New Life in Christ" (3:1–17) and the duties of Christians in 3:18–4:1. Is Paul reflexively describing the ideal family as it might have existed in the garden had the command of God been obeyed? Of course elsewhere we have similar household codes (Eph. 5:21–6:9 contains identical expressions as here), and most commentators point out the difference between the household of the Greco-Roman world and what Paul is describing in Colossians (and elsewhere). But in this case, the sequence wives, husbands, children, slaves tracks with the decrees of Gen. 3. Their effects are now reversed because a new life has been made available in Christ. Wives submit to husbands as is fitting in the Lord, as against them both acting independently in disobedience. Husbands love their wives and do not seek to assign them blame. Children (Eve is the mother of all) are to obey parents and not unleash the tragic violence we see in Gen. 4–11. Toil is now not under curse but can be serving the Lord with proper hopefulness of inheritance (Col. 3:24). This would also explain why Paul does not include the Galatians pairing in Col. 3:11 ("neither male nor female"), for here the context is one of a proper new Adam in Christ and the conditions of being male and female in him. He means to get to that after his description of the "new man that is being renewed in knowledge after the image of the creator" (3:10). And he does, still speaking of the slave but defining his toil in a different world than the world east of Eden.

3:1 **since then you were raised with Christ, seek the things that are above, where Christ is, seated at the right hand of God**—As there is nothing in doubt here, the translation "since" is to be preferred to "if" (RSV, NRSV). "Since" does not prevent the exhortative nature of what Paul is saying, but may indeed drive the point home. It is wrong to classify this as realized eschatology in the manner of Lindemann and others.[5] As Sumney puts it: "If resurrection with Christ in 3:1 means that the eschatological reservation always present in Paul's thought has collapsed . . . there would be no need for the exhortations that follow" (2008: 176). Paul's rhetorical purpose is underscored with the character of his "be who you are" address, consistent with what has been said to the Colossians thus far about Christ's accomplished work on their behalf.

It is of course ironic and probably intentionally so that, having denounced inflated visions and the heightened religious experience of angel worship that puff up and so threaten Christian faith (2:18), here Paul tells us that there are indeed things above worthy of our seeking. What is above is the risen and ascended Christ himself. He is not one high thing among others, nor is his height a matter of philosophical speculation (he is an angel or a power or a plenipotentiary of some rank) or religious ascent so as to experience personally and differentiate

---

first created man, when he said, 'let us make man in our image and likeness'" (Gregory of Nyssa, *On the Making of Man* 30.33–34).

5. Andreas Lindemann, *Der Kolosserbrief*, Zürcher Bibelkommentare: Neues Testament 10 (Zürich: Theologischer Verlag, 1983), 53.

oneself in consequence. His height is without comparison, and it is a fully public and accessible truth, available to all by faith. It is also not an ascendancy he earned by moral striving such that it is now our vocation to catch him up. He returned to where he always was, having become poor for our sakes.

This is made clear by the language Paul uses here, one more descriptor in his arsenal to fill out the picture provided already in 1:15–20 ("image," "firstborn," "before all things," "beginning"). To be seated "at the right hand" is to say in other words "one in the identity of God." Angels stand about the throne or bow down before the throne. They are not at the left hand or the right. The Son does not stand or bow, but is seated in the closest space architecturally imaginable, "at the right hand." The "right hand" is a virtual hypostasis in Old Testament usage. It is the manifestation of God's self in action in respect of creation. We know that "right hand" to be none other than Jesus Christ the eternal Son. He descended "for us and for our salvation" and has returned and taken his seat again, now wearing the glorious scars.

Commentators in search of Old Testament allusions are right to make note of the language of Ps. 110: "The LORD said to my Lord, 'Sit at my right hand.'" Does Paul make creative use of this specific Old Testament passage, or is the idea already present in the tradition, such that he merely—or importantly—seconds it here, relating it to Christ's present ascended reality? The question may be too narrowly tuned. Psalm 110 is hardly the only place where the general idea of divine agency and plenipotentiary authority combine to give us a grammar capable of ontological extension for "of one substance" talk in its noncreedal, biblical idiom (for samples, see Bauckham 1999: 25–42). "Giving the name above all names" in Phil. 2 makes clear that YHWH extends the name to enclose the Son, effecting a new way of speaking about what was always a reality in the Godhead: "That at the name of Jesus every knee should bow, to the glory of God the Father."[6] God has highly exalted the Son. He is at what the Old Testament called "the right hand of preeminence"[7] from whence he came ("he did not think equality with God a thing to be grasped"—but equality it was in eternity). Luther sought to capture this ontological reality in his translation of Ps. 110: "Der HERR sprach zu meinem HErrn." "HERR" is the one LORD (YHWH). He speaks within his own eternal identity to the Son. The Son is David's ("my") 'adonai ("Lord"). The Holy Spirit gifts David to comprehend two eternal persons, capacitating David to declare the Lord "*my* Lord." "HERR" and "HErrn" are Luther's way of trying to reproduce in German the eternal relations of Father and Son, yet in one undivided Godhead YHWH. He follows the same tack in Ps. 2 as well and at other points in the Psalter.[8] He works with the dogmatic understanding that the Holy Spirit is

---

6. David S. Yeago, "The New Testament and Nicene Dogma: A Contribution to the Recovery of Theological Exegesis," *Pro ecclesia* 3 (1994): 152–64.

7. The core text is the Song of Moses (Exod. 15:6), with the range encompassing earthly kingship (1 Kgs. 2:19) to God's placing his Son on the sole place of authority (Ps. 2:6).

8. Christine Helmer, "Luther's Trinitarian Hermeneutic and the Old Testament," *Modern Theology* 18 (2002): 49–73; Christopher Seitz, *The Character of Christian Scripture: The Significance of a Two-Testament*

an eternal person in the triune life of God, moving from the "who spake by the Prophets" confession of the third article of the creed. He does this to defeat the claim of some that the creeds are postbiblical, philosophical abstractions and can be dispensed with (Servetus), on the one hand, and to challenge the view that the Holy Spirit emerges in the declarations of church councils in a more full way than scripture itself attests (Eck), on the other. Luther declares the anteriority of the Holy Spirit prior to the church of Jesus Christ in time, as what the church's creed itself claims. David spoke by the Holy Spirit. The Holy Spirit showed him the eternal persons of the Father and the Son within the old scriptures that declared this. Colossians here reproduces the dogmatic verity as everywhere present in the scriptures with which Christ is "in accordance."

3:2 I remarked above on the difficulty of separating the present unit (3:1–4) from either what precedes or what follows. Some commentators see this text as the conclusion of the "theological section" preceding and speak of an "ethical section" beginning at 3:5. But neither such a division nor its categories can be sustained; their division is foreign to Paul's thinking. The term *zēteite* in 3:1 means "to seek," and the TNIV's "set your hearts on" (imperative) is chosen to capture the sense of "orient yourself according to" and to parallel *phroneō* in 3:2, which it renders "set your minds on." Paul is speaking of centering ourselves in this world with our attention on Christ at the right hand of God (cf. Rom. 8:5; Phil. 3:19). "Seek" may also be a way of displacing the energy implied in the visionary quest. "Seek instead things above where Christ is." This is an ethical injunction grounded in a theological fact. The victory of Jesus Christ over death and all principalities and powers is crowned by his present sovereignty: he is above all things, and he and God the Father are in fullest conceivable conjunction. This is a fact, and it is meant to orient us and provide us with our compass through life's struggles. It has the capacity to fund our right choosing and our living in the new life provided by Christ for us, who have died in him.[9] Paul is describing that our orientation point provides "paths for us to walk in" by means of Christ's assault on darkness and death, burying us and giving us a new life in this life. Because of this we find one of the rare instances in Colossians where Paul pauses to repeat himself: **Set your minds on things above, not on earthly things**. The imperative form (now *phroneō*) and its object "things above" are reiterated to make the theological/ethi-

---

Bible (Grand Rapids: Baker Academic, 2011), 84; idem, "The Trinity in the Old Testament," in *The Oxford Handbook of the Trinity*, ed. G. Emory and M. Levering (Oxford: Oxford University Press, 2011), 28–40; and H. Assel, "Der Name Gottes bei Martin Luther: Trinität und Tetragramm—Ausgehend von Luthers Auslegung des fünften Psalms," *Evangelische Theologie* 64 (2004): 363–78.

9. A good illustration might be watching a sporting event that was tape delayed and then finding out the final score before the end of the broadcast. Does knowing that your team won hinder enjoyment of the game? No, it means that, even if your team fumbles the ball, all would still be well. In the same way, great exertions toward Christian victory were unmarred and declared themselves warranted and all part of living toward the higher victory already assured. The higher victory did not create moral lassitude but brought energy as one could now lean into the higher triumph in this life. I am indebted to the homily of my friend John Barr for this example.

cal point. The positive is restated and set in contrast with the "things on earth," a likely counterpart to "things of the flesh" in the lengthy account in Rom. 8. Philippians 3:12–14 also shows Paul focused on things above.[10] Here he emphasizes the present possession of the prize, even as he exhorts the Colossians to lay hold of and orient themselves around it so as to receive its benefits.[11]

3:3 for you have died and your life is hidden with Christ in God—We return to the fundamental claim made in 2:20: the Colossians have died to the elemental spirits of this world. Dead previously in sin (2:13), "estranged and hostile in mind, doing evil deeds" (1:21), they were buried with Christ in baptism and raised to a new life with him "through faith in the working of God who raised him from the dead" (2:12–13).

The pairing of hidden/revealed found here and in the following verse ("when Christ who is our life appears") corresponds generally to apocalyptic conceptions. Something is true but remains hidden and is perceived only by special revelation. Daniel sees something that has already taken place in visionary time, even though its time for historical unfolding is later: "The vision concerns a time yet to come" (Dan. 10:14; see also 7:16; 8:17; 9:25). Daniel is however confused, even to the point of sickness, and must be reassured as to the framework for what he sees; it does not conform to his own time. The difference in Paul's language in Colossians is apparent. What is hidden with Christ makes sense of the present time and provides a sure marker for the hope that is to be embraced. Another nuance of "hidden with Christ" (*kekryptai syn tō christō*) may be that of security and protection. We know of the Psalms references to being hidden as a sheltering in God's care (27:5; 31:20). When God hides his face from Israel, as a counterpart, his Torah and testimony are hidden and preserved for a latter time (Isa. 8:16–17), when comprehension is to be granted to the faithful (43:8–13).[12] The true servant Israel is hidden in the shadow of God's hand (49:2), and it is he that properly perceives the accomplishing plans of God, now being disclosed as in intended fulfillment, even across generations of time and, in time, to be perceived by the nations themselves (52:15). The Isaiah remnant has been told what God will surely do; the servant witnesses that doing; in his own sacrifice, nations are enabled to perceive the hidden truth of God's accomplishing word and work. The same notion is at work in Paul's proclamation, but now is to be widely comprehended and embraced. This too was the vision of Isaiah, when he saw the servants of Israel joined by servants more broadly from the nations: "I was found by those who did not seek me" (60:1–2; 65:1–2).

3:4 In Colossians Paul links the conception seen in Isaiah to the specific dying of Christ and our death in him. We are hidden in the eternal plan of God: Jesus Christ. We have been enclosed in this plan by his death and resurrection and

10. Paul also uses *phroneō* in his exhortation in Phil. 3:15: "Let those of us who are mature be thus minded."

11. "Orient yourselves also toward that which is on high" (Barth and Blanke 1994: 390).

12. Christopher Seitz, "Isaiah 40–66," in *The New Interpreter's Bible*, ed. L. E. Keck (Nashville: Abingdon, 2001), 6.376–78.

ascension. Because of this, Paul discloses an eternal truth by means of his present proclamation: **when Christ who is our life appears, then you also will appear with him in glory**. Like the faithful around the prophet Isaiah, the Colossians are given a clear picture of what will happen in God's time, even as they live now between the in-time eschatological accomplishment of Christ and its temporal denouement, "when Christ appears" in final judgment. What is accelerated in his description is our actual death. This is given only in a figure in Isaiah: there, it is the dying of identification with a word that will go unheeded in its generation (8:18–22), but that will nevertheless bear fruit. Here, Jesus Christ bears the death of all time and incorporates those who believe in him into that death. And so Paul rightly speaks of the life of the Colossians as Christ himself, "who is our life." The fourfold repetition of the word **Christ** (instead of the proper pronoun) in these three short verses serves to underscore the christological focus of Paul's proclamation. In Gal. 2:19–20 Paul can say of himself: "I have been crucified with Christ; it is no longer I who live, but Christ who lives in me." To be sure, in Galatians he predicates that life as a life "in the flesh by faith in the Son of God," but the distinction is immaterial. Colossians 2:12 says virtually the same thing when Paul writes: "through faith in the working of God." What he has said of himself he here says of the Colossians as a whole. The prophet Isaiah will find himself joined by faithful servants who accomplish what God intends in their own flesh. The movement from individual to collective witness is unmistakable. It is there in First Isaiah with the prophet and his children, and it is there in Second Isaiah in the servant and the servants.[13]

Then you also will appear with him in glory must be understood in part as an explanation of what it means that we are presently hidden with Christ. To have our life hidden with Christ in God means that our "new man" is not fully known even to us. Paul will speak later of being neither Jew nor Greek, neither circumcised nor uncircumcised (3:11), and this is because we have put on "a new man that is being renewed in knowledge after the image of its creator." The declensions set out in the table of nations (Gen. 10) belong to the orderly purposes of God after the disobedience of Adam (the fall) and the evil culminating in the generation of Noah (the flood). Overcoming them by human effort is neither possible nor properly warranted (Gen. 11). The call of Abraham and the election of Israel are to serve that divine purpose, by means of which blessing may come to the nations. But now those purposes are wrapped up in the work of the one cross by the one new man Jesus Christ. So a new humanity is in his gift, and he gives it. We know what it is not. It is not in the inevitable gravitational pull of the old Adam, though it is in the process of "being renewed in knowledge in the image of its creator." Equally, it is not a humanity of disembodied ideas or religious advancement: wife and husband, father and children, master and servant remain for Paul (Col.

---

13. Ibid., 460–61, 472–74; W. A. M. Beuken, "The Main Theme in Trito-Isaiah: 'The Servants of Yahweh,'" *Journal for the Study of the Old Testament* 47 (1990): 67–87.

3:18–4:1). But inside older categories we are bearers of a new humanity in our bodies in Christ. And in those categories we are being renewed in Christ in ways that are hidden to our own knowledge or what we would call our "self-identity." We have no essential self-identity. To create declensions of our essential selves after the work of the one man and the one cross is to encroach on what Paul here calls "our life hidden with Christ in God." If there is anything essential to set our minds on, it is that a degree of hiddenness in our self-knowledge is there by design in Christ. It is built into our present reliance on him and his life. It cannot be overcome in the nature of the case, and it extends to sexuality, health, knowledge, science—all will yield their deepest realities only partially, and none will make any higher sense than the one new man.

3:5–6 therefore put to death what is earthly in you—We now enter the subsection of the text dealing with behaviors/orientations to put off/to death (3:5–11) and to put on (3:12–17). "What is earthly" picks up 3:2 ("things that are on earth"), and the theme of the coming of Christ (3:4) anticipates the concern of Paul for the wrath of God "coming on account of these" (3:6). Usually New Testament research speaks of virtue/vice lists.[14] This means either the lists found in Stoic literature of the period (where moral exhortations take the form of virtues contrasted with vices) or the basic moral contrasting of two ways in Jewish sources. One thinks of the book of Proverbs or Ps. 1 as an example of such conceptions ("blessed is the man who has not walked in the counsel of the wicked / ... the wicked are like chaff"; the way of wisdom and the way of folly; the wicked and the righteous in Ps. 37).

Given that such examples (or combinations of them) exist and are circulating at the time, the question becomes whether Paul is adapting them in some specific way given concerns he is aware of in the Colossian community. Do they arise here because, for example, sexual sins (Col. 3:5) and foul talk of various descriptions (3:8) plague the Colossian church in special ways? Alternatively, Paul is concerned simply to set forth proper conduct expected of those who have died in Christ without trying to address any particular conduct known to him on the ground. Because the lists of virtues and vices (the "desires of the flesh" and the "fruit of the Spirit" in Gal. 5:16–25), or the lists of one or the other independently,[15] are not uniform in the New Testament, it is clear that Paul is not just recycling fixed and well-known lists but thinking about the rhetorical purpose in each individual instance. But that is a different matter than saying his achievement is what it is because he has information on the ground that directs his selections in their particularity. The reference to covetousness as the embodiment of idolatry is a peculiarly Jewish way of thinking, and so Paul is closer to his own scriptural

14. For full discussion and bibliography, including the question of Jewish and Stoic influence, see Lohse 1971: 137–39; Dunn 1996: 212–17; and Moo 2008: 254–60. For specific examples, see A. Malherbe, *Moral Exhortation: A Greco-Roman Sourcebook* (Philadelphia: Westminster, 1986), 138–41.

15. E.g., vices in Rom. 1:29–31; 1 Cor. 5:9–11; 6:9–10; Eph. 5:3–4; virtues in Phil. 4:8. The Pastorals and General Epistles also contain such lists.

inheritance than to virtue/vice listings observed in Aristotle and other contemporaneous sources.

More needs to be said about the Colossian location of this material. Paul has condemned the path of worldly regulations and false asceticism (2:16–23). He has also spoken of the need of the Colossians to orient themselves according to "things that are above" because their life is now to be found in Christ. The wrong conclusion to be drawn would be that such a life has no concrete form in this world. Not only does the new life take concrete ethical form, it does so according to well-known regulations and specific virtues. The negative prohibitions are those that would appear very high in Paul's own Jewish and scriptural priorities for how to live obediently under God and also, for the observant Jew, how to distinguish oneself from the surrounding pagan culture. Paul is not making the Colossians into Jews, but as elsewhere, he is taking the world imprinted by his scriptures and addressing the new in-Christ men and women in Colossae with "blessings and curses" such as Deuteronomy set forth in a different day.[16] To be hidden away with Christ is to set one's mind on the things of fragrance that distinguish the new Israel. A fivefold assembly of things to put to death in the members (3:5) has its counterpart in the fivefold concern with proper conversation in the church (3:8). Part two (3:12–17) sets out a fivefold collection of virtues, complemented by the practices in the worship life of the church where these find their proper and fitting manifestation in the praise of God.

While it is now part of the vocabulary of New Testament research to speak of virtues and vices lists, the actual form here in Colossians does not preserve that. The two fivefold enumerations are interrupted. The first list has its own twofold commentary before we move to the second list. On account of the vices first listed the wrath of God is coming (or presently comes, in the nature of the case). More significantly, these vices are said to mark off what was a former way of life. In that sense, they speak of a form of life that cannot now exist in the same company as what we know to be peculiarly Jewish/scriptural condemnation of those Gentiles in the world around them. This condemnation is grounded in the scriptural witness, and Paul sees it marking off as well the new man in Christ. The second list picks up only when this initial list and its commentary are rounded off. Included alongside them ("put them all away") are kinds of wrong speech and speaking. That is, they appear to be a crucial set of prohibitions of their own

16. For those who believe the author of Colossians has chiefly in mind correcting Jewish false teaching, a conclusion like Dunn's is necessary: "Paul did not want his readers to follow the Colossian Jews in their ritual and worship, but their ethical standards were to be Jewish through and through" (1996: 214). I believe the sounder approach is to ask what Paul is doing rhetorically in the light of the letter itself, and especially in view of his addressing a church he has not planted and does not know firsthand. That the ethical standards are "Jewish through and through" has to do with Paul's handling of the scriptures for a church needing their address in Christ. The new Adam gives a new way of life to the new men and women he is making. Do sexual sins and false speech get the priority they do because of their centrality in Gen. 2–3 and the influence they may have in consequence on Paul's formulation?

kind. But they do not mark off something especially true of the Gentile condition. They belong to an old nature with its practices and are wrong on account of this. In that sense, they are wrong wherever they make themselves present and were not special components of being outside the covenants and commonwealth of Israel. In light of this, Paul then moves to conclude there is no longer Greek or Jew, circumcised or uncircumcised, and so forth. The new man is the new man in Christ who conforms to the image of God prior to the disobedience that, in its wake, caused distinctions to be made in God's own plan of salvation, in which a special role is given over to Israel. Paul does not confuse the two lists and he also does not conflate them.

Therefore put to death what is earthly in you means, in the terse phrasing of Lohse: "Let the old man, who has already died in baptism, be dead" (1971: 137). Romans 6:11 states it in this form: "Consider yourselves dead to sin and alive to God in Christ Jesus." The Greek has literally "the members that are on earth," as those instruments or faculties by which sin is committed. This is not a condemnation of our corporeality but the concrete way in which sins—in this case sexual sins—make their character known. The faculties of the old Adam are prone by habit in the direction Christ has come to deaden in our new man. Now we have in Greek four words in a row: *porneia, akatharsia, pathos, epithymia*. To the last term is added *kakēn* because "desire" by itself is neutral; here, then, "evil desire." The first term refers to sexual contact that is prohibited. Adultery, prostitution, and sexual activity prior to marriage that the betrothed male would recognize as illegitimate (Deut. 22:13–30) are all obvious cases of *porneia*. It is also probably the case, given the central place given to virginity in scripture and in Jewish practice familiar to Paul, that the term **fornication** is closest to what is intended.[17] The juxtaposition with the next term also underscores this interpretation. **Impurity** often spills into the sexual context, though it can mean cultic impurity more specifically. According to Gal. 5:19 it is a "work of the flesh" and so not a nonsexual cultic infraction more specifically. **Passion** likewise has the nuance of shameful or uncontrolled passion in Rom. 1:26 and 1 Thess. 4:5. It would be the sort of passion that demanded fulfillment in a state of being uncontrolled. **Evil desire** completes the picture.

While Stoic systems may have empirically determined the nonvirtuous and undesirable character of these kinds of conduct, Paul's frame of reference is scriptural. This is made fully clear in the fifth element: **and covetousness, which is idolatry**. The Greek word here means "more desiring" or "insatiable desiring." It is the restless demand always to have more, which is an addiction of the flesh and spirit. In the context of our list it is "the ruthless unsatiableness evident when the

17. See the rejection of Bruce Malina's position ("Does *Porneia* Mean Fornication?" *Novum Testamentum* 14 [1972]: 10–17) in Sumney 2008: 189, and also the view of Moo 2008: 256–58 and Lohse 1971: 138. Philo assumes virginity to be the ideal for men and women both (*On the Special Laws* 3.64). Sumney concludes: "Given that Colossians is within the Pauline tradition, it seems clear that *porneia* here refers to any sexual intercourse other than that with one's own spouse within marriage" (2008: 189).

sexual appetite is unrestrained in a man with power to gratify it" (Dunn 1996: 215). Precisely because the need always to have more is, for Paul, an indication that God has ceased to be the giver of what we need, as he bestows it of his grace and mercy, it is associated with idolatry. The pagan world appears to Paul and his fellow Jews as one of unrestrained sexual license, and that can be explained as due to its inherently idolatrous existence. "To be without God in the world," as Paul means that, is to be left to one's own desires and appetites. By contrast, Jews knew what God demanded even when in their disobedience they suffered God's judgment, or precisely in the light of that. So reflexively Paul speaks of his worldview when he adds **on account of these things the wrath of God comes**. It is not to be denied that Paul likely has in view the final judgment of God, in which his holiness in confrontation with evil manifests itself to us as wrath. But the coming judgment of God in the form of wrath pertains to a present reality that Paul knows on the basis of a past referent of fulfillment. God has manifested his wrath in confrontation with sinful desire and excessive idolatry—because he has, he does and will do. A translation "on account of these things the wrath of God is coming [*erchetei*]" does not of course rule out present manifestations of that. But Paul has spoken in 3:4 of a future appearing and of our life in that appearing, and so he likely contrasts that here with a future of wrathful judgment whose seeds are, however, being sown in the present misconduct.

3:7 **in these you once walked, when you lived in them**—The language hearkens back to 2:6–7. The Colossians are walking in Christ "rooted and built up in him and established in the faith." The former life they lived was "in these once walking"—walking apart from him. Previously Paul spoke only of walking. Here he speaks of walking *and* living because he has introduced the positive reality of dying and rising to new life in Christ in the interim (2:13; 3:3). Now we are in a good position to see how the language of New Testament research (virtue and vice lists) is only broadly appropriate in the Colossians context as set forth in 3:5–17. The Colossians once walked and lived in the fivefold world of *porneia* and its associated idolatries. This world cannot exist in Christ. It must be put to death. In a similar way, the council in Acts 15 describes those things that must be abstained from, minimally, if the Gentiles are to be Christians in one body with Christians of Jewish background. Richard Bauckham and others show that the four necessities (no pollutions of idols, no blood, nothing torn by beasts, no *porneia*) are those things laid down for the "sojourner in the midst" when Israel came out of Egypt (see Lev. 17–18 for the four requirements, in the identical order as in Acts 15:29). "Gentile" laws existed in the law revealed to Israel.[18]

In Col. 3:5–17 we do not find a single list of vices followed by a single list of virtues. Rather, we find first those things that must be put to death. Gentiles walked

18. R. Bauckham, "James and the Gentiles (Acts 15.13–21)," in *History, Literature, and Society in the Book of Acts*, ed. Ben Witherington (Cambridge: Cambridge University Press, 1996), 154–84; idem, "James and the Jerusalem Council," in *The Book of Acts in Its Palestinian Setting*, ed. R. Bauckham (Grand Rapids: Eerdmans, 1995), 415–80.

in these things, so to live now in Christ they must be eliminated altogether. In 3:8 we begin a new fivefold series.[19] Its true counterpart is found in 3:12. The first series comprises things to be "put away" and the second things to "put on." Both have brief extensions attached to them (3:9–11 and 3:13–17). The second extension, following the positive virtues to put on, is longer because it elaborates on what is good and worthy of Christ and the new man. It speaks of love, harmony, peace, fellowship, and thankfulness. The series represented by 3:5 speaks of threshold conduct and bearing. These five realities, known in the Gentile world, are toxic and must be put to death altogether. They cannot exist with Christ. They represent a Gentile way of life that must die if Christ is to live and the new man in him.

One might think of an analogy. If there are things in my house that are lethal and dangerous, they must be removed and sequestered or destroyed. Equally, there are items that must be put on the curb, week by week, and "put away" by those in charge of removals. The first corresponds to 3:5–7, and the second to 3:8–11. Both must be dealt with seriously, but the first are deadly. The second "putting away" is also happening in relationship to something positive, the "putting on" of virtues especially fit for the new man. The argument here is not that each item in 3:8 is matched with a single counterpart in 3:12. Rather, the counterpart to "anger, wrath, malice, slander, and foul talk" as a whole is "compassion, kindness, lowliness, meekness, and patience." The counterpart to lying in 3:9 is forgiveness in 3:13. The transitional material in 3:10 explains that we are in the process of being renewed. This renewal aims at nothing less than the restoration, in Christ, of the Adam that God had intended men and women to be and that Christ has restored in his own new Adam. The categories that emerged in consequence of sin, some providentially decisive and good, are however now coming into a fresh reconfiguration (3:11). We are no more these things. Our new identity is hidden with Christ in God. But it is being renewed as we put off and put on what Paul sets forth in 3:8 and its counterpart in 3:12, once the deathly conduct known in the Gentile walk is dealt with by becoming dead through the work of Christ himself and submission to him.

Now we have the key to the precise narrative form of what Paul accomplishes in 3:5–17. It is not the simple counterpart to Gal. 5:16–25 ("works of the spirit" and "works of the flesh"), and it does not purport to be. It deals rather with the threshold reality of a deathly walking and living being put to death and then speaks of things to be put away and replaced with new things put on. This is a renewal with its focus on Christ the new man and his provisioning of a new Adam. It may be that the sexual sins of Gen. 3 (desire) and the prevarication of the first couple influenced Paul in what he says in Col. 3:5 and in 3:8, but this would be to focus far too narrowly on a range of behaviors already well rooted in scriptural

---

19. Sumney notes in passing: "There is a case to be made that the vices of v. 5 derive from common Jewish accusations about Gentiles, but no such case can be made for the list in v. 8.... The vices in v. 8 include conduct that other moralists of the first century would have condemned" (2008: 196).

condemnation of Gentile conduct and the first-century form these take. It has already been noted, however, that the (seemingly) abrupt transition to concern with wife-husband-children-toil does comport with the negative decrees of Gen. 3 and their new reversal in Christ.

3:8 but now rid yourselves as well of these things: anger, wrath, malice; slander and foul language from your mouth—I adopt the view held by most that *panta* means the things to follow. This is consistent with the position I take on the form of the material as presented in Colossians. The final reference to **mouth** might conceivably refer to the entire list (things that take the form of public speech, including angry, wrathful, malicious conversation), but it is more likely the first three vices reinforce one another and the last two are vices of the mouth more specifically. Anger and wrath "are often used virtually interchangeably in Scripture, and they probably cannot be distinguished here" (Moo 2008: 263).[20] Paul is referring to attitudes and emotions that can lead to **malice** (*kakia*) or the settling of grudges in the community. Anger and contempt are rarely bottled up and usually boil over into public comment of some destructive kind. So the first three are closely related in this series. The final two give characterization of what then comes from the mouth, **slander** (*blasphēmia*) and **foul language** (*aischrologia*; literally, "shameful words"). At issue is defamation in coarse terms. It cannot be ruled out that this includes cursing in the name of God (e.g., "g-d him/them/you"). The imperative Paul uses is *apothesthe* ("rid yourself" or "put off"). It can refer to the shedding of garments, but this is rarer than the general sense of the verb as rendered here.[21] This being said, its counterpart at 3:12, *endousasthe* ("put on"), specifically refers to being clothed, and in Rom. 13:12, 14 (compare Eph. 4:22, 24) we have the same pairing ("cast off the works of darkness" and "put on the Lord Jesus"). This underscores again our understanding of how the form of the entire unit has been constructed in the case of Col. 3:5–17.

3:9–10 An elaboration is offered regarding the prohibitions of 3:8. In so doing, they also anticipate the positive "clothing" series in 3:12. Something is being stripped off, so that something new can be worn. Paul continues his concern for wrongful speech in the Christian community by moving to lying: **do not lie to one another: you have taken off the old man with its practices**. The Greek deploys two participles ("taking off" in 3:9 and "putting on" in 3:10) that can be rendered causally ("because you have") or with the participial form retained ("having put off").[22] Why a specific concern with lying? The idea that Paul is getting

20. Moo remarks further in respect of the third item: "Paul's purpose is not to single out three specific sins but to use the three words together to connote the attitude of anger and ill will toward others that so often leads to hasty and nasty speech" (2008: 264).

21. P. T. O'Brien, *Colossians, Philemon*, Word Biblical Commentary 44 (Waco: Word, 1982), 186; and J. Gnilka, *Der Kolosser Brief* (Freiburg: Herder, 1985), 184, believe the verb points to garments being removed.

22. Lohse 1971: 136 wants an imperative and so translates "put off." Paul is rather moving between exhortation and the grounding for it, which is imperatival by its very reality.

some detailed report from Epaphras makes a kind of general sense, but the letter does not tell us this. My view is that Paul begins with a list that refers to Gentile conduct and its elimination. Then he moves to vices in emotion and in speech, for which he offers a positive counterpart in 3:12. Here he is transitioning with the provocative image of the old man and the new man. Because I believe Gen. 2–3 is making its force felt with the language of clothing and image and knowledge in the articulation of Col. 3:5–17, I prefer to make that clear in the translation (so also Lohse 1971: 136, 142).

To speak of "old self" or "old nature" in English translation also raises questions of anthropology. What is a self and what is a nature? If the Genesis language is allowed to make its force felt, Paul is speaking of humankind as God created it—male and female. The subtle flexibility of range for Hebrew 'adam, from "man" to "humankind" to "Adam," is undisturbed. This is man (and woman) as a totality, and not some abstraction in modern psychological terms ("nature" or "self"). The language Paul uses here is clear in Greek: *ton palaion anthrōpon* and *ton neon* (*anthrōpon*). The "new man" is Christ, or us in him; the "old man" is Adam. The context reinforces this interpretation, with its language of "stripping off" and "clothing oneself in" (*endysamenoi* in 3:10; *endousasthe* in 3:12) and being "renewed in knowledge according to the image of its creator [*kat' eikona tou ktisantos auton*]." We are being renewed in a knowledge—not of the tree of knowledge—that brings about renewal, as the garments of our old Adam are being replaced by the garments of Christ the new Adam. The garmented fellowship enjoyed by Adam and Eve before the fall is here intimated, as Christ restores the fellowship for us that he enjoys with the Father, "highly exalted" in consequence of his sacrifice on our behalf.[23] "Knowledge" here is the form of Christian provisioning that stands in contrast to the deathly knowledge in disobedience. It is knowledge of God, not self-knowledge of our loss of God.

Do not lie to one another—Some hold that this special attention to the lie (*mē pseudesthe*) is because it summarizes what has been said in 3:8. This is not particularly clear. It does seem that the independence of the command means a discrete concern. One possibility is that lying is a particular form of "not loving the neighbor as oneself" and is related to that command "do not lie" in a series in Leviticus, where it is glossed, "do not deceive one another" (Lev. 19:11, 18). Lying could also be a way of speaking of the Decalogue's prohibition of false testimony (Exod. 20:16; Deut. 5:20) and so of its use in Christian application. It may be a concern in the context of reference to Genesis, as a form of Adam's dissembling or the serpent's devious questioning. This all belongs to the context of the old Adam, and this is being put off now in the Christian community. Beyond this it is difficult to say. One thing is obvious. It allows for the introduction of putting

23. Moo puts it this way: "It is therefore our 'Adamic' identification, with its servitude to sin, that we have 'put off' in coming to Christ; and it is our 'Christic' identification, with its power over sin, that we have 'put on'" (2008: 268).

off and of renewal (*anakainoumenon*): **and have put on the new man, which is being renewed in knowledge after the image of its creator.** Lying was one of the practices (*praxesthen*) in the ambit of the old Adam.

3:11 **here there cannot be Greek and Jew, circumcised and uncircumcised, barbarian, Scythian, slave and free man, but Christ is all, and in all**—These are categories of the old Adam. They remain as renewal is taking place, but they are no longer determinative. They cannot have the place of priority they once had. A new denominating is in place. In my view "male and female" are not in the list here because Paul will be speaking about them very shortly. In the case of Gal. 3:28, Paul is in the context of Abraham and his offspring, not Gen. 3.[24] I supplied **and** in the reference to **slave and free** because it is an obvious pair on the same order as the first two. **Barbarian** and **Scythian** are the two oddities. Barbarian is an onomatopoeic word used by Greeks to specify non-Greek speakers; Scythian refers to someone living north of the Black Sea. The reputation of the region's inhabitants, in sources from the period, is routinely that of barbarians without equal. Sumney (2008: 206) raises the question as to whether this duo is not a further stipulation of uncircumcised (non-Greek and non-Jewish) peoples, but instead is a contrasting pair: those from the extreme north and those from the extreme south, that is, world encompassing.[25] This reading is attractive not just for consistency in the verse, but also for underscoring that the new Adam is a universal reality, without border. This matches well the reversal of conditions in Gen. 1–11 as a whole. Christ alone makes the promise to Abraham a fulfillment. The repetition of **Greek/Jew** in the form of **uncircumcised/circumcised** may emphasize the most proximate character of what Christ has wrought and its significance in a letter to the Gentile Colossian church. On slave and free Paul will have more to say shortly. To underscore the point he is making in the entire unit, Paul can do no better than conclude with **but Christ is all, and in all** (*alla ta panta kai en pasin christos*). In this context, Paul is referring to the all-encompassing work of Christ as the new Adam, affecting every citizen under heaven.

3:12 And so now the citizens in Colossae are addressed in the imperative as those Paul has now in mind: **Put on then, as God's elect, holy and beloved, compassion, kindness, lowliness, meekness, and patience.** The new elect of God is not the Israel of his purposes after the Tower of Babel, in the calling of Abraham. Set apart and elected and beloved are those claimed by Christ in the new Adam of his purposes. They are to be clothed in the baptismal robes of new life through a circumcision not made with hands (3:11). These robes consist of a fivefold tailoring. The clothing to be worn is for the one body the church. The church without the denominations of the old Adam (3:11) and the church that is the elect of God as was Israel is now one body called from every nation. Colossians

24. First Corinthians 12:13 also lacks the pair. There may be no single tradition when it comes to Paul's use of the motif.

25. The choice then is between an emphasis on totality or on extreme depravity unable to disqualify the grace of the cross.

3:15 forms an inclusio to this opening imperative address, as it hearkens back to the first address of the Colossians as holy and faithful (1:2).

If this list is the true counterpart to 3:8, one does not just rid oneself of bad conduct in the realm of speech and emotion through hard work (or attention to regulations Paul has condemned as ineffective in 2:22). There is the redeeming renewal of Christ himself at work, as the intervening verses make clear (3:9–11). Or, to return to the previous illustration, the continual "putting on the curb" of our vices in emotion and speech happens as we make an exchange. As we take something off, we put something on. It is the clothing of Christ for the man and woman God made according to his created purpose. Perhaps unsurprisingly, **humility** (*tapeinophrosynēn*) is mentioned in this list, and it is the same word that appears in Paul's condemnatory catalog in 2:23. Humility can be put on if Christ is the one provisioning it, because he has modeled that garment and alone is able to dispense it in accordance with his purpose. We do not weave this garment through "rigor of devotion" or through severe disciplining of the body (2:23). We put on the garment Christ has woven and worn, "not counting equality with God a thing to be grasped, he humbled himself [*etapeinōsen heauton*]" (Phil. 2:8). He took the form (*morphē*) of a servant and garmented himself for our salvation. He makes these garments available and in our size.

The fivefold weave is a seamless garment in counterpart to what we take off and rid ourselves of. As in Hebrew *rehem*, Greek *splanchna* ("compassion") points concretely to the bowels as the seat of emotion and tenderness (paired here with *oiktirmou*, so "bowels of mercy" or "love shown in mercy"). God is himself "full of compassion and merciful" in his most essential self (Exod. 34:6), and the "compassionate formula" of Moses's encounter at Sinai forms a virtual leitmotif in the book of the Twelve. It is the ground of God's life with Israel and the means of its ongoing renewal through judgment and forgiveness.[26] In Christ this essential self is modeled in the cross. It is the virtue Christ most desires to clothe us in, and it heads this list. Kindness is also an attribute frequently associated with God in the New Testament (Rom. 2:4; 11:22; Eph. 2:7; Titus 3:4), and it has the same range in the Old Testament. God tells Moses he cannot see him; rather, he will let his goodness pass before Moses (Exod. 33:19), which consists of his name in first-person address ("I will have mercy; I will have compassion"). The obviousness of this Old Testament figure for Christ himself requires little commentary. We are garmenting ourselves in his goodness for our sakes. Humility is Christ's self-abasement in taking the form of a servant for our sakes (Phil. 2:7–8). It is hard to hear of **gentleness** (*prautēta*), the fourth item in the list, without thinking of the yoke Christ offers to those who are weary and heavy laden in Matt. 11:29;

26. Christopher Seitz, *Prophecy and Hermeneutics* (Grand Rapids: Baker Academic, 2007); R. C. Van Leeuwen, "Scribal Wisdom and Theodicy in the Book of the Twelve," in *In Search of Wisdom: Essays in Memory of John G. Gammie*, ed. L. G. Perdue, B. S. Scott, and W. J. Wiseman (Louisville: Westminster John Knox, 1993), 31–49; and N. B. MacDonald, *Metaphysics and the God of Israel: Systematic Theology of the Old and New Testaments* (Grand Rapids: Baker, 2006), 117–38.

we take his yoke and learn from him, because he is "gentle" (*praus*) and "humble" (*tapeinous*). Does Paul know of the tradition of putting on a yoke that is Christ's, and so has adapted it for similar purpose here? It is doubtful that such a question can be answered. Galatians speaks of fruits of the spirit and includes many of the virtues listed here, including patience, kindness, and gentleness (5:22). Easier to conclude is that Matthew records a tradition of putting on a yoke whose point is complementary to what Paul enumerates here. And finally Paul speaks of **patience** (*makrothymia*) as rounding out the list. Close to hand is the depiction of God as "slow to anger." God is patient and forebearing. So must be therefore the elect of God in the one body.

3:13 In the negative list above we found an elaboration that focused on lying in the community. In the one body Paul here describes, lying is replaced with forbearance and forgiveness: **forebearing one another and forgiving each other, if one has a complaint against another; as the Lord has forgiven you, so you must also forgive**. Notice the exact same pattern in the foundational narrative in Exod. 32–34. Israel sins. God judges. Moses intercedes. God declares himself a God of mercy and compassion, slow to anger, abounding in steadfast love, *and forgiving*. That is his "virtue list." The point of the narrative turns on the reliability, for Moses and Israel, of being able to continue the journey with God, given their sinful weakness and his holiness and justice ("by no means clearing the guilty"). Will God go with them? Or must he use an agent? The answer Moses receives takes the form of the recitation by God of his own attributes, which his name YHWH bespeaks. His name is the reliability Moses and Israel seek, grounded not in promises of their perfection but in his compassion, mercy, slow-to-anger, abounding-in-vast-love character. This takes the concrete form of forgiveness and constitutes as such God's forbearance through time. So too here, by the very acknowledgment of the crucial place forbearance and forgiveness must hold in the one body, is also the acknowledgment that the Israel of God will not be perfect in the wearing of Christ's garments. Complaints will emerge that need forgiveness in the body to ensure the body's sustaining life. The threefold repetition of **forgive** matches the density that will be necessary and the commitment God has to it: "as the Lord has forgiven you, so also you must forgive." Reflexively Paul speaks of "the Lord" (*kyrios*). No space exists between Christ and YHWH when it comes to the one divine character in which all these virtues are grounded and from whom forgiveness is possible and available in the one body.

3:14 and above all put on love, which binds everything together in perfect harmony—Typical of translations available, I supply the imperative "put on" here from 3:12. The Greek is simply "and upon these love [*agapē*]." One question, therefore, is whether we have Paul speaking of yet a sixth virtue to be added to those named in 3:12, or whether love is a special garment worthy to be referred to on its own, the "top hat" of Christ's provisioning. The NJB is perhaps a little overdetermined when it renders, put on love "over all these clothes." Still, the separation of the verse from the preceding list surely intimates the significance of this virtue. It is one among others, but it has the special attribute of being able to bind things together perfectly. One thinks here of 1 Cor. 13 and the encomium to love there. Love is what is able to effect harmony because of its special capacity to bind together.

3:15 and let the peace of Christ rule in your hearts, to which peace you were called in the one body. And be thankful—It is hard to avoid the impression that Paul is simply generously piling one hoped-for outcome on another as he seeks to bring his concerns to conclusion. The positive (3:13–15) lends itself to further elaboration and extension in distinction to the negative (3:9), and Paul appears to have trouble saying all he wishes to say. At the same time, the reference to **hearts** (*kardias*) leans forward toward the next two verses, where Paul speaks not of virtues so much as the practices they give rise to and the habits that support them in return. **Peace of Christ** (*hē eirēnē tou christou*) parallels "word of Christ" (*ho logos tou christou*) in the following verse. If this is a proper understanding of what Paul is saying, then the peace that is to rule "in your hearts" is not an abstraction, a gifted interiority, or a free-floating virtuous acquisition, but takes actual form given the practices of the body. The thankfulness Paul speaks of in lapidary summation in 3:15 lives in thankful hearts through psalm singing and song singing and mutual accountability in the body, such as 3:16 describes.

That the "peace of Christ" is not an interior disposition one cultivates or possesses is also made clear by the verb with which it is attached here. Paul uses the verb *brabeuetō*, which is associated with the role of an umpire in adjudicating affairs. One translation therefore renders "let the peace of Christ arbitrate in your hearts" (Dunn 1996: 211). **Heart** refers to the seat of the will and center of a person's decision making and is not an individual emotional location separate from mind and will. Christ's peace is to be the umpire in our affairs in the one body. This is the peace he has left with us, as John 14:27 formulates. Ephesians 2:14 declares Christ himself "our peace." Lohse states compactly: "'Peace of Christ' actually describes the sphere in which man as the new man exists" (1971: 150). Therefore Paul can also say the peace "to which you were called in the one body." The new man is not an individual but is new in the context of the body as a whole, where Christ's peace exists and arbitrates the life of the church. **And be thankful**, as I indicated above, refers not to an individual disposition we are to have or cultivate, but consists of our life in the body, taking the form described in the following verse. "Rather the community should give thanks by acknowledging in its praise" what God has done in Christ; not only "be thankful" but also "be the ones who give thanks" (Lohse 1971: 150). Lohse, anticipating 3:16, writes: "Appropriate thanksgiving, which v 15b encourages, occurs in the hearing of and reflection upon the word and in the songs sung by the community to glorify God" (1971: 150). Impossible with a negative list, here Paul must transition to the practices of the newly garmented virtuous life of Christ, by speaking of the forms appropriate in worship and the fellowship of the one body.

3:16 let the word of Christ dwell in you richly, through teaching and admonishing one another with all wisdom, singing psalms, and hymns and spiritual songs with thankfulness in your hearts to God—The word of Christ is translated by Moo "message of Christ" (2008: 285–88) as an effort to give an interpretation of this otherwise rare expression (appearing in qualified form only in Heb. 6:1). Usually we read the far more common "word of God" (e.g., Col. 1:25) or "word of the Lord" in the New Testament. Moo means "the message about Christ" and not "the message Christ proclaimed," though it is hard to know whether this is correct given so few occurrences of the phrase. The phrase is parallel to "peace of Christ" and so might carry the nuance: everything left behind and conveyed to the church as his legacy. Given that this is bound up with the scriptural word in its entirety, it would seem artificial to declare the "word of Christ" something distinctive over against the more comprehensive "word of the Lord" or "word of God" even as Paul is here trying out a new expression. My translation is an effort, along these same lines, to say that the rich dwelling of the word of Christ in the body occurs in the form of teaching and admonishing, which cannot be separated from the singing of the psalms and other hymns. The worship practices of Israel continue as before—and as they continue today—with the psalms central to the "word of Christ" in its rich dwelling in the body. It is axiomatic that to be thankful in worship is to join in the thanksgiving of the saints who have gone before. The one body was prefigured in the one Israel, and the praises of God found in its rich life are praises to the LORD/YHWH with whom Christ is in fullest identity. These continue and are augmented with hymns of specifically Christian orientation as the one God is praised via the doxological rubric we can imagine associated itself with the psalms very early in the body ("glory be to the Father, and to the Son, and to the Holy Ghost, as it was in the beginning, is now and ever shall be, world without end"), and so clarifying their literal and extensional sense. Isaiah spoke of a "new song" (42:10), perhaps a song to join the old praises of Miriam as a new exodus unfolds. This dynamic is built into the praises of Israel and cannot be restricted to a single type-antitype in the very nature of the case.

To teach and admonish in all wisdom ought to register with us as close readers of Paul's letter thus far. In Col. 1:28 it referred to the vocation of Paul (in his first-person-plural fellowship), the goal of which was the presentation of every man mature in Christ. This happens via admonishing and teaching (*nouthetountes* and *didaskontes*). So we have some good idea to what Paul is referring. What he does is teach and exhort and admonish. He uses his scriptural inheritance to guide his address as he translates it into a new idiom to proclaim Christ as Lord (teaching) and to speak of the new garmenting in Christ and the new life of the body (admonishing), reclaiming the intention of God at creation in the first Adam. As he has done as teacher and admonisher, so they are to do, with himself and the scriptures as guides for what is the "word of Christ" in proclamation in the body.

It is worth repeating the hermeneutical parameters that are suggested by Paul's activity in the letter, especially as this entails his use of the scriptures in a new idiom of address. We may imagine this use in terms of noting, with the help of a concordance, how Paul cites or otherwise alludes to a scriptural heritage. We may then puzzle out how his audience might pick up allusions and appeals to this universe of signification. But this is of course all to the side of how Paul himself operates and also how we might imagine his act of communication to Gentiles without knowledge of or clear access to the scriptures. Paul does not "quote from scripture" as if consulting a book and looking up proof-texts, much less doing concordance searches. In Colossians we have no scriptural citations anyway. It is my position that Paul reflexively moves from the world of his scriptural DNA. He may do this with studied effort, or it may be an unconscious and inevitable consequence of living so deeply in the world of the scripture's patterns and language that he has no choice (and would not want one). In my view he does not do any of this in an effort to see whether the audience will follow his careful allusional genius or otherwise hope his efforts succeed in this regard. He is a pastor trying to marry his world of scriptural truth with the frame of reference he believes the Colossians inhabit, and he does so with conviction that the one cross will make all horizons converge.

But it is also my view that Paul would never have considered that his scriptures would somehow cease delivering up their riches, much less that he had said all that might be said of their literal and extensional senses. The latter view might suggest that we need to be experts in how Paul uses scripture rather than in letting him lead the way as he gets out of the way. We modern non-Jewish readers are like the Colossians in one sense. We were never Jews. We come to the scriptural heritage that flows in and out of Paul's life as outsiders. But we are also unlike the single Colossian church of an imagined first reception of his letter, for we know that the scriptures that were Paul's have in fact remained our own. If we are wise in such things, we will know how central the (old) scriptures were in the church's life as Christian scripture in a two-testament witness. We read Paul and can see, sometimes provisionally and at times more clearly, how his mind appears to be working when it comes to this legacy. I would like to believe we have become the church he hoped the Colossians would be—a church that would read scripture after him, that sought to be taught and admonished from these scriptures. That the old scriptures continue to exist in the form that Paul read them and was formed by them, and that his letters now sit astride them as a new scriptural witness, is a development Paul may never have thought possible, though it is a grand outcome on two levels at the same time: Paul as scripture (a surprise for him) and scripture as retained (something he would never have doubted). The question is what to make of the character of Christian scripture as containing the old in a form essentially unchanged and the new, juxtaposed and uncollated, sitting alongside it. We cannot freeze the horizon and ask what did the Colossians think Paul was doing when they read his letter, because his letter was only the first invitation to read a scripture after him that would not for them be old, but utterly and entirely new. The real and serious dilemma of the law for Paul would become their dilemma too, insofar as they read sympathetically of life under the law and sought then to hear that law in all its literal seriousness. If this were to happen, they might also understand the pathos of a Paul trying with all his creative care to speak into their world and our world, to the point of seeing his life as afflicted for their sakes, a sharing in the sacrificial work of the one cross of his Lord, who was Lord of a new Adam now being renewed according to the eternal purposes of God.

Paul speaks of singing psalms, hymns, and spiritual songs with thanksgiving, teaching, and admonishing. A **psalm** is the unbroken praise of Israel teaching and admonishing the body.[27] The **hymns and spiritual songs** are the "new song" the old scriptures spoke of (Isa. 42:10) as it reflected on its own former-latter deliverances of God's mercy and judgment within its own temporal scope. The psalm and the song are like the scriptures of the Christian church. One we learn to sing alongside Paul because of Christ, and the other Paul is taught to sing by Christ, which he gladly sings on tune with the new man everywhere being raised up and renewed in the one body. His vocation may be drawing to a close but in other ways it is only beginning.

Paul has warned the Colossians about false religious practices. But he has not done so without speaking of what true worship looks like. It is the place where genuine thankfulness manifests itself, in the one body. It is a place of true teaching and admonishment, patterned on his own vocation. It is not a place of ranks and distinctions and boasting of ascents, but of spiritual praise of God in one body, where all wear the garment of Christ's fivefold weaving. Paul tells the Colossians what to avoid and then what to put to death and then what to divest themselves of. Stripped for the waters of baptism in this way, Christians are then robed in the garments of Christ as the first couple in their unbroken fellowship with God in the garden. The renewal Paul speaks of in 3:10 ("in knowledge according to the image of its creator") takes place over time, in the one body, in the forms of fellowship and worship he has been here describing. At this point Paul offers a summation.

3:17 and whatever you do, in word and in deed, do everything in the name of the Lord Jesus, giving thanks to God the Father through him—As in Phil. 2:11 and the passage it brings to conclusion, we have here the basic ingredients of what will in time take the form of the church's trinitarian faith. **The name of the Lord** is a constant refrain in the Psalter as Israel gives thanks to God by blessing

---

27. To note that the term "psalm" can apply to compositions other than those in the Psalter or to observe that the terms "song" and "hymn" might refer to actual "psalms" seems to confuse the issue (Josephus can use *hymnos* and *ōdē* when speaking of scriptural Psalms). If Paul wanted to refer to any sung composition and by that exclude a reference to the Psalms of the Old Testament, he went about it in a very odd way in referring to "psalms, hymns, and spiritual songs." He may be trying to be comprehensive but he can hardly be speaking of compositions apart from the Psalms. The more natural reading is to assume that in his own frame of reference, the Psalms are musical compositions par excellence, and they are being augmented in the light of Christ. The canticles of Mary and Zechariah are themselves closely allied with the older scriptural compositions. The Israel of God is praising the birth of Jesus and John as a continuation of Moses, Miriam, Hannah, Hezekiah, David, Habakkuk, and others.

his name (YHWH). "The name" (*hasshem*) will become a virtual metonym for the sacred name YHWH. "The LORD" (*yhwh*) will in time be referred to by a sacred gloss, in Hebrew *'adonai*. Rather than speak aloud the name in the context of recitation of sacred scripture or in worship, the acoustic icon YHWH is guarded by saying aloud instead *'adonai* ("the Lord") or *ho kyrios* in Greek translation. Philippians 2:9–10 carefully describes how the "name above every name" (*to onoma to hyper pan onoma*) is given by God to Jesus, so that in turn, at his name, "at the name of Jesus" (*hina en tō onomati iēsous*), "every knee shall bow." Paul's scriptural text is Isa. 45:23. It consists of a solemn declaration made before all the ends of the earth, by God in first-person address: "I am God and there is no other" (45:22) follows and seconds the preceding "I, YHWH, and there is no other *'elohim* beside me" (45:21). The solemn oath can be made only in his own name ("by myself I have sworn"), and it will not return (empty). It is "to me every knee shall bow and every tongue shall swear, 'only in YHWH are righteousness and strength'" (45:24). Philippians 2:10–11 sees the solemn oath fulfilled in Christ, and the "name above every name" being given to him so that now, at the name of Jesus, "every knee shall bow / every tongue confess." To clarify the scope of what Christ has accomplished as God's own Son and work, the hymn in Philippians speaks of every knee bowing "in heaven and on earth and under the earth."

The crucial thing to note is that, as this "name above every name" is given and a new spoken (unglossed) name, Jesus, receives worship and homage—as was only appropriate in respect of YHWH (the same Isaiah text being called upon makes this point urgently)—Paul will of necessity conclude: "To the glory of God the Father" (Phil. 2:11). Here the biblical version of the later creedal confession makes the point clearly with its terse but unmistakable, incipient trinitarianism (the confession can be made only in and by the Holy Spirit). To bow to the name of Jesus gives glory to the Father. To speak of Jesus as the Lord (*ho kyrios*) is to give glory to God the Father. In Col. 3:17 Paul concludes his positive appeal to the one body to do everything in the one name, "the name of the Lord Jesus." As in Phil. 2:11 he therefore closes with, "giving thanks to God the Father through him."

Does Paul's rhetoric soar a bit here in an effort to speak of comprehensiveness (**whatever you do, in word and deed, do everything**), or does he have something more specific in mind? The question arises because of the location of the verse. The preceding verse spoke of worship and admonition, and the verses prior to that of the proper conduct in the one body. So does **name of the Lord Jesus** conclude a series with "peace of Christ" (Col. 3:15) and "word of Christ" (3:16), indicating that all conduct and speech as set forth in 3:12–16 is to be done in the one body in the one name of the Lord Jesus? **Word and deed** would therefore encapsulate all that Paul has mentioned in the foregoing, in the territory of compassion, forbearance, forgiveness, thankfulness, teaching, and worship. But equally, the verse can point ahead to 3:18–4:1, where the duties of the new Adam are set out, the first one being predicated "as is fitting in the Lord" (3:18). "Fitting" gives way to "pleasing the Lord" (3:20), which passes on to "fearing the Lord" and "serving the Lord" (3:22–23) and concludes by returning to service of "the Lord Christ" (*tō kyriō christō*).

Modern commentary has focused on the illuminating parallels between Paul's admonitions in 3:18–4:1 and what are called "household codes" from the Greco-Roman milieu. Both Aristotle and Plato discuss the household unit and its critical place within a stable society. The Roman household was the cornerstone of society and the means by which peace and stability were to be effectively maintained. The paterfamilias had specific responsibilities for upholding the "chain of command" in the family (wife, children, slaves) and rights and privileges accrued to them in the light of that. What is immediately clear, in view of 3:18–4:1, is how thoroughly distinctive is Paul's own understanding. The sixfold reference to *kyrios* in the space of nine verses can hardly be accidental. Moreover, Paul concludes by telling the master of the slave, and presumptive head of the Christian household, that a master in heaven is over him. The point is clear enough, but the Greek is even clearer given the repetition noted. The *kyrioi* ("masters") have a *kyrios* in heaven. As we leave the present section with its emphasis on doing everything in the name of *kyrios iēsous* (3:17) and enter the space Paul sets aside to describe the new Adam household—with its sevenfold reference to *kyrios* (including the finale in 4:1)—the difference between the contemporaneous household and the one familiar to the Colossians in the old Adam could not be more striking. Doing everything in the name of the Lord Jesus includes what is fitting, pleasing, and reverent to the Lord, within the family of his new designing. Proper service and proper justice are within the single domain of the Lord Christ (3:24). The final verse at 3:17 serves to link the "word" of 3:12–16 with the "deeds" to follow in 3:18–4:1.

IN DEED

(3:18–4:1)

Modern commentary frequently begins by noting the self-contained and independent character of this section of Colossians. It may then proceed to ask about the prior life of the unit and its relationship to "household codes" as these are available for study and comparison. Some may even speculate that a letter without the code once existed. Either as part of the letter or as added, the code is said to domesticate true Pauline gospel or it otherwise represents the sober business of living in the world, in a Christian adaptation of what the world itself has thought, or what Hellenistic Judaism previously adapted for its own context. The limits of the form-critical approach have also been a topic for discussion. How might we imagine Paul coming upon these codes and remanufacturing them for the Colossian church? Did he read Aristotle and Plato in something of the manner of our consulting them today, via texts?[1] Was he aware of the rules of the household from observing Greco-Roman culture and then fashioned his own alternative? Was his own manner of life within Judaism the same as what we find in Philo (*Hypothetica* 7.1–14; *On the Decalogue* 165–67) and Josephus (*Against Apion* 2.190–210), for example?

The other such discourse we have on this topic is found in Eph. 5–6. Interestingly, it is introduced with almost the exact same language as we find in our letter, and it is another instance where Ephesians and Colossians obviously overlap: "Addressing one another in psalms and hymns and spiritual songs, singing

---

1. Aristotle (*Politics* 1.2.1–23; 1.5.1–12) discusses the household management (*oikonomia*) in three classes: master-slave, husband-wife, father-children. Philo and Josephus (in Hellenistic Judaism) speak of household rules so the general idea was certainly in circulation for someone like Paul, whose Judaism was Pharasaic. "In Palestinian Judaism and especially in Rabbinic literature there are no 'rules for the household'" (Lohse 1971: 155n8). See also Plato, *Laws* 3.690a–d; 3.6.771e–7.824c.

and making melody to the Lord with all your heart, always giving thanks in the name of our Lord Jesus Christ to God the Father." Then follows a description of the Christian household (wife, husband, children, slaves) in a longer form than in Colossians (Eph. 5:21–6:9). The putting-on motif of Colossians then follows this in Ephesians, with the image of "the whole armor of God" (6:10–17). The appeal for prayer (6:18–20) and the dispatching of Tychicus complete the intriguing parallels to Col. 4:2–9. The mention of the slave Onesimus and the extended section on slavery in the code of Colossians (lengthier than the single references to wife, husband, children, masters) are beguiling when we consider the relationship of Colossians to Philemon, which concludes with similarly named personal greetings. Is Paul preparing the Colossians for the return of Onesimus with this section of his letter, to be seconded by their anticipated reading of the letter to the Laodiceans (now called "Ephesians")? Having told them of the proper conduct of masters and slaves in the new Christian household, he would then in Philemon appeal for an even better way. All this is intriguing but will remain hidden from our view.

Several reasons can be given to oppose the view that we have a preexistent household code in the form we now read it in Colossians: (1) the sevenfold repetition of *kyrios* is integral to the discourse and closely associated with Col. 3:17; (2) the reference to "word and deed" picks up the preceding "word of Christ" and kindred concern for proper speech and worship (cf. Eph. 3:19), while easing the transition to the concern with duties ("and deed") in the Christian family; and (3) the form-critical conception of a preexistent household code may be questioned.[2] Why are Colossians and Ephesians rhetorically and structurally different if a prototype were available in a preexistent form? In my view Paul has been working with the themes and patterns of Gen. 1–3 in the garmenting section above. The garments of the new Adam made in Christ, the image of the creator, the knowledge that renews, proper conversation and manner of life—all of these can be related to Paul's reflections on a new creation in Christ, in contrast to the disobedience of the first couple and the sinful wake it produced. This new creation and new Adam are male and female. So the movement to discuss the "household management" is far from unrelated to Paul's larger argument. In many ways, it is expected.

Commentators observe that one distinctive of the household *topos* in Colossians (and elsewhere in the New Testament) is the direct address to subordinates. They are customarily referred to in the third-person in the lists we can consult. And the obvious focus is on the paterfamilias who exercises *patria potestas* in the family and in relation to outsiders, where his reputation is at issue.[3] The list in Colos-

2. With reference to David Balch's "Household Codes," in *Greco-Roman Literature and the New Testament*, ed. D. Aune (Atlanta: Scholars Press, 1988), 25–50, Sumney concludes: "The codes probably draw on a preexistent topos, a 'paraenetic scheme,' but do not rely on a precise literary form" (2008: 230).

3. In the handy list in Lohse 1971: 154–57 (who provides quotations from Polybius, Hierocles, Epictetus, Diogenes Laertius, and Seneca), the orientation is clearly that of paterfamilias and all others

sians begins with the wife, then the husband, then children and (both) parents, slaves and master. Each is addressed directly about the relationship between them. Given the Gen. 1–3 background of so much of this letter—in my view going back at least to the decrees of the writ against us in Col. 2:13; and before that, to the relationship of the Son to the invisible God in 1:15–20 ("image," "firstborn of creation," "beginning"); and before that, to the fruitful multiplying of the gospel in 1:6—it is difficult to leave this unit out of the same general pattern. The woman is first addressed in the decrees over the old Adam (Gen. 3:16), and the focus is childbearing and the husband's rule.[4] Next is the man (3:17) who wrongly listened to his wife and with her ate the forbidden fruit. The focus of the judgment over him is toil and difficult servitude. If Paul has been speaking about a new creation and the garmenting in Christ of a new Adam, it would be natural for him to speak of life in the new household of faith, which is also the place of worship (a theme close by in 3:16).[5] Paul may have in mind the vexed relationships that exist in consequence of the fall and is here speaking of a new household in Christ. The various integers in the household are directly addressed again, but now with the sevenfold orientation around the Lord of the household, the *kyrios*, who is Christ the Lord (Col. 3:17). I noted above the absence of the pair "male and female" in the list of 3:11 as appropriate if anticipating the address to the new family here. We will need to give thought therefore to Paul's seeming dialectic when it comes to the slave-free reality. Presumably he means that the slave is now no longer a slave as the world means that or as existed in the old Adam's world of harsh toiling, but is a slave under the regime of a new master in heaven (4:1). Given this, Paul can be anxious that Onesimus be known to the Colossians (including Philemon) as both "faithful and dear brother" as well as "one of yourselves" (4:9), that is, as a Christian brother belonging to their new household. He can therefore also speak of him as a "son" (Phlm. 10) and appeal to them that, upon the return of Onesimus to them, he be treated "no longer as a slave . . . but as a dear brother" (Phlm. 16). In that sense, the household code is not a conservative retreat to the ways of the world, but belongs fully to the new creation Paul is seeking to articulate in realistic terms. It is radical precisely because its spirit opens onto the kinds of possibilities the Pauline letter collection at its final book makes clear are available for the new Christian family. Paul's imprisonment is the shared context of a new and radical reflection on life in the world.

3:18–19 The Greek text has five sentences, each beginning with an addressee (wives, husbands, children, fathers, slaves). A final sentence at 4:1 opens similarly, *hoi kyrioi* ("masters"). As often noted, what is unusual is the three-verse elaboration

---

in relation to him: friends, allies, gods, parents, brothers, country, strangers, and "acquired relationships" (i.e., son, father, brother, citizen, wife, neighbor, fellow traveler, ruler, subject, children, slaves). They are not addressed directly, and they exist from the standpoint of the single, central paterfamilias.

4. In Gen. 3:20, Eve is named as "the mother of all humankind."

5. True of Roman households as well (Sumney 2008: 231–32). Within the New Testament, see Acts 12:12; Col. 4:15; Phlm. 2.

for the slaves (who are being addressed directly and more extensively). The addressees of 3:18–22 move logically from one relationship to the next. **Wives, be subject to your husbands, as is fitting in the Lord** therefore immediately resumes with **husbands, love your wives, and do not be harsh with them**. In my view "as is fitting in the Lord" really pertains to both sides of the equation, as it is not possible to read the exhortations of this code as formally paterfamilias centered. We see a similar styling in 3:20–21. It is further my contention that "be subject . . . as is fitting in the Lord" has in view the reversal of life in the garden, just as "love your wives" intends the same contrast with the disobedient patterns of Adam and Eve. "Be subject . . . as is fitting" uses language (*hōs anēken*) similar to what one sees in the popular philosophy of the period, to be sure.[6] But its attachment to "the Lord" alters what is the more general appeal to empirical testing and experience as one seeks the tranquil life of good citizenship anchored in the display of authority and power by the paterfamilias vis-à-vis others. The predication "as is fitting in the Lord" also prevents one from taking Paul's counsel here in the sense of timeless truth capable of communication in maxims of two dimensions. Paul is describing life in the new Adam. To "be subject . . . as is fitting in the Lord" is to live in full relationship of transparency and love of a kind that aborted in the garden. But equally true, the exhortations are grounded in the notion of order. The Lord is to be over all and his manner of life put on. Only inside of that can one speak of derivative orders and accountability. To be subject is not to be subjugated. It is the rejection of separate and independent thought and action of the kind easily exploited by the serpent (Gen. 3:1–4). This separation leaves us wondering how Eve knew what she knew in her part-accurate, part-exaggerated ("you shall not touch it") response to the serpent (3:2–3). Where was Adam that he is not there, but suddenly is "with her" after all (3:6), and so shares in the distance and proximity both of a relationship neither loving nor subjected?

In none of the household codes will one find the husband/man commanded directly on the same terms as all the others of the house. And one will not find a command to love. For Paul, the "head" of the house is "head" insofar as the love that Paul previously said must be over all (Col. 3:14) is in fact evidenced in him toward his wife. Only in that context of the love of Christ can subjection or submission find its divinely ordered purpose. Widespread are the cautions about a wife managing the household above her husband and the disorder this causes—whether in scriptural sources or popular philosophical ones. The alternative however, in the Christian household, is one managed in love.

We can see here the hermeneutical challenge of contextualization and comparative evaluation. To be aware of philosophical sources of the period is not the same thing as knowing what Paul knows, prioritizes, and seeks to communicate

6. Though the language of the Hellenistic synagogue, which is held to replicate this, is not identical; Aristotle speaks of "the fitting" (*to kathēkon*), and Pseudo-Phocylides of "it is fitting" (*kathēkei*); see discussion in Lohse 1971: 158.

in the form we find it in Colossians. The tendency is to speak of "origin" and "adaptation" of something culturally imbedded as if we can be sure this is how Paul too is thinking, instead of it being a reflection of the logic of our own point of orientation.[7] Relied on too strongly, it abstracts the presentation of the Christian household from its literary context. In Colossians, we do not hear Paul's address on these matters until after we pass through the virtues (and vices) set forth in 3:5–17, which are to govern the Colossian church. The measure of overlap between household and church is such that we cannot think of them in Pauline terms as distinctive spheres of life. In this sense, the transitional verse describing worship is in a logical location (3:16). Husband, wife, children, slaves are under the rule of Christ's peace (3:15), whose distinctives Paul has been at pains to set forth. To say that a wife is to be subject to her husband and that he must love her as his chief responsibility stands under what Paul has stated thus far. The submission of the wife is not the obedience of the child, which is in turn due both parents equally. Paul adds to the exhortation to love the charge not to be harsh, for this is inconsistent with the fivefold garment set forth in 3:12 with its elaborations in 3:13–16.[8] Overreach in power and governance is harshness and provocation (3:21). It cannot exist in the new Adam.

3:20–21 children, obey your parents in everything, for this pleases the Lord and its counterpart fathers, do not provoke your children, lest they become discouraged form the next relational pair. In Eph. 6:1 the same verb appears (*hypakouete*) as well as the same plural object (parents). The obedience of children is toward father and mother equally, another departure from the household codes. But for Paul, this matter is grounded in the Decalogue itself, and in Eph. 6:2–3 "rightness" (*diakaion*; Colossians has "pleases," *euareston*) is clarified in the following verses with a citation of the fifth commandment: "'Honor thy father and mother' (this is the first commandment with a promise), 'that is may be well with you and that you may live long on the earth.'" Ephesians then concludes with a note about not being harsh, similar to Colossians, but with the exhortation to raise the children "in the discipline and instruction of the Lord." This is yet another place where the differences between the two codes has to do with their respective locations within the letter and not some genetic factor of borrowing and adapting. Colossians has already set forth the expectations of the new Adam/one body and so is able to speak out of that frame of reference quite succinctly. Ephesians does not have the same introductory material and so clarifies that the commands regarding children, parents, and fathers are rooted in the Decalogue and the wisdom one sees in Proverbs and kindred texts. Though it is true that the ancient household could include children who were married, Ephesians clearly speaks of children as such. We have no good reason for doubting that the same is

7. See the otherwise fine review of "the household code" in Lincoln 2000: 652–54.
8. Eadie compactly observes: "The implication is, that the submission of the wife is gained by the love of the husband. Though the husband is to govern, he must govern with kindness. This duty is so plain that it needs no enforcement" (1856: 258).

true in Colossians. Without unrolling another theory about how to explain the relationship between the two letters, I adopt the older perspective of the tradition and assume a generally complementary character, especially when the language is so obviously similar. The father is to avoid harshness and provocation. It is an obvious downside to hyperstrictness that it inhibits growth into maturity and the gaining of true adulthood as "pleases the Lord." Ephesians states this positively in the terms supplied by the Decalogue: here is the first command with a promise! It promises "to be well with you" in the good land of encouragement and long life. Equally, this life of promise needs the care of the father not to be squandered by attention to his own responsibilities in the new household of Christ.

3:22–4:1 We now come to the section that is considerably longer, dealing with slaves (*hoi douloi*). They are addressed as "you" (plural) for four verses (3:22–25), concluding with the resumptive comment at 4:1 (linking *kyriois* in 3:22 and *kyrioi* in 4:1). The repetition of "Lord" is striking and has already been noted (3:22–25). The clear rhetorical effect is given through consideration of the verses as a whole. Masters are "earthly" (*kata sarka kyriois*). There is a master who is heavenly, bearing the same Greek nomenclature (*kyrios*). The first verse dealing with slaves sets out this contrast (3:22) and in case we miss it, it is dwelt on and clarified in 4:1, where the masters are themselves addressed (*hoi kyrioi*) and told they have a master in heaven (*kyrion en ouranō*). The only really difficult interpretive question in 3:22–4:1 is 3:25, which seems to sit there on its own. Some believe it refers to the wrongdoing of the masters, but the difficulty is having the issue raised before they are actually addressed. Some believe its position allows it to move in two directions at the same time: the wrongdoing of the servant and the master stands before a final judgment. I take the view that 3:25 continues the directives to slaves and has in view concern over the misconduct (compare Eph. 6:8). Its positive point is in insisting that the slave is an accountable human being on par with everyone else in the household; there is no special exemption ("there is no partiality") given the condition of servitude. The Christian slave is a Christian first and foremost.

That said, the thrust of the four verses as a whole is to emphasize the provisionality of earthly masters and the centrality of the Lord. To conduct oneself always with an eye toward the earthly master encourages fawning, disingenuous and servile conduct. The slave is being addressed personally and extensively because in Christ his personal and extensive existence has been reconfigured. The "fear of the Lord" (3:22) is the beginning of wisdom, and it is a wisdom fully available to the slave on the same identical terms as husband, wife, children, each in the new household with new responsibilities and accountabilities. "Singleness of heart" is not an impossibility for the servant, but is possible in Christ. Service is no longer to men, but to the Lord. If wrong is done, it will face judgment and recompense. In 3:25 is an assurance to the slave in the sense that no partiality will be shown (cf. Eph. 6:8), even as it both warns the slave and forms the backdrop for the direct address to the masters in Col. 4:1.

Slaves, obey in everything those who are your earthly masters, not with eye service, as men pleasers, but in singleness of heart, fearing the Lord—A new perspective and point of orientation has been made available. Rather than "eying the master" (*ophthalmodoulia*) and working only on those terms in order to "please" (*anthrōpareskoi*) Paul describes a different manner of life. To "fear the Lord" is to be released into a different understanding of labor and its place, now in the Christian household of the new Adam. A Christian master has a new set of marching orders distinguishing him from the world's understandings of slavery and his role in relationship to it. They are earthly masters with a heavenly master whose law is love and the fivefold garment of its manifestation. It is difficult to balance the concern with direct address in this unit as a whole with the reality that every addressee stands under the commands taken as a whole and received as a whole. **Whatever your task, work wholeheartedly at it, as serving the Lord and not men.** "In everything" of 3:22 joins "whatever" of 3:23 and in so doing hearkens back to the general exhortation made to the entire church at 3:17: "In whatever you do . . . do everything in the name of the Lord Jesus." The wholehearted service of God can be known and fulfilled in the work of the slave in the Christian household: **Knowing that you will receive from the Lord an inheritance as a reward. You are serving the Lord.** It is tempting to link the language of inheritance to the promised reward of the Decalogue as Eph. 6:3 refers to that. Proper service gives an inheritance from the Lord. But given the context, the closer referent is probably the "hope" Paul refers to in Colossians itself. This is the "hope laid up in heaven" (1:5), "the hope of glory" (1:27), and the "things that are above" (3:1–4). The slave has an inheritance alongside the earthly master and it is one and the same: **For the wrongdoer will be paid back for the wrong done, and there is no partiality.** As indicated above, 3:25 sets forth a general principle. Heard by slaves, it applies to them in something of the same sense as Eph. 6:8: "Knowing that whatever good anyone does, he will receive the same again from the Lord, where he is slave or free." Equally, in the phrasing of Colossians, "whatever wrong anyone does" will be recompensed. But no partiality exempts the master in his role, nor the servant in his. All stand before the same "master in heaven." So Paul brings the unit to a close on this same note: **Masters, treat your slaves justly and fairly, knowing that you also have a heavenly Lord.** The key word here is **also** (*kai*). Lohse translates: "Realize that you too [*kai*] have a Master in heaven" (1971: 154). Justice and fairness are the standard for the masters under the Lord himself in the new household of God.

Paul of course presides as head over his own kind of household, one might say, in the imprisonment he is about to reference (4:3). He has brothers he is about to mention (4:7–17) there in his "house," alongside Timothy, whom he has already called to our attention (1:1). The letter to Philemon speaks as well of this household of fellowship and of the special place of Onesimus the slave in it. He is Paul's child, "whose father I have become in my imprisonment." Paul greets his sister Apphia there (Phlm. 2), just as he mentions Nympha here (Col. 4:15).

Philemon is the Colossian master of the servant Onesimus. Paul wants Onesimus to be received as he himself would be received. Paul is "slave [*doulos*] of Christ Jesus" as the superscription over Romans (and likely over all the letters to follow) puts it: *Paulus doulos christou iēsou*. His fellow worker in the gospel, responsible for bringing the "word of truth" to the Colossians, is our beloved "fellow servant" (*syndoulou*) Epaphras (Col. 1:7). So Paul is not simply reconfiguring what is meant by "master" but also what is meant by "servant." The roles referred to in 3:18–4:1 cannot be read without attention to the larger reality of the new Christian family. It is not my view that 3:18–4:1 (and kindred texts in the New Testament) is at odds with Philemon, but opens onto the possibilities Paul in Philemon earnestly hopes for. He is a servant of Christ, and Onesimus is his "faithful and beloved brother" (4:9). He is "slave" but in the context of the new Adam household, he is a fellow servant, brother, son, and "one of yourselves" in the household church Paul is here addressing.

It would be intriguing to speculate what Paul's actual understanding of slavery is and whether the horizon of the Old Testament casts its own kind of shadow over cultural realities in the pagan world around him, making him reflexively aware of the different "codedness" of his own frame of reference. Chattel slavery is foreign to the Old Testament. Laws for the redemption of slaves exist in a form unknown in antiquity. Kidnapping warrants the death penalty. Israel did not exist in a time capsule, and it rubs elbows with its surrounding culture in every bit the same jostle as would the new household of Christ. Its failure to be anything like the major warring powers of the day (Assyria, Babylonia, Persia) meant that the existence of slavery was considered differently simply as a cultural fact on the ground, leaving aside how it was handled theologically. Perhaps here too Paul was an eccentric member of the world of household codes and so never had to cast off their limitations or tailor-make a robust account of the new life in Christ to conform to them. His own frame of reference, insofar as it was inscripted by the oracles of God entrusted to the Jews, provided different lenses and different resources for thinking about the new household family, including the slave. Unsurprisingly, when he speaks of the roles of parents and children in Eph. 6:1–2, he moves reflexively to the fifth commandant of the heart of the law (Exod. 20:12; Deut. 5:16). That same Decalogue grounds the Sabbath life and its provisions for Israel, sojourners, male and female servants alike in the remembrance that all of Israel "were slaves in Egypt" and it was the LORD "who brought them out with a mighty hand and outstretched arm" (Deut. 5:15). The servants are to share the same rest as Israel in the household of the Sabbath life of liberation and service. For Israel had the memory of past slavery and the present life of redemption in the LORD who delivered them. It cannot be far from Paul's view that as "slave of Christ" he was in an altogether new household of faith, reconfiguring patterns given in the world in the same way the LORD established a new life for his people and those blessed in their midst.

GOODBYE

(4:2–18)

We come now to a section of text (4:2–6) interpreters are not confident in declaring attached either to what precedes or to what follows. Partly at issue is attention to the character of letter correspondence in its antique form. A similar passage appears in Eph. 6:18–20, and there it seems to offer final remarks closely associated with the letter's ending: "And pray in the Spirit on all occasions with all kinds of prayers and requests. With this in mind, be alert and always keep on praying for all the Lord's people. Pray also for me, that whenever I speak, words may be given me so that I will fearlessly make known the mystery of the gospel, for which I am an ambassador in chains. Pray that I may declare it fearlessly, as I should."[1]

It may be an artificial judgment to have to make, however I hold that Paul has concluded the main body of Colossians with his description of the new household of Christ, and he now begins to wrap up his discourse. The reference to prayer in 4:2 is not so much the start of a new topic as it is a way to introduce first-person concerns that will dominate the letter's content until the final adieu: "I, Paul, write this greeting with my own hand. Remember my chains" (4:18). Paul speaks of devoted prayer because he is about to speak of prayers to be entreated on behalf of himself.[2] His situation in prison is brought to mind, and we never leave this until the close of the letter. Because he refers to a special prayer that he and his colleagues might effectively gain a hearing for the gospel in the context in which they find themselves, he also speaks of opportunities of like nature for the Colossian Chris-

---

1. Eph. 6:18–20 is but four verses from the conclusion. Like Colossians it moves to speak next of Tychicus and the anticipated exchange of greetings and experiences. Then it concludes.
2. Of course the reference to "being watchful with thanksgiving" (*grēgorountes en autē en eucharistia*) may pick up the language of 3:17 ("being thankful in all things") but the association is a general one. Paul is summing up in general terms what he has said as he begins to bring his discourse to a close.

tians (4:5–6). Paul is easing himself out of the specific Colossian context and putting them in mind of his own circumstances because he is about to envision a personal exchange with the Colossians concerning the fellowship he enjoys in prison and the details of that, conveyed by Tychicus and Onesimus. Prayer is the means whereby consistent and devoted attention can be given to one another across distance and circumstance. It will not cease once Paul's ambassadors arrive, from either side of the exchange. So that is where he begins his final and closing comments.

4:2–4 devote yourselves to prayer, being watchful and thankful, and pray for us as well that God may open a door for our message, that is, speaking of the mystery of Christ, for which I am in bonds: that I may make it manifest, speaking as I ought—That this is one sentence in Greek is sometimes obscured in translation. The prayer that is to be earnestly prayed pertains to the work of Paul and his colleagues. This work is **our message**, which consists of **speaking of the mystery of Christ**. Paul asks that they pray to God to open a door and that in turn Paul might clearly walk through it, so to speak, in proper announcement of the message for which he is God's steward. Ephesians 6:19–20 gives a very similar version as Colossians; there Paul asks for prayers for boldness and proper words to convey the mystery of Christ, for which he is "an ambassador in chains."

To be sure, the reference to thankful and sustained praying by the Colossians picks up themes with which the letter opens ("thanksgiving" and "unceasing prayer" in 1:3–12). But now the Colossians are requested to do what Paul has indicated is his own practice toward them. There he was opening up a discourse with a church he had no experience of, and here he is winding one down as he makes a final request of them. The language of opening a door for the word (*thyra ton logon*) is reminiscent of 1 Cor. 16:9 and 2 Cor. 2:12, where it has to do with positive reception by those Paul has addressed with the gospel. In the context of Col. 4:3, where Paul speaks of his imprisonment, it would appear to refer to opportunities for his proclaiming "the mystery of Christ" in spite of that, or because of it. Philippians 1:12 speaks of imprisonment as a surprising means by which "to advance the gospel." Upon inquiring of the reason for Paul's imprisonment, they learn that it is "for Christ," which Paul declares to be its own proclaiming of the gospel ("it has become known throughout the whole pretorium"). Given that in this letter the "mystery" refers to the special vocation of the gospel in respect of Gentiles (Col. 1:27) and given that Paul will refer to the vocation of the Colossians to "outsiders" in 4:5, I conclude that Paul is here referring to the gospel's hidden-and-now-revealed address to and inclusion of the wider world beyond Israel. Paul's imprisonment is the working out of Christ's afflictions in his own fleshly existence in respect of the Gentile mission (1:24).[3] He asks that his message pass through the door God opens. The objectivity of this word is not

3. "One can well envisage the 'apostle to the Gentiles' in prison reflecting on his life's work as more and more of a key feature of the eschatological and cosmic scenario with which God's whole purpose for creation and humanity would reach its climax" (Dunn 1996: 263).

however as independently active as what Paul gives thanks for in 1:6 (compare Moo 2008: 322). Paul may not walk through the door God opens, but the word to be proclaimed is inextricably linked with his own personal embodiment of the mystery of Christ "for which I am in bonds." Paul asks that their prayers enable him to be the vehicle for a proper manifestation of the mystery of Christ. In whatever way God will see to that, Paul asks that the Colossians pray for its accomplishment in him.

4:5–6 with wisdom conduct yourselves toward outsiders; make the most of the time—At the very beginning of the letter, Paul wanted the Colossians to know that he and his fellow workers had "not ceased to pray for you, and to ask that you be filled with the knowledge of God's will in all spiritual wisdom and understanding" (1:9). Here at the close, he likens his vocation to the Gentiles to the conduct they are themselves also to manifest toward "outsiders" (*pros tous exō*). The term is a general one meaning, in this case, non-Christians. The wisdom in order here is referred to as also "making the most of the time." Wisdom means knowing when *kairos* reflects a specific opportunity in God's time. It is not that time is evil (Eph. 5:16) or short (1 Cor. 7:29), but precious in wise appropriation and opportunity. So Col. 4:6 stipulates the context: **Let your speech be regularly gracious, seasoned with salt, so that you may know how to respond to everyone**.

In the rabbinic literature salt is associated with wisdom. This would appear consistent with the context here, since wisdom is mentioned in 4:5. The Christian will confront outsiders, and in the nature of the case they will come from manifold and distinctive backgrounds. Their questions to Christians about their faith will not be capable of address via a tract or a memorized formula. Proverbs contains maxims that on the face of it are in tension with one another (does the young man speak with confidence, or does the young man hold his tongue?). Therefore wisdom is needed to know how to apply what the maxims entail. The "art of steering" is a gift of wisdom (*tahbuloth*) because it indicates the choppy waters and varying weather conditions that must be carefully negotiated. One can think here of gracious speech that is at the same time compelling, truthful, engaging, properly seasoned so as to match the circumstances within which the Christian will be called to speak. Not far from the sentiment here, which brings the address of Paul to the Colossians as such to a close, is the counsel of Peter in 1 Pet. 3:15: "Be always prepared to give an answer to anyone who calls you to account for the faith that is in you; do this however with gentleness and with respect."

Excursus: The Finale and the Question of Paul as Author

For premodern commentary it would surely have been registered as deeply counterintuitive to have a "letter of Paul" with the thickest of personal attachment and testimony regarded as a candidate for pseudepigraphy. Only Rom. 16:1–23 contains more in the way of final greetings (whatever one might make of that in the modern period of critical evaluation). Fully seven named individuals are commended or otherwise referred to by a first-person voice claimed to be Paul's. Two more in the Colossian and Laodicean churches (Nympha and Archippus) are personally referred to by Paul. The Epaphras of Paul's commendation in Col. 1:7 appears here in closing (4:12) as the man of steadfast prayer Paul again holds up for their reflection and consideration, if not emulation (4:2–6). The emissary Tychicus, who appears as well in Eph. 6:21–22, and the Onesimus of Phlm. 10 are mentioned specifically by Paul as those dispatched to give a report of affairs in Paul's context (Col. 4:9) and "to encourage your hearts" (4:8). To make all this comprehensible as consistent with the genre of pseudepigraphy (or something else) requires the (considered reliable) list of Phlm. 24–25 (Epaphras, Mark, Aristarchus, Demas, and Luke) to have been utilized for the purpose of augmentation, so that a letter not by Paul might be considered reliably authored by Paul, with the (now no longer extant) city of Colossae chosen as its (flexibly adaptable for another purpose) recipient. Even Käsemann, who wanted to lodge Colossians on other grounds in a deutero-Pauline context, had to concede the parameters were tight: "If genuine, as late as possible, because of the content and style; if not genuine, as early as conceivable."[4]

It is not a conservative or maximalist instinct that would argue against a conclusion of non-Pauline authorship. At some point it is simply more prudent to conclude that we may not know what authorship actually means at the period in question; or that Paul is in fact the most credible candidate for whatever we do mean by authoring a letter, in his name and in the name of those mentioned as his colleagues.[5] The alternative must look at the thick account of personal greeting and the listing of colleagues and other details from "Paul" and judge these to be a contrivance, constructed so as to elicit a credible hearing by a wider audience than the one the letter addresses, who would believe this to be the real Paul in the circumstances of personal dictation, which the letter itself sets forth and sees as a crucial aspect of its total communication.[6] I have dealt with the change in perspective the letter assumes as consistent with Paul's wider understanding of the nature of the church, given his location and the gospel's

4. Ernst Käsemann, as cited in Lohse 1971: 166n18 and Dunn 1996: 19n1.
5. Hardly a conservative scholar, Barclay points to the scholarly impasse and notes the following: "Even when allowing for the influence of the Colossian situation on Paul's mind, and the necessities of his confrontation with the 'philosophy' there, it is plausible to argue that some aspects of the theology of Colossians have moved too far from Paul to be credited to him. But it is harder to prove such a claim. The problem is that both sides in this debate are able to argue 'Heads I win, Tails you lose.' On the one side, the similarities with Paul are taken to argue for authenticity, and the differences indicate only his flexibility of mind, differences which a careful imitator would hardly introduce. On the other, the similarities with Paul show the extent to which the imitator was steeped in Pauline thought, but the differences indicate the operation of a different mind. But it is hard to see how such an argument can be resolved" (2004: 28–29).
6. I am well aware that the argument for a benign (nonduplicitous) form of antique pseudepigraphy exists. The audience is meant to know that such a form exists and so is not bothered by the deployment of this genre. It is just that the actual character of the literal sense portrayal of the letter, with its details and thick account of Paul and his associates, does not naturally give the impression of such a genre. And if it does want to be this, why go to the effort to create all the details if the presumed audience does not actually need them? Ephesians and Colossians are really rather different at this point. And it is still my assumption that Ephesians is the work of the same author of this letter, but as a fully and intentionally composed circular letter.

taking hold in a church he has never visited. The same can be said of the style of his address, consisting in longer and more complex sentences. This and the vocabulary he uses to speak of possible false trails exist together in the new idiom Paul is striving to construct, as he brings the world of scripture to those who do not know it in language and imagery they will find compelling and that he will find true to the "oracles of God entrusted to the Jews."

An imitator of Paul would have signed Paul's own name at the close of the letter ("I, Paul, write this greeting in my own hand. Remember my fetters. Grace be with you") in the exact manner in which we know Paul to have truthfully signed off on letters he had dictated and about which there is no modern scholarly debate (Gal. 6:11; 1 Cor. 16:21). The same person would have constructed and claimed as Paul's associates the long list of names in Col. 4:7-18.[7] He would have included the details about Paul's affairs in prison and how these were to be conveyed personally by Tychicus and Onesimus ("they will tell you of everything that has taken place here"). The deeply personal and sympathetic tone adopted in the opening chapter of Colossians, with the emphasis on Paul's individual and corporately shared concern for them, would have been created by this same person. The "Colossians" would have been chosen as the Christian community to be addressed because it was no longer in existence, having been destroyed by earthquake in the early 60s, a letter not by Paul to a community not really Colossae with names of people not really in Paul's association as Colossians describes this.[8] Or, if it did exist and if Tychicus and Onesimus did make their way there, as the letter assumes, and they greeted Philemon, Apphia, and Archippus in Colossae and Nympha and "the church in her house" in Laodicea, the report they brought of Paul was one

7. Sumney envisages a variant account of the pseudonymous scenario for Colossians. He acknowledges that the greetings section is "more extensive than in any Pauline letter except Romans, and the longest in relation to the size of the letter" (2008: 266). The point of the section is to "lend plausibility to the attributed authorship" and to link the letter to Philemon as the setting for Paul's ministry. Sumney refers to the view of Hans Hübner (*An Philemon, an die Kolosser, an die Epheser* [Tübingen: Mohr, 1997]), who concludes that those being cited are "not only living but also have given permission for their names to be mentioned" and that if this is so the letter is not the work of a single author but "the project of the Pauline circle" (Sumney's phrasing). On this account, then, the named individuals from a genuine Pauline letter (Philemon) and others (Tychicus) agree to allow their names to be used in a letter attributed to Paul but one that they have written, in which Paul is the main figure, while they in turn appear in the guise of having "Paul" send greetings on their behalf. They are depicted in glowing terms and as fellow prisoners. Both Sumney and Hübner concede that this is all speculation. One wonders how plausible such a scenario really is. Why would it not simply be a deceit? Further along, in speaking of Tychicus, Sumney remarks that he "is not just a brother but also a *beloved* brother. This makes his association with Paul more personal" (2008: 207). Does he mean "makes it so" (when it is not so), or is he speaking of an actual reality and not a "project of the Pauline circle" to insinuate themselves into the letter? This is a further difficulty in having to keep track of the various details of the pseudonymous theory so as to know when we are reading an artifice and when we are reading what is actually the case.

8. Colossae was inferred to have been destroyed by earthquake in AD 61 in the light of remarks by Tacitus. He speaks of the Lycus Valley having been wracked and of Laodicea having recovered, but without any mention of Colossae (*Annals* 14.27). Orosius in the fifth century may corroborate this, when he writes "in Asia three cities, Laodicea, Hieropolis, and Colossae, have fallen by earthquake" (*Historiae adversum paganos* 7.7.12). See also Eusebius, *Chronicle* 1.21-22.

simply created imaginatively but also realistically by an imitator of Paul, and it exists in the fictive world of the letter only. If on the other hand they did bring a report of Paul—this letter as it now sits before us with its details about Paul and themselves—it was a report they and the imitator agreed on ahead of time, in light of the Paul so depicted being a fictive personality.[9]

A proponent of Colossians as pseudepigraphy seeks to provide an explanation for its purpose if indeed composed on those terms.[10] Mark Kiley speaks first of it as a "letter of recommendation for Epaphras" (1986: 103). Presumably, the Epaphras named in the letter is therefore a real person (he is also mentioned in Philemon), and he uses a pseudepigraphic letter as a form of recommendation for himself. The phrasing is presumably careful: "On the simplest level, the presentation of Epaphras in the letter may allow us to say that, in some sense, Colossians serves as a letter of recommendation." Does this mean that a purpose for the letter lay at hand, or was that the reason the letter was written as such? The letter does not actually show Epaphras as leaving the prison fellowship of Paul, so is that to make him appear more laudable? Who wrote with this intention, and why spend so much time on other matters?

Perhaps because of the thinness of this explanation, another one is elaborated. Kiley picks up the suggestion of C. L. Mitton that Colossians is "Paul's message for today" (of course, it is not that in the strict sense of the word), intending to "present Pauline teaching in its universal and eternal aspect" (1986: 106–7). The letter is not addressed to Colossae only but will find a reading in Laodicea. An earthquake destroyed Colossae, and it did not exist when the letter was written. So, "the letter could have been read with force in other communities because of the precedent of letter exchange established by 4.16. (In this scenario, the letter might have been presented as having survived the earthquake.)" (1986: 104). As for the desire to present Pauline teaching "in its universal and eternal aspects," Kiley comments on the conflict material in Col. 2 in a manner actually congenial with my own view:

> Many of the elements of the portrayed heresy constitute what looks like a warning against possible future distractions from Christ. The evidence for that assertion lay principally in the statements of Col to beware if someone (unnamed) should do so-and-so (not stating that it is actually happening), and the inability of present research to identity this particular heresy with any known group. If Col is indeed a warning against possible future developments, that would fit well with the already noticed tendency of the letter toward making Pauline teaching relevant to more than the community he founded at one particular period; indeed, the heresy warning could be part of the program in Col to say that Paul's teaching survives the vicissitudes of time. (Kiley 1986: 104)

9. Barth and Blanke 1994: 476 remark on the final greetings in 4:7–18 that, if the names are simply supplied from Philemon and others added, "such a procedure at the close of the letter might be the result of deliberate deception. It can be assumed as a serious possibility in regard to the Pastoral Epistles (cf. esp. 2 Tim. 4:9ff). But it should be considered only when the other contents of the epistle pose the most serious questions about the authorship of the Epistle. For Col., in our opinion, this is not the case."

10. Kiley 1986. Compare L. R. Donelson, *Pseudepigraphy and Ethical Argument in the Pastoral Letters* (Tübingen: Mohr, 1986).

And again:

It wants to show that Paul's teaching is not strictly limited to the exigencies of time and place. (Kiley 1986: 107)

All of this is hermeneutically valuable, but the obvious question remains whether such a subjunctive and speculative account is more economically and realistically available on the terms given by the letter's own plain sense.[11] What the pseudepigraphical account may well see is what we would call the letter's canonical intention. It belongs to the character of God's word and its grasping of Paul and his historically real situation that the universal and eternal aspects of the gospel are opening themselves up to him in his historically defined place of standing. The letter does not create a Paul who undergoes this grasping—by observing the gospel taking hold in a church he did not plant, or by seeing the implications of the one scripture's hidden-but-disclosed word, or by seeking to comprehend his suffering and affliction in the light of the one cross and his own peculiar vocation as steward of the mystery of Christ, or by coming to understand who Christ is in relationship to Yhwh's lordship in time—but rather is, on the terms of its own deliverances, Paul's own deeply personal account of this as his own profound will and testament. The letter itself describes an exchange of letters and a concern that reaches beyond a single audience at Colossae to Hieropolis and Laodicea as well, and indeed "for all who have not seen my face" (2:1). Its final sentences describe a fellowship of associates in prayer and communion rich in range and background and theological perspective. The "universal and eternal" aspect of Paul's message is the universal and eternal truth of the gospel itself as it bears in on him and reveals its scale and scope and majesty and the deep scriptural unfolding of this one gospel in God's time in Christ the Lord.

The final greetings are hardly standardized in character. First, they introduce the letter's couriers, Tychicus and Onesimus. These two are spoken of in terms of high praise. The first has a commission both to tell the circumstances of Paul's imprisonment fellowship and also to encourage them. Onesimus they know already. He will also, with Tychicus, "tell you of everything that has taken place here."

11. One may therefore wonder about the rhetorical character of Lincoln's own final remark (he holds to a view of Colossians as pseudonymous and the final lines as supplied by the real author so as to "add verisimilitude to his taking on the persona of Paul"): "For those who disagree with such a stance on authorship, all that is necessary in most of what follows is, of course, to make the mental substitution of 'Paul' or 'Timothy' or both for 'the writer'" (the term he will use) (2000: 583). But is this actually possible? How can a theory about the letter to the Colossians that informs the commentator's presentation be simply severed from the interpretation of Colossians in which every reader finds whatever referent he or she wants for its main figure and makes a "mental substitution" of it? If mental substituting is optional here, why is it not optional everywhere else? Here one can distinguish the hermeneutical "critical realism" of Barclay (who says he is not confident the issue can be resolved given what we have before us) and the postmodernism of Lincoln. He sets out his position and claims it explains the evidence, but then avers that one can proceed to make mental substitutions because that is "all that is necessary." I am not convinced it is true to the genre of Paul's letters or the scriptures in general to concede this kind of general hermeneutical lassitude.

Next the roll call of those with Paul is indicated. These are Jews and non-Jews, six in total number. Epaphras is in the latter group, and he is the founder of the church already referred to above (1:7–8).

Then comes the request of the Colossians that they greet the church in Laodicea meeting in Nympha's house. They are to see that the letter borne by Tychicus gets read at that church as well, and in turn they are to read the letter that the house church in Laodicea possesses.

Finally, a special directive is given to Archippus, and then Paul "picks up the pen" and signs his name, with final greetings. To that final portion of text we now turn.

4:7 concerning all my affairs Tychicus will inform you. He is a beloved brother and a faithful minister and fellow servant in the Lord—The first person mentioned here—and highly regarded by Paul in his commendation—does not appear in the letter to Philemon, generally regarded as authentic and (for those who dispute Pauline authorship) the alleged source for names being used at the end of Colossians as a means to "strive for verisimilitude as part of the device of pseudonymity" (Lincoln 2000: 580). One may suppose such a device (the provision of names for the purpose of verisimilitude) was not without its risks, in that, for example, Tychicus is known elsewhere and may quite reasonably be expected to be alive or known by others who could vouch for him and the account given here of him. Presuming it not also to be a device in Acts, Tychicus is mentioned as part of the retinue who accompanied Paul eastward on his journey from the province of Asia to Jerusalem to deliver "the collection" at the close of his third missionary journey (20:4). Aristarchus, who is also a "fellow prisoner" with Paul (Col. 4:10 and Phlm. 24), is mentioned alongside this same Tychicus in Acts, accompanying Paul if not also arriving with him in Jerusalem.[12] In Titus 3:12 he is sent by Paul to Crete, and in 2 Tim. 4:12 he is mentioned as dispatched to Ephesus. He is also named as the courier bringing the letter we refer to now as Ephesians to that part of proconsular Asia (Eph. 6:21). Here he is called "beloved brother" and "faithful minister" and "fellow servant," and in Ephesians the first two commendations appear as well. The purpose of his visit is the same in both places. He is to bring the letter and along with it, to provide news and support: "That you might know how we are and that he might encourage your hearts" (the phrasing is identical in Eph. 6:22 and Col. 4:8).

One can understand the high praise of the courier in threefold form—rarely so lavish—if the purpose in part is to assure a good reception of him in the churches of the Lycus Valley and to warrant his capacities for being an encourager alongside his courier role. Not to be left out, of course, is that he is spoken of this way

---

12. Lightfoot 1997: 120 wonders if Tychicus is the delegate appointed by his church, like the others in Acts 20, to take the offering to the poor in Jerusalem according to Paul's injunctions (1 Cor. 16:3–4) and so may well be the "brother who is famous among all the churches for his preaching of the gospel" (2 Cor. 8:18). This is impossible to determine of course, but it is not inconsistent with the high praise Paul gives him in Col. 4:7.

because Paul believes it to be a true account of him. It does not require a lot of imagination to consider the hours spent alongside a traveler bound for Rome or an otherwise active agent of Paul's dispatching.

If the Tychicus here mentioned is not a fiction (for the purpose of verisimilitude, including invented details), it is tempting to piece together the details of his journey to Asia Minor based upon information in Ephesians, Philemon, and Colossians. He and Onesimus, the runaway slave, bring this letter to the church at Colossae. It is 120 miles away from Ephesus, so they would stop there en route and deliver that circular letter, or if it is actually the general epistle Paul commands to be read in Colossae that we have come to associate with Ephesians, then it would be dropped off at the church in Laodicea prior to arrival (it is a short distance to the west of Colossae). He would also be bearing the letter to Philemon, a member of the Colossian church, along with the slave who is now returning to him with Paul's commendation and also his direct appeal as that letter makes it. The letter written for the Colossian church would then be subsequently exchanged with the one at Laodicea, with greetings exchanged with "Nympha and the church in her house" there (Col. 4:15). The church at Hierapolis, a short distance to the north, would also come to hear about the prayers of Epaphras on their behalf, as these congregations learn of that in 4:13 and pass the news of him on. Archippus, a member of the congregation in Colossae with a special ministry, would receive a personal directive from Paul (4:17), and the same "fellow soldier" and Apphia "our sister" would again be singled out in Phlm. 1–2. Tychicus's role as courier and bearer of news and encourager would be warranted by what the churches read at Col. 4:7. Like their own Epaphras (1:7), he is regarded by Paul as fellow servant and beloved (4:7). That he is reckoned a "faithful minister" (*pistos diakonos*) may well mean that Paul envisages a genuine ministry role for him there in the churches. In every way the Colossians will read that this is a true colleague of Paul, a trusted emissary, and one commissioned to tell them of Paul's own affairs (*ta kat' eme' panta*; literally, "all the things concerning me").

4:8–9 I am sending him to you for this exact purpose, that you may know how we are, and so that he may encourage your heart—The thought is repeated here, but now with the first-person plural, "that you may know the things concerning us" (*hina gnōte ta peri hēmōn*). That the phrase is general certainly gives the honorable Tychicus scope to speak of this as he sees best.[13] Paul's not giving details must be explained by Tychicus being empowered to render the news of affairs himself, and Paul is giving him the license to do that by this terse and simple indication. Equally so in respect of his ministry of encouragement, we might

13. I wondered if any of the minor implications of Paul's terse phrasing might appear in the tradition and found this from Chrysostom: "Admirable! How great is the wisdom of Paul! Observe, he does not put everything into his epistles, but only things necessary and urgent. In the first place, he doesn't want his letters unnecessarily long. Second, his messenger will be more respected if he too has something personal to relate. Third, in this way Paul demonstrates his affection for Tychicus; if he did not feel this way, he would not have entrusted him with the news of his affairs" (quoted in Gorday 2000: 56).

fairly conclude. Tychicus is a "faithful minister" and able to do his job without instructions from Paul that the Colossians will read and attend to. The "things concerning us" properly follows the reference to "my affairs" in 4:7, because Paul is an apostle in the midst of associates, and that is ingredient in the discourse as it opens in 1:1 and continues to 1:14. He is also about to name them. And further, he is about to name a very specific member of his prison congregation, which may come as a surprise to them. Onesimus, the slave of Philemon, is one of the first-person-plural fellowship of Paul and more than that, he is accompanying Tychicus: **and with him Onesimus, the faithful and beloved brother, who is one of yourselves**.

Paul has chosen his words carefully here we might assume. This is the slave of Philemon, a member of their own church. He has spoken as highly of the courier bearing the letter of Paul as he can. He has described his ministry. He has asked this Tychicus to speak of him and of the things pertaining to him and all his associates as he sees fit.[14] Onesimus is named as one of these colleagues, and it is he who is accompanying Tychicus. He is not described as slave, nor are the circumstances of his finding his way to Paul, or now to them, mentioned. He is simply called "the faithful and beloved brother," and the language is allowed to find its own fit. As though to let them know that he knows just who this is, he adds the otherwise unnecessary **who is one of yourselves**. Paul does not say of Onesimus what he does say of the thrice-commended Tychicus—that he is a fellow slave (*syndoulos*). If the letter to Philemon is read alongside Colossians, that is a matter that will need working through. **They will tell you of everything that has taken place here**—Does that not leave a lot hanging in the air, and perhaps properly so? Doubtless there is much to say on this score, and Paul leaves it for the two emissaries, "slave and free," to speak of this as they will. Onesimus has a lot to report, but inside of that, he has further a story to tell about his time with Paul and his new life in Christ. How will that all be received, if that is what is being intimated here? Paul had spoken of wisdom and of speech seasoned with salt as his last comment to the Colossians (4:5–6). In a manner of speaking, two outsiders will stand before them as that language hits their ears. Of course Paul's comment refers to something else, but one can suppose it will also have its own manner of insinuation for those who hear the whole letter in the presence of those who bear it.

4:10–11 We now come to the list of persons present with Paul in his circle of fellowship. It is difficult to bring more precision to the context than that. Some conjecture that the rare term **fellow prisoner** (*synaichmalōtos*) refers to actual turns of imprisonment to share Paul's lot or even to help reduce his sentence. It is applied only to Aristarchus here, Epaphras in Philemon, and Andronicus and

14. Theodoret comments: "Paul would have been reluctant to send Onesimus to the Colossians on his own, since he was an escaped slave and therefore offensive to them; thus Tychicus was more suitable for teaching and instruction" (quoted in Gorday 2000: 56). At issue is not so much Onesimus as an ineffective or unsuitable teacher, but Tychicus being sent and mentioned before the runaway slave.

Junia in Rom. 16:7.[15] It is probably not simply a metaphorical term, or it would not be applied selectively (as here), yet more than that is hard to say. The others **of the circumcision** are called **fellow workers** (*synergoi*), so Paul is in obvious working association with them. One supposes we are to imagine something on the order of house arrest, especially if Acts 28:16 is permitted to be brought in to complete the picture ("and Paul was allowed to stay by himself, with the soldier that guarded him"). As "prisoner" (*desmois*) he is nevertheless able to receive "the local leaders of the Jews" (28:17). At his lodging (*xenian*) great numbers came, and there Paul preached "openly and unhindered" (28:31). Acts refers to a two-year period of this activity, during which time "he welcomed all who came to him" (28:30). Is this how we are to imagine Paul's imprisonment as he recounts it in Colossians? Certainly Paul believes that his imprisonment is a travail and a sharing in the afflictions of Christ, however much opportunity it nonetheless affords him, as he refers to above: "That God may open a door for our message, that is, speaking of the mystery of Christ, for which I am in bonds: that I may make it manifest, speaking as I ought" (Col. 4:3–4).

We can conclude that Paul is able to have genuine fellowship with the Jewish Christians he names as well as with the uncircumcised believers named here (Epaphras, Luke, Demas). He speaks of fellow labor, of encouragement, and of the prayer and work of the Colossian church leader, Epaphras. So he is far from a prisoner in solitary confinement or a man on death row or even a typical criminal awaiting trial or serving a sentence.[16] Most importantly, he is able to undertake his apostolic ministry by means of letter construction and dictation. He has received the good news from Epaphras that a church in Colossae has been born and the gospel has taken firm root there. When Paul speaks of "fellow work" in the context of these six persons, and of two about to depart for the churches of the Lycus Valley, he can surely also mean his own letter compositions. What a "seminar room" that prison lodging—however we imagine it—must have been. In addition, if the coming and going described in Acts is an accurate account of life as Paul presently experienced it, his ministry continued, and this likely included the work undertaken by Jewish and Gentile Christian brothers, among whom are six named individuals here. Paul speaks of there being only three Jewish members of his prison fellowship engaged in the "fellow work" for the kingdom of God.[17] Again, this notice finds an oblique confirmation in the denouement of

---

15. Epaphras is taking his turn in Philemon, and Aristarchus is doing his stint here.

16. In Phlm. 22 he speaks (perhaps wistfully) of visiting the Colossians one day. Is this a realistic hope or a way to remind them of the seriousness of his appeal on behalf of Onesimus? "Kindly get the guest room ready."

17. The syntax is capable of a different interpretation, but this seems to be the most sensible way to understand the verse in context. See the clear discussion in Moo 2008: 340–43. Compare the rendering of Lohse 1971: 170, for example, which is closer to NET and NJB: "these are the only ones among my fellow workers . . . workers for the kingdom of God . . . who came from the circumcision," which Moo clarifies in comment: "It is noted that they are the only Jewish Christians who have remained faithful to the Apostle as fellow workers for the kingdom of God" (2008: 172). The third possibility is that of

Acts. Paul has been relentless in always returning to the synagogue context, even when against his own will. Only at the very end do we see the apparent, rather mournful, relenting of that high purpose, as Isaiah is cited on the same terms as its original deliverance (Acts 28:26–27). Yet all the same we read of disagreement among the Jewish brethren, and Acts will not fail to report that "some were convinced" all the same by what Paul proclaimed from the scriptures (28:24). Surely the reference to a door opened by God was not now exclusively directed to Gentiles only. The reference to three coworkers represents something of the same note of persistent hopefulness.

Greeting you are Aristarchus my fellow prisoner, and Mark the cousin of Barnabas (concerning him you have already received instructions; if he comes to you, welcome him), and Jesus called Justus. These are of the circumcision, the only ones among the coworkers for the kingdom of God. They have been a comfort to me—The Greek text begins with the verb "greets" (*aspazetai*) and is then followed by three names. The Thessalonian **Aristarchus** is mentioned alongside Tychicus from Asia as a companion of Paul's en route to Jerusalem (Acts 20:4); he is with Paul during his lengthy Ephesian ministry (19:29). He is also mentioned as beginning the journey to Rome with Paul in 27:2. Presumably he arrived and remained with him. However we understand his **fellow prisoner** stint, Paul himself calls Aristarchus and the other Jewish Christians a comfort to him. They share his prison conditions, just as we know Paul considered his afflictions a sharing in Christ. **Mark** is presumably the John Mark of the checkered career we read about in Acts 12:24–25 and 15:37–39. A reconciliation has presumably taken place (2 Tim. 4:11). He ends up with a ministry in Rome according to 1 Pet. 5:13. Mark may well have written his gospel in Rome. Should he pass through Colossae, they are to greet him warmly and receive him. Indeed, **instructions** (*entolē*) have apparently already been conveyed on this matter. If this is a detail for the purpose of gaining plausibility for the letter as Paul's, it is extremely oblique. Paul refers to instructions from some other source that presumably Epaphras or Onesimus told him had been issued.[18] Paul is reconciled to him, in case there is any doubt about that, and yet he does not indicate any firm intention of Mark to visit them, only its possibility. **Jesus Justus** is the third Jewish coworker. As the name Jesus was widely used within Judaism at the time, it was customary to provide a second name. Two other persons in the New Testament have this additional name (Acts 1:23; 18:7).

I stated above my preference for the translation regarding the Jewish Christians as the only ones, not of their total number, but of those who are **coworkers**

Dunn 1996: 274 and KJV. Dunn renders: "They are of the circumcision, these alone fellow workers for the kingdom of God, who have been a comfort for me." This interpretation has the work for the kingdom of God undertaken by the Jewish Christians, with a distinction then being made with those named subsequently.

18. Lightfoot 1997: 122 thinks these are Paul's instructions but the text could have made that clearer without any trouble.

(so RSV, NIV, ESV, NKJV). But equally the point is not lost that three Jewish brothers can convey only a tinge of the bittersweet. Paul speaks of them being a **comfort** (*parēgoria*) to him, and we are left to ponder why he mentions this in respect of these three in particular. Certainly their shared life as Jews and now as Jewish Christians must have been in Paul's mind. They would have a common life that was turned in a new direction by Christ, and a common scriptural heritage, and they would equally share the poignancy and disappointment concerning their own brothers (Rom. 9–11). They are fellow workers for the kingdom of God, and so that is its own special comfort for Paul.

4:12–13 Greetings to you from Epaphras, one of yourselves, as servant of Christ Jesus, who always struggles earnestly for you in his prayers, that you may stand mature and fully assured in all the will of God. For I bear him witness that he works tirelessly for you and for those in Laodicea and Hierapolis—Again we have the verb for greeting in first place. It appears again in 4:14 to introduce Luke and Demas. This is due to the lengthy and singular remarks appended to the person of Epaphras. He founded the church, as we know. He is the "beloved fellow servant" of 1:7; the "faithful minister on our behalf" of 1:7; and the means by which Paul and his fellowship came to know of "your love in the Spirit" (1:8). Paul spoke of his praying together with them all on behalf of the Colossians (1:9). He spoke of his own individual *agōna* on behalf of the Colossians, those at Laodicea, and "those who have not seen my face" (2:1), and now he attributes these qualities to Epaphras as an individual, praying as if in **competition** (*agōnizomenos*) and working tirelessly on their behalf. His goal is the goal Paul himself referred to at 1:28. However we are to understand the details of this labor, Epaphras is being commended on the same terms as Paul seeks in this letter to the Colossians to describe himself. Nowhere is mention made of his returning to them or to him having had a falling out with them that Paul now seeks to repair. He is Paul's present associate in prayer and in fellowship.[19] That is what they are to know and to take encouragement from. Laodicea and Hierapolis have already been mentioned as cities close by Colossae. The former was a prosperous administrative center in the Roman province of Asia twelve miles to the west. The latter will be known in time as the home of Bishop Papias of Hierapolis around 125. It was six miles north of the more influential Laodicea, with the three cities forming a rough triangle. They were all on Roman roads. It is likely that Epaphras founded all three churches and so is mentioned here as laboring for them all.

4:14 greetings to you from Luke the beloved physician and Demas—The idea that the third evangelist was a **doctor** (*ho iatros*) is to be traced to this lapidary and incidental detail in Colossians. The name **Luke** appears two other times, in Phlm. 24 (with Mark, Aristarchus, and Demas, as here) and in 2 Tim. 4:11

19. Literally, "he has much labor/exertion." The reference is not to his having worked hard to found the church but rather to his presently laboring for it alongside and in the pattern of Paul himself, as described in the letter they will hear read aloud.

("Luke alone is with me"). Tradition has it that the first Roman imprisonment is represented by the conclusions of Philemon and Colossians (and referred to in Acts 28), and a subsequent one, leading to his execution, is mentioned in 2 Timothy. It is likely that the same *loukas* is referred to in these three passages. Less straightforward is the traditional view that this Luke is the author of the Third Gospel and Acts.[20] Of course it was an obvious enough inference, as Acts closes with the author speaking of himself together with those he accompanies in the "we" sections of that work, and the final chapters speak of their arrival together in Rome. So it was naturally assumed that Luke remained with Paul in the period of his Roman imprisonment. Did Paul have or need a personal physician? This we cannot know.[21] But if we are not to assume that a different Luke is intended here or that this detail was generated to create a verisimilitude of Pauline authorship, it was surely a remarkable collection of individuals. Demas remains however an obscure individual.[22]

4:15–16 Give my greetings to the brethren at Laodicea, and to Nympha and the church in her house. And when this letter has been read among you, have it read also in the church of the Laodiceans; and see that you in turn read the letter from Laodicea—We now read of a letter exchange. Chrysostom mentions the view that the letter **from Laodicea** (*ek laodikeias*) was not one from Paul to them, but one from them to Paul.[23] This view has all but disappeared in modern commentary (the learned Calvin holds to it). Of course the significance of Paul writing a letter that he intended to speak to more than one congregation is obvious enough, as it implies a different range of theme and subject matter. My view is that the letter to the Laodiceans is what is now referred to as Ephesians, whose

20. Papias represents the view as recorded by Eusebius. Theodoret is typical of the early tradition when he remarks in passing: "The former [Luke] also composed the divine gospel and the story of Acts" (2001: 102). Chrysostom on 4:14: "This is the Evangelist" (2004: 314).

21. Lightfoot 1997: 123 puts forward the idea that when Paul fell ill in Galatia (Gal. 4:13–14), Luke decided to join him and provide medical attention. This was something of a commonplace view earlier. Eadie still represents it: "The health of the apostle, as they [the Colossians] might know, had been signally benefited by his medical skill, and that this might be at all times available to his patient, Luke attached himself to his person, accompanied him in several of his missionary tours, was with him in his voyage to Rome, and remained with him in the Italian metropolis." He continues: "Sir Thomas Browne, however, in the first chapter of his Religio Medici, says, that 'several circumstances might persuade the world he had no religion,' and among them he mentions—'the general scandal of my profession.' It was, indeed, a common saying, *ubi tres medici, duo athei*. Luke might have been an example to the profession. His physico-spiritual character is happily delineated in the following epigram: *Pandit evangelii et medecinae munera Lucas/Artibus hinc, illinc relligione valens/Utilis ille labor, per quem vixere tot aegri/Utilior per quem tot didicere mori*" (1856: 295). It was ever so much more fun to write a commentary before the rise of the Tübingen School!

22. The Demas of 2 Tim. 4:10 is set in contrast with Luke.

23. See also Theodoret: "The divine apostle, however, did not say, the one to Laodicea as well, but *the one from Laodicea as well*: they had written to him about some matters; it was likely that they made an accusation about what happened in Colossae, or they were afflicted with the same malady as they. Hence he said this letter had to be read by them as well" (2001: 102).

circular character and resemblance to Colossians are both readily attested. The only question would be why this letter is referred to here as if it is presently already at Laodicea. So this is one of the mysteries that the New Testament holds before us and refuses to budge on, and it retains the final word. What is not in doubt is that Paul conceives of a single letter having the capacity for further address. Galatians, to be sure, is also addressed to "churches." But this reference in Col. 4:16 "provides the clearest evidence for the intentional distribution of Pauline letters beyond their original addressees" (Sumney 2008: 280), and I hold to the view that this was Paul's own conscious intention and that it informed the way he composed what he has said (see the introduction).

Paul asks only for the church at Laodicea and not Hierapolis to be greeted. He could mention specifically their greeting the Laodicean church because of the letter exchange he is calling for, as the context for this passing of greetings (there is no such exchange for "those in Hierapolis"). It cannot be ruled out that Paul composed two letters and sent them by the hand of Tychicus, the first one being dropped off at Laodicea (twelve miles to the west) and the second at Colossae. They are kept separate initially because the letter to Colossae mentions the church planter Epaphras, who is a Colossian, and it is more appropriate that it go to them first (4:12). The letter to them can also be read with profit at Laodicea (and elsewhere in the region, one presumes, and eventually everywhere!) and vice versa. Epaphras is known to both congregations and is likely the man responsible for the gospel coming to all three cities (4:13). By writing two letters (whose similarity in style is obvious, including repeated phrases), he can address two congregations at the same time. The letter we refer to as Ephesians most likely circulated in more than one church in Asia Minor because it was actually written for widest circulation and never just for one church.[24]

The "church of the Laodiceans"—this notice allows us to see—is **the church in the house of Nympha**.[25] Perhaps the "brothers in Laodicea" worshiped in more than one house as it was a prominent city. But 4:16 appears to suggest that a "church of Laodicea" is one house church in particular that Paul is referring to.

4:17 and say to Archippus, "See that you fulfill the ministry you have received in the Lord"—This is the same man referred to in the greetings at the start of the letter to Philemon, together with Philemon and Apphia "our sister." He is termed a "fellow soldier" (Phlm. 2). Given this obviously positive moniker, it is logical to assume that the final personal greeting of Colossians is also positively intended. Archippus, Paul tells us, has a "ministry" (*diakonos*) "in the Lord." Before he signs off, Paul wants to be sure he conveys this message to him. Perhaps Epaphras has mentioned something of importance to him, and Paul recalls it here. As with

---

24. The apocryphal Letter to the Laodiceans was obviously written at a later date and sought to fill what was regarded as a blank space available for such a composition. By this time, Ephesians was the secure title of the fifth letter in the thirteen-letter collection.

25. A text-critical variant makes the female Nympha a man instead. This is the more difficult reading and so now widely preferred in modern translation.

the lapidary comments characteristic of the final greeting section as a whole, Paul says just what he needs to say and no more. Sometimes less is more. He appears to assume Archippus will know all he needs to know with these seven words.

4:18 *I, Paul, write this greeting with my own hand. Remember my fetters. Grace be with you.*—The details of the final greeting section of Colossians—incidental, significant, personal, elliptical—are of such a nature that is hard to imagine them as simply manufactured so as to lend plausibility to a letter purporting to be Paul's that is not. Would not just a name or two have done the job? Why mention so many odd particulars (the instructions already given concerning Mark, read the letter from Laodicea, tell Archippus to fulfill his ministry) when the point is simply to add a layer of basic verisimilitude? The letter to the Ephesians is regarded as non-Pauline for the same reasons as are argued to be relevant for Colossians. Yet it is concluded with nothing like the final notices and greetings we have in Colossians. Apparently the verisimilitude cloaking was deployed unevenly. On my view one of the most difficult hindrances to the idea of pseudepigraphy is the character of the last twelve verses of this letter.

In the final verse Paul ceases dictating and puts his own signature on what he has composed. At the close of Galatians he speaks of the large letters of an untrained amanuensis, and in 2 Thess. 3:17 the script of his "own hand" is the guarantee of authenticity ("it is the way I write"). There is no good reason to doubt the same bona fide signature and its intention to claim the letter as Paul's as we find here.

In the light of the total achievement that is the letter to the Colossians, the final words in Paul's own hand speak for themselves. He speaks of his imprisonment in concrete terms. And having said what he wanted to say, to the Colossian Christians and their fellow Christians in the Lycus Valley, he now asks God's grace to have the final word. The first-person plurality that characterizes the first part of the letter is joined here by a second-person plural at the close. Paul's final **grace be with you** will of course have in view the Colossian Christians he has been addressing. It will be a grace heard and received by the Christians at Laodicea when they hear the letter read to them. But it will also reach to those Paul may be beginning to imagine or to intend will be recipients of his letters as a greater work now forming a collection of more than one letter, the means by which his ministry extends itself beyond its earthly terminus. That includes therefore the present reader, you and me, and every reader in every church throughout the world in time and space. In this way Paul exercises the ministry of the gospel to which he referred in 1:23: "Which has been preached to every creature under heaven, and which I, Paul, became [and we might now add, remain] a minister." Such is the great accomplishment of this "I, Paul."

APPENDIX

PAUL IN HIS OWN WORDS—A PARAPHRASE

A Letter to the Churches of God in Christ

(by the hand of Tychicus to accompany the letter to the Colossians and the letter to the saints who are also faithful in Christ Jesus)

Paul, called by the will of God to be an apostle of Jesus Christ, to all the saints in the church of God, all those who call on the name of our Lord Jesus Christ, both their Lord and mine.

Grace and peace to you from God our Father and from the Lord Jesus Christ.

Those of you who know me from my letters will see in what follows a departure from my usual manner of letter writing. The large letters with which I now write indicate that I have decided not to dictate a letter to a secretary, as is my normal practice, and have decided instead to take pen in hand. "See with what large letters I write when in my own hand." Also, because I have learned so much from him and from his orderly accounts of the gospel and of the early church—he has given me a key role in the latter—I concluded there was some value in adopting my brother Luke's own style for the occasion of this communication. You will know much about me from the letters I dictated and sent to churches I have visited, and others I learned about from coworkers in Christ, but nowhere will you find a record where I describe what I was trying to do as apostle and letter writer. Luke never even mentions me in that latter role! But I learned much from him here in prison in Rome, and you will see the influence his own style has had on me in my letter to the Colossians and Ephesians, as well as in this cover letter. I intend this cover letter to accompany those two epistles, and equally it would serve well to introduce the larger letter collection I am now in the process of assembling. My education centered on memorization and recitation, and I am proud to say I can quote from memory the scriptures, both in Hebrew and in Greek. But I am new at this manner of communication so kindly bear with me.

My intention here is to provide a brief account of how I see my role as apostle and letter writer, given that it has been some time since I first began this aspect of my ministry in Jesus Christ, in my letter to the Thessalonian church. When you read any of the letters I have composed thus far, or Luke's account of me in his Acts, though I do on occasion speak personally, my chief concern is proclaiming the gospel of Jesus Christ and giving pastoral counsel to the churches—not on letting you know about the details of letter writing. But as time has moved on, I have given more thought to what started out as something of a surprise in my career, this letter-writing ministry, and what God intends for it in a larger sense. Like the prophets of the old scriptures, my chief responsibility has been to convey the truth of God's word in Christ to the churches, the Israel of God. But like Jeremiah, the mission God has given me has from the start been one intended to be played out on a very wide canvas. Jeremiah was a prophet to the nations, and so too am I. To the church in exile he wrote a letter of encouragement and guidance, using as always his faithful assistant Baruch, much in the manner of Tertius, my loyal scribe. His ministry of suffering and affliction has of late given me much thought, as I reflect on the decade and more of my own active ministry in Israel, Asia, and Europe.

But unlike Jeremiah, letter writing has become the main form of my apostolic life. Initially I thought that the letter was the best way to convey myself into churches I loved and cared about, but was absent from. My travels have taken me far beyond my wildest dreams. But as with my hands-on ministry—again, described well by brother in Christ, Luke—this vocation requires a pouring out of myself into the churches, over and over again, and so too in like manner one letter has been followed by another. In this, moreover, I have been constantly reminded of the once-for-all immeasurable love of our Lord Jesus himself. I speak in the letter you are about to read of Christian affliction and how proclamation of the gospel—in letter form, in prayer, in personal teaching and preaching to churches, in prison and under trials innumerable—is a participation in Christ's own self-offering and a means to further that and to complete what is lacking in my own participation in Christ by means of my apostolic life. What began as individual letters to churches I knew and cared about, and visited, and longed to see again, began to change. What could I have imagined about the numerous journeys I have taken to proclaim Christ, and so too, I suppose, what might I have known would become of this particular aspect of my—letter-writing—ministry in him?

I mentioned Jeremiah and the prophets, and I have had occasion recently to think about the means by which they make themselves known to us. We have their words of truth and witness and judgment and encouragement, delivered under this king and to that occasion. On occasion, as with my own letters, we learn about the prophets more personally, and we can even get glimpses of how their messages were passed on to the wider Israel of God, limited though these are. In the Minor Prophets we have individual witnesses, much like my own letters, though authored by different hands, a "goodly fellowship of the prophets"—as I heard it referred to the other day in worship. But we also know that in those twelve voices we have a choir and not twelve soloists. Their "letters" of divine speech are addressed to specific occasions, but as I so often say in my own letters, the church I am addressing I speak to "together with all those who in every place call on the name of the Lord." As with the letter to the Colossians, I can ask that what I have written to them be passed on to the church nearby in Laodicea, and theirs read in Colossae in exchange. I have now composed enough letters to realize that what started out as specific address has matured into something far more expansive. Once there was Amos and Hosea, but in very little time they found themselves surrounded by a host of cooperating witnesses, whose words would address the time and also march through time and extend the proclamation, by virtue of their form and character, and also because they are in association with other kindred witnesses. Suddenly a goodly fellowship of the prophets had a word to say to generations yet unborn, because of the character of the prophetic word as time-bound and timeless and, as such, God's word.

In my own case, I have thought it prudent simply to arrange the letters by length. Or, at least that is my present thinking. So they are not in chronological order and that on purpose, just as the Minor Prophets are not in strict order of history but of something else more penetrating. So too, of the Major Prophets, Isaiah comes before Jeremiah and Ezekiel in many orders probably because it is the most comprehensive, and I feel that way about my letter to the Romans. This lack of chronology—we all like to find things in an order we can follow—is partly remedied by the expedient of placing Luke's second work close by. Acts gives one searching for a time line something to work with. But it is very basic and was not drawn up to give precise information about my letters in a straightforward way. I do think it purposeful to have Acts end with my arrival in Rome, then to be followed by the letter I wrote from Corinth several years earlier, as though the open proclamation I undertook in Rome, as brother Luke puts it, now takes the form of the letter I wrote to them so as to make myself present as ambassador for Christ and the gospel; I got there after all, though the fears I had at the end of Romans were realized and Luke leaves nothing out on this score. But Acts also serves as a useful introduction to the epistles of Peter, James, and John, so I suspect it can serve more than one purpose in the larger literary witness to Jesus Christ.

Even a side-by-side placement of Acts and my letters would not resolve all problems for the reader who cannot but think sequentially, any more than providing a sacred history from Joshua to Kings makes vanish any and all questions about the order and setting of the prophets of Israel (I do think there is an analogy here: Former Prophets is to Latter Prophets as Acts is to my letter collection). Rather, it reminds the churches that to understand one letter is to read it in association with the others and with Acts, and not to isolate it and read it "in proper chronological order"—much less determine which letters from a later period, which have a different style, cannot be from my own authorizing self. The form of the letters in a collection is also a medium of communication, indicating where the emphasis is—and is not. I decided that Romans was the lens through which I wanted the other letters heard and indeed composed it for this purpose. Of course it is intended to be comprehensible to the specific audience who first opens and reads it, but anyone reading it will understand it is a mature letter summarizing much of what I have said, thought about, proclaimed, and argued with others about these many years, and so I always intended it to communicate the gospel of Jesus Christ in mature form (including my reflections on the mystery of Israel and the church) into churches beyond that one only, significant though it is. The longer prologue of the letter I composed because I want it to serve as a prologue to the entire collection I am assembling and not Romans only. I assume Romans will be read in conjunction with what is becoming a letter collection, and not as a letter whose sense is declared when someone knows everything about the Roman church situation. As with the Colossian church, I only know about the church situation in Rome secondhand, from Priscilla and Aquila, but was not constrained even by that when it came to my letter-writing intention.

Let me add one further comment on this. I am speaking here of the movement in my own conception, from the dictation of an individual letter to a written letter collection, and lately have been comparing that in my mind with what "the oracles of God entrusted to the Jews" set forth when it comes to the prophets of Israel. But the comparison does not mean that I set out to imitate something like "the logic of the prophetic canon" in my own contribution. I had far too much going on in my ministry for Christ and had far less an idea of where this would all lead—the journeys and trials and church planting, and the letter writing as an increasingly critical component of that. What I believe I am discovering through the obedience to Christ and where that has taken me is something of what he called forth as well from his agents of proclamation of old. I am beginning, in other words, to see how the contribution I have been called to make as apostle, in person and in written testimony, appears now in something of the same form as held true for the prophets of Israel as a collaborative witness. Why is that? It is the same God doing work by Christ in me that leads to the parallel, as God the Holy Spirit has occasioned this in the scriptures of old and now in my own apostolic testimony. When I speak in Colossians and elsewhere of a mystery, and of a plan whose purpose is only now being revealed, hidden as it was before, I could easily be speaking of the testimony that now takes form as my legacy as Christ's apostle in a growing letter collection.

And where, after all, did the idea of a hidden plan, a former and latter thing, a new thing only now being uncovered, come from but Isaiah himself, who could speak in similar terms in his own day? There is indeed a mystery here, a sacrament of God's deep planning and accomplishing, because on the one hand the hidden thing was truly hidden before, but the revealed scriptures provide the way in which one understands the conception itself, grounded in the word given, disclosed by God to Israel—or as I put it at the end of my letter to the Romans: "according to the revelation of the mystery that was kept secret for long ages, but is now disclosed and *through the prophetic writings* is made known to all nations." Hidden of old but proclaimed by the prophetic writings all the same, by the power of God the Holy Spirit. When I wrote those lines I was trying to convey what I am now describing in fuller detail when it comes to my apostolic—newly prophetic—vocation as letter writer, where the mystery is the means by which my own written legacy has taken something of the same remarkable form as was unanticipated and initiated both, in the individual prophets of old, and in the untimely vocation it has been my joy to follow.

More flows from this as well. Because the revelation of God to Israel speaks of Christ and a promise to be fulfilled in him, under its own peculiar form of testimony, in prophecy, type, and moral judgment, I have been at pains in my letters to cite the scriptures and show how they preach Jesus Christ. I want my brethren to hear from their own sacred words the one gospel of salvation, and so it has been my custom—as brother Luke puts it—to argue from the scriptures in the synagogues of the Jews, for three weeks in Thessalonica or for two years in a rented hall if necessary, that is, in any and every place I have been, so that others might overhear and also be persuaded.

But one ought not be misled by this. This preaching is not a mechanical matter of proof-texting, as I must genuinely persuade this audience and then that one—here Jew, here Gentile, here proselyte, here a fellow Jew of a kind I myself must guess at, being educated as a Pharisee in Jerusalem—and must allow the old word itself to do its new work, getting out of its way as I preach both it and the cross of Christ. Oftentimes in the dictation of letters I have a rough idea of what I want to draw from in my privileged education of scripture memorization (I have like Ezekiel truly swallowed the scroll). I do the best I can, moreover, to let the church know what sacred voice I am citing, when so moved by God. But on other occasions I suspect I allow it to speak its voice without being fully aware of it. All this matters little as the message of God in Christ is the overriding burden of my proclamation.

I suspect in my letter to the church in Colossae people will hear echoes of scripture that I would agree are that, but that I am unsure I intended in some precise way. I also suspect that Israel's own prophets had the experience of delivering intelligible messages of judgment and of hope, but of also being inspired in such a way that the final horizon of their proclamation was under the superintending hand of God alone, and not fully within their grasp or that of their audience. At least initially. That is why in all my letters I pray that what comes through is the larger declaration that God's word is without tether or limit. Do not follow me. Follow the one Lord who inspires the scriptures and me through them, and allow them to speak over my own head. I encourage the Colossians and all who in time will read the letter sent to them to "let the word of Christ dwell in you richly." That is the word of scripture that is coming to its wonted end: "disclosed and through the prophetic writings is being made known to the nations."

Those far off being brought near are, I pray, to hear in my struggle as a member of the covenants, not an event in my rearview mirror and without meaning for them (namely, the "law" is now dead and has nothing to say), but rather, in our one Lord Christ, a struggle that has its own form in the Gentile condition as well, and can inform it, in Christ, when the scriptures "entrusted to the Jews" are opened up and permitted to sound their notes in Christ for those once "without God in the world." I point the way from my own place in God's providence, as a Jew with a mission to Gentile and Jew both, when I cite these scriptures. But I believe that God will speak to the church I have spoken to, and will continue to speak, when, as I fear and hope both, the gospel will begin to find its readiest reception beyond the sacred precincts of the beloved saints of Israel.

I have just now cited the language ("without God in the world") I used in the letter I authored almost alongside the one I am sending by Tychicus to Colossae. I call it simply "the letter to the saints who are faithful in Christ Jesus," which gives you a sense of my present thinking. He will carry that letter as well. You will appreciate that as I await my trial before Nero I have ample time to reflect on my apostolic ministry, consider the future, and also communicate by letter with churches. This is because of the conditions of my house arrest, which allow me much exchange with visitors who relate to me the conditions of churches I both know and do not know, as well as more extended fellowship with fellow coworkers in Christ. I have mentioned Luke. I also have the company of those of my own Jewish brothers in Christ, though their number is lessening. You will read of them at the close of the letter to the Colossians.

I mention two members of the church in Colossae who are here with me. Epaphras was converted by me during my lengthy preaching ministry in nearby Ephesus. He traveled the distance—it's not that far, 120 miles or so—to listen to my proclamation of Jesus Christ, and though the scriptures of Israel were unknown to him, as with many Gentile believers he has become an ardent student of God's word and my exposition of it in the cause of Christ. In Epaphras I have also discovered another aspect of the mystery of God's plan. The gospel is spreading and taking hold—in fulfillment of God's promise in creation, now in a new creation under that new man in the image of God, Jesus Christ—without my personal planting or encouragement. My apostolic office is spilling out into a next generation, in this case without my explicit design or plan. The mantle of Elijah has been passed on, but without his own hand on it. Epaphras planted a church and has come to Rome to tell me about it, eager for my acknowledgment of this great mystery, and also with the kinds of concerns a true pastor in Christ wishes to share and seek guidance about and pray over. I am unsure when he will return to Colossae, but my letter will in any event go ahead of him. You will read it below.

I have also asked that after it has been read in the worship service of that congregation, it then be carried over to the church in nearby Laodicea. Epaphras has also told me about that fledgling congregation and its concerns. I gather that Laodicea is a bigger and more impressive place than Colossae. I can remember the prominent woman Nympha, who also heard me in Ephesus, and I am overjoyed to hear that the church in Laodicea is resident in her very house. I am sending a letter to that church as well, via Tychicus, and though the themes and language are very similar, I am asking that the letters be exchanged. As you learn below, given developments in my own thinking, I composed that letter as one fully able to circulate widely, so much so that I simply headed it "to the saints who are faithful in Christ Jesus."

A brief word about my decision to circulate my letters in this way. Initially my concern in writing letters was quite specifically local, pastoral, and practical. You can read in the letters to the Corinthians of my concern, urgency, even anxiety as I try to minister in one place but also pastor churches I know about and love beyond my present circumstances of teaching and preaching Christ Jesus. You will also gather that the business of letter writing was governed by the pastoral vocation and nothing more; that is enough. Letters I wrote eventually got lost; that was no matter. But eventually I realized that letter writing was itself an apostolic vocation. So I began to take care to have copies made. The horizon of the letters began to expand as I considered the implications of this vocation of letter writing. When I write to the Colossians I am generally aware of the situation on the ground there, insofar as Epaphras's visit and report were the occasion for my dictation.

But it is not simple vanity that has made me aware of the afterlife of individual letters, and also the effect of a collection of letters, and how such a reality will serve the cause of Christ and the mission of the gospel. I have not been to Colossae or Laodicea. To be sure I have an idea of the religious life in the region from my travels and especially my long stay in Ephesus (I also know the concerns on Epaphras's heart). But this fact alone no longer seems as decisive to me. I have learned that the gospel has its own power of conversion, its own independent character of mission and new life. Just as Epaphras is at work in the cause of Christ without my commission or its necessity, so too my letters carry the gospel cooperating with and reaching out beyond my explicit intention or design. One reading the letter at a distance will become a member of the church I am addressing, simply by sympathetically seeing themselves as one addressed by the gospel, as they are in their own place, and seeking to understand the inroads the gospel can make by analogy in their own lives and own specific conditions. We often do not even know the problem Christ is seeking to address, until the power of his gospel grasps us in mercy and forgiveness, and then addresses us in deeper ways our whole life long. So I begin by saying, exchange the letters that are at Laodicea and Colossae, but the larger conception follows from that.

I had some inkling of the significance of this when I was in Corinth, writing the letter to the Roman church (which I also knew about only secondhand). My intention at the time was to visit the congregation eventually, though I would never have guessed the reason that would occasion that journey or the conditions of my present stay here. At that time I was intending to visit Rome because God was calling me to proclaim Christ to the ends of the earth and, as they say, "all roads lead to Rome." I also had it in view to go all the way to Spain. I am no longer sure that is possible, given circumstances here. But more importantly, I am no longer sure it is necessary. My letters will go there for me. What I have learned here in my imprisonment for Christ is the power of Christ at work as resolutely as the command of God at creation: "be fruitful and multiply and fill the earth." The new Adam, the head of the church, is making that happen as the gospel word is growing and bearing fruit in all the world, as I put it in the letter you will shortly read. To God the Father be all praise and glory.

That is why I decided to write this cover letter. To explain that a letter to Colossae is always a letter to all the churches of God in Christ. My opening salutation above seeks to make that clear. It is the same one I used in the letter I wrote to the Corinthian church.

I mentioned two men from Colossae here with me and thus far have spoken only of Epaphras, our beloved fellow servant. The presence of the second one underscores a different aspect of this mysterious extension of the gospel word of Christ. Again, when I was preaching in my two-year stay in Ephesus, I made a convert from the Phrygian region—that was all I knew about it at the time, for many people came to hear me preach Jesus Christ, from throughout Asia—whose name, as it turns out, was Philemon. I have learned from Epaphras that he was not only a disciple and fellow servant of Christ but had indeed become a coworker for the gospel, like himself. The church was meeting in his house. He reminded me of two others I had converted, Apphia and Archippus. All this came as welcome news and a confirmation of this marvelous extension of the gospel, the consequence of my preaching but more to the point, the fruitful multiplying of the gospel word by Christ himself. Epaphras mentioned many other good works undertaken by Philemon and his company and of his affection for me personally and my fellow workers.

So imagine my surprise—why should this any longer be my bearing?—when a runaway slave appeared one day at my lodgings and was allowed entrance. He had learned of my presence in Rome and was accompanied by other brothers in Christ Jesus. He had heard the gospel of Christ. He had also discovered that I knew his master Philemon. I am happy to say he is no longer a slave of anyone but Christ Jesus and is now a brother in the Lord. So after consulting with Luke, Mark, Aristarchus, and Demas, I dictated a letter also to be sent to Colossae to Philemon. A church I never visited or preached to finds itself here on my own very doorstep, all of us as it were fellow prisoners of Christ. I have asked him, gently but firmly, to receive Onesimus, as he is called, back as a fellow brother in the Lord. I have also asked that a guest room be prepared for me in this lovely hamlet in Phrygia, which I hope to visit after my trial here.

So close have I become, in such a mysterious and unplanned way, with fellow workers in Christ there.

I have assured those in Colossae and Laodicea of my ongoing prayers for them, and send greetings from friends they know who are with me, and other highly respected leaders of the church sharing my life here. We are "fellow prisoners in Christ." Imprisonment is nothing new to me of course. Brother Luke in his account tells of various episodes when I was hauled before officials of various kinds and placed under arrest, the first time overnight at Philippi. In other letters of mine I mention the terrible trials I have endured, and in this very Colossian letter I reflect about my own mature sense of that—the life of affliction and suffering—in Christ. Due to various political and religious circumstances, fomented by false accusations against me in Jerusalem, I was for two years in prison in Caesarea. It would have been a comfort to me to have had there the kind of fellowship I am allowed here in Rome, as well as the freedom to compose letters. At the time I was simply too unsure of my fate and what energy I did have I used in prayer and personal reflection—all of which served me well in my defense before Jewish and Roman officials. Since I wrote Philippians earlier in prison, it will be my instinct to place these "prison letters" together in my collection. The letter to "the saints who are also faithful in Christ Jesus" which I intend to see circulated in the wider region outside of Ephesus, going first to Laodicea by the hand of Tychicus, although a bit longer than Galatians (and so ought to precede it), I am placing at the head of the three prison letters. Philemon, because so small, I will probably place at the end of the collection on the same principle of descending length.

The fellowship I enjoy here in the open circumstances of my house arrest in Rome is one of the greatest surprises of my (now fifteen-year-long) life as an apostle of Jesus Christ. Imagine the fellowship in Christ one has in men like Mark and Luke, from whom I have learned much about our Lord. I have been able to share my letters to Colossae, Laodicea, and Philemon with them, and the content of these letters is no doubt now as much more a community prayer and common labor than letters I dictated in my earlier days.

One of the aspects of my missionary journeying Luke has captured well in his Acts—and this likely is influenced by our mutual reflections—is the tension in my own understanding of my special apostolic vocation. In my speech recorded by him before Agrippa, and at other places in his orderly account, I make clear my vocation from Christ himself as apostle to the Gentiles. But never do I seek to leave my own people to the side, even when my instinct leans in that direction. In Ephesus I was discouraged by the reception of those in the synagogue and so even hired out a private hall to speak in, for five hours every day for two years. But my own people followed me there, and the audience that heard me was composed of both Jews and Greeks. This happened again and again in my life as ambassador for Christ. Luke has his own way of describing this reality in his orderly narrative.

When in his final episodes we, all of us, at last arrive in Rome—after trial on land and shipwreck and near death at sea—I asked my fellow Jews in the capital city (there are converts from their own number from as far back as Pentecost itself) what word they have received about me from Jerusalem. I tell them briefly of my hardships with my fellow Jews in Jerusalem, worried that they will be biased against me, but it transpires they have received no news of any kind. They do seek to hear about the way of Christ, though they describe it as a sect about which nothing good has been said. So a day is set aside for them to come to me at my lodgings, which they do in great numbers. All day long I preached to them and explained Christ from all of the scriptures (as Luke reported our risen Christ himself had done). The results were only partially successful; some were convinced, others disbelieved. Though I quote Isaiah I could as easily have mentioned Ezekiel or others of the prophets of old. What is unheard or unheeded by Ezekiel's own people ironically—God says—would be grasped by those without the election language of God's people. So Acts ends with the sad declaration that the open speech conducted from then on out would be to Gentiles, although I never assumed the final verdict was in anyone's hands but the Lord God himself. That was the conviction I was grasped by when years before from Corinth I had spoken of the mystery of God's plan.

I mention this because some main themes in the letter to the Colossians are only available to my understanding and assent as a result of time moving on. The truth began to bear upon me that the outreach to the Gentiles was not simply a tragic spilling out for an unintended first or second audience, but that the Lord God of Israel had in Christ a hidden plan of redemption. The plan did not undo election and covenant—as my own people charged, and as I once thought so even in my life as a Christian—but disclosed their inner purpose. I will have more to say about this mystery in the letter to the Colossians, and it fits alongside insights I was privileged to receive from the Spirit in my letter to the Romans, and that finds expression in the first of the three prison letters I am placing together. I mention this here because my conversations with Luke in particular have been invaluable in perceiving the truth of this great mystery. Like all such things, the great light can blind before one can see its marvelous life-changing truth.

It falls only to mention at the last my dearest companion Timothy. I feel justified in not dwelling on his role alongside me because I intend letters I have written to him on previous occasions to be edited for inclusion in the letter collection. They will give evidence of his crucial role alongside me and as I anticipate, after me. I should think they would fit best after the brief Thessalonian correspondence, and together with a letter to Titus, prior to Philemon. I have been so blessed by the confidence that the work I have begun God will himself bring to fulfillment—as I have learned in the Colossian ministry of Epaphras—that it is important to give evidence of this formally in the transition of the letter collection: from letters that emerged from the common ministry Timothy and I shared, to those that show him taking the service he has received from me and shared with me and moving out under God's grace and guidance in his own ministry in Christ Jesus.

When last I had occasion to speak in Jerusalem with the apostles Peter, James, and John, they commended my ministry and especially mentioned my letter writing. I sensed even a bit of envy, if brothers in our Lord are permitted that, and urged them to take up the vocation themselves. Peter mentioned that if he did, he would always be sure to put in a word of commendation on my behalf and urge the churches of his own address to read my letters. How marvelous the plans of God.

Glory to God whose power working in us can do infinitely more than we can ask or imagine; glory to God from generation to generation in the church, and in Christ Jesus forever and ever.

Amen.

BIBLIOGRAPHY

Frequently cited works are listed here. Other works are documented in the footnotes.

Aquinas, Thomas. 2006. *Commentary on Colossians*. Translated by Fabian Larcher. Edited by Daniel Keating. Naples, FL: Sapientia.

Barclay, John M. G. 2004. *Colossians and Philemon*. T&T Clark Study Guides. New York: T&T Clark.

Barth, Markus, and Helmut Blanke. 1994. *Colossians*. Anchor Bible 34b. New York: Doubleday.

Bauckham, Richard. 1999. *God Crucified: Monotheism and Christology in the New Testament*. Carlisle: Paternoster.

Beetham, Christopher A. 2008. *Echoes of Scripture in the Letter of Paul to the Colossians*. Atlanta: Society of Biblical Literature.

Bray, Gerald L., ed. 2009. *Commentaries on Galatians–Philemon: Ambrosiaster*. Ancient Christian Texts. Downers Grove, IL: InterVarsity.

Calvin, John. 1996. *The Epistles of Paul the Apostle to the Galatians, Ephesians, Philippians, and Colossians*. Translated by T. H. L. Parker. Edited by David W. Torrance and Thomas F. Torrance. Grand Rapids: Eerdmans.

Childs, Brevard S. 1984. *The New Testament as Canon: An Introduction*. Philadelphia: Fortress.

———. 2008. *The Church's Guide for Reading Paul: The Canonical Shaping of the Pauline Corpus*. Grand Rapids: Eerdmans.

Chrysostom, John. 2004. "Homilies on the Epistle of Paul to the Colossians." Vol. 13/ pp. 257–321 in Nicene and Post-Nicene Fathers. Peabody, MA: Hendrickson.

Dunn, J. 1996. *The Epistles to the Colossians and to Philemon: A Commentary on the Greek Text*. New International Greek Testament Commentary. Grand Rapids/Carlisle: Eerdmans.

Eadie, John. 1856. *Commentary on the Greek Text of the Epistle of Paul to the Colossians*. London/ Glasgow: Richard Griffin.

Gorday, Peter. 2000. *Colossians, 1–2 Thessalonians, 1–2 Timothy, Titus, Philemon*. Ancient Christian Commentary on Scripture: New Testament 9. Downers Grove, IL: InterVarsity.

Kiley, Mark. 1986. *Colossians as Pseudepigraphy*. Sheffield: JSOT Press.

Lightfoot, J. B. 1997. *Colossians and Philemon*. Edited by Alister McGrath and J. I. Packer. Wheaton, IL: Crossway.

Lincoln, A. T. 2000. "The Letter to the Colossians." Vol. XI/pp. 551–669 in *The New Interpreter's Bible*. Edited by L. E. Keck. Nashville: Abingdon.

Lohse, Eduard. 1971. *Colossians and Philemon*. Translated by W. R. Poehlmann and R. J. Karris. Edited by Helmut Koester. Hermeneia. Philadelphia: Fortress.

Moo, Douglas. 2008. *The Letters to the Colossians and to Philemon*. Pillar New Testament Commentary. Grand Rapids: Eerdmans.

Sumney, Jerry L. 2008. *Colossians: A Commentary*. New Testament Library. Louisville: Westminster John Knox.

Theodoret. 2001. *Commentary on the Letters of St. Paul*, vol. 2. Translated by Robert Charles Hill. Brookline: Holy Cross Orthodox Press.

Trobisch, D. 1994. *Paul's Letter Collection*. Minneapolis: Fortress.

Wright, N. T. 1986. *Colossians and Philemon*. Downers Grove, IL: InterVarsity.

SUBJECT INDEX

abasement, 137–38
Abraham, 66, 67, 78–79, 91, 106, 120, 152, 160
accorded testimony, 47
Adam, 91, 128, 129, 132, 145–46, 152, 157, 159, 170, 171, 172
adaptation, 173
admonishing, 164
admonishment, 166
'adonai, 69, 149, 167
adoption, 112
adultery, 155
affliction, 34–35, 87, 102–3, 104, 187
agency, 97
alienation, 105, 146
allegory, 90, 136
allusions, 38, 43, 44–45, 65, 142, 149, 165
Ambrose, 147
Ambrosiaster, 27, 36, 141n17
Amos, 46
Anderson, Gary, 129, 145, 146
Andronicus, 186
angels, 33, 123, 137, 149
anger, 158
Anointed One, 117
anthropology, 159
apostleship, 33–35, 58, 62, 74–76
Apphia, 175, 181, 185
Aquinas, Thomas, 22, 27, 112n5, 116, 124, 130, 131, 132
Archippus, 41, 60, 62, 180, 181, 184, 185, 191–92
Aristarchus, 40, 49, 180, 186, 188
Aristotle, 154, 168, 169, 172n6
Arius, 93, 94, 95
art, 99

ascension, 131
asceticism, 142, 154
Athanasius, 10, 93n8, 99n16
atheism, 112
atonement, 131–32
audience, 32, 33n22, 44, 64, 88, 91
Augustine, 11, 12, 27, 114, 136–37
Aulen, G., 132
authenticity, 24, 47, 77, 192
authorial intention, 20, 44
authority, 49, 98, 99, 125–26, 149
authorship, 22, 25, 36, 47–50, 55, 61, 179–84

Balthasar, Hans Urs von, 11
baptism, 126–27, 132, 136, 145, 146, 147, 166
barbarian, 160
Barclay, John M., 26, 49, 51, 52, 61n7, 76, 115n3, 123n4, 180n5, 183n11
Barth, Karl, 11, 43, 46, 61n7, 129, 182n9
Baruch, 58, 60
Basil, 97n13
Bauckham, Richard, 100–101, 156
Beale, Greg, 43
Beetham, 38n27, 43, 44, 45, 65n14
beguiling speech, 113, 115
Bernard of Clairvaux, 10–11
Bible. *See* scripture
blamelessness, 106
Blanke, Helmut, 43, 61n7, 129, 182n9
blessings, 154
body, 126, 133–34, 136, 143
boldness, 178
bond, 130–31
bondage. *See* imprisonment; slavery

SCRIPTURE INDEX